ENGAGE

"Management is about arranging and telling.
Leadership is about nurturing and enhancing."
— *Tom Peters*

INSPIRE

"You get the best efforts from others not by lighting a
fire beneath them, but by building a fire within."
— *Bob Nelson*

EMPOWER

"Leaders become great, not because of their power,
but because of their ability to empower others."
— *John C. Maxwell*

BE AN
INSPIRATIONAL
LEADER

- ☑ **ENGAGE**
- ☑ **INSPIRE**
- ☑ **EMPOWER**

DAN NIELSEN
WITH EMILY SIRKEL

Copyright © 2017 by Dan Nielsen

Published by
Dan Nielsen Company
www.dannielsen.com
contact@dannielsen.com

Printed in the United States of America.

All rights reserved. No part of this book may be reproduced or transmitted in any form or by any means, electronic or mechanical, including photocopying and recording, or by any information storage and retrieval system, without permission in writing from the publisher, except for brief quotations in critical reviews and articles.

Readers should be aware that internet websites offered as citations or as sources for further information may have changed or disappeared between the time this book was written and when it is read.

ISBN: 978-0-9898150-4-8

This book is dedicated in honor and deep eternal respect for Max Coppom and Dr. Talmadge Johnson—without question, two of the most effective and impactful inspirational leaders I have ever met.

— **Dan Nielsen**

CALL TO ACTION

This book is intended to be more than merely an interesting or informative read. I wrote and designed this book to be an encouragement and resource for you on your journey toward becoming a more inspirational leader. The fact that you have opened this book and are reading these words right now is itself a testament to your desire to *Be an Inspirational Leader!*

So with that in mind, I encourage you to proceed with openness and expectancy, ready to discover, learn, and immediately apply any insights and principles that resonate with you as you read. Take notes as you read, underline ideas and perspectives that stand out to you, and don't be afraid to re-read sections and dig deep as you explore these important principles and fascinating stories of inspirational leadership.

Commit now to learn something from this book, and then to take action and leverage what you learn. With commitment and determination, you can and will *Be an Inspirational Leader!*

CONTENTS

PREFACE XI

PART I: THE CRITICAL NEED FOR INSPIRATIONAL LEADERSHIP

1. **WHAT IT IS AND WHAT IT ISN'T** 3
   What Does Inspirational Mean?
   Which Leaders are Inspirational?
   Common Misconceptions about Inspirational Leadership
   So What Does It Really Mean to be an Inspirational Leader?
   Are You a Leader?

2. **WHY IT WORKS** 15
   The Ultimate Strategy for Success
   Motive Matters

3. **WHAT IT MEANS FOR YOU** 21
   Strength Training
   Fatal Flaws
   Call to Action

PART II: ATTRIBUTES OF AN INSPIRATIONAL LEADER

9 KEY CHARACTERISTICS 33

4. **BE ACCOUNTABLE** 35
   Take Responsibility
   Offer Explanations, Not Excuses
   Express Remorse, Not Self-Pity
   Take Corrective Action
   Follow Through
   Earn Trust
   Share Credit, Shoulder Blame
   Hold Others Accountable

5. **BE AUTHENTIC** 53
   Don't Compartmentalize Yourself
   Beware of Accidental Inauthenticity
   Know Yourself
   Avoid "Buddy-Buddy" and "Big Boss" Syndromes
   Lead with Humility and Confidence

6. **BE TEACHABLE** 65

       Retain the Mindset of a Beginner
       Be Expectant and Eager to Learn
       Learn from Your Mistakes
       Be a Lifelong Learner

7. BE APPROACHABLE 83
       Redefine "Open Door"
       Treat Everyone with Respect
       Demonstrate an Approachable Demeanor
       Be Fully Present

8. BE RESPONSIVE 101
       Be Alert, Available, and Proactive
       Follow Up and Follow Through
       Prevent and Resolve Conflict
       Look Outside the Box
       Maintain Your Energy

9. BE FLEXIBLE 117
       Be Innovative and Open to Change
       Be Adaptive
       Choose People Over Policy

PART III: THE STRATEGIES & TACTICS OF AN INSPIRATIONAL LEADER

3 CRITICAL HABITS 133

ENGAGE

10. BUILD CONNECTIONS 137
       Cultivate Authentic Relationships
       Ask Questions and Take Notice
       Promote a Connected Culture
       Articulate a Meaningful Mission

11. MAKE INVESTMENTS 153
       Provide Relevant Training and Education Options
       Create Opportunities for Individual Growth
       Nurture a Culture of Leadership
       Show Appreciation and Recognition

INSPIRE

12. CREATE VISION 177
       Answer the "What" and the "Why"
       Paint a Vivid Picture
       Share Passion, Build Excitement, and Maintain Enthusiasm

13. DEMONSTRATE VALUES 191

Establish Core Values
Avidly Promote Integrity at All Levels
Lead by Example

EMPOWER

14. FACILITATE GROWTH 205
Equip Beyond the Essentials
Give Frequent Feedback
Build Confidence as Well as Competence
Prepare for Future Opportunities

15. GIVE AUTHORITY 219
Avoid Micromanaging
Encourage Appropriate Independence and Autonomy
Extend Trust and Grace

PART IV: A CALL TO ACTION

16. LEVERAGE THE POWER OF HABIT 231
Make a Commitment to be Intentional
Identify and Select the Right Habits
Start Small but be Consistent

17. CREATE YOUR PERSONAL SUCCESS SYSTEM 243

ACKNOWLEDGMENTS 248

ABOUT THE AUTHORS 252

KEYNOTES 254

RESOURCES 255

NOTES 256

PREFACE

I remember as if it were yesterday. At 11:00 pm, just two hours after my high school graduation ceremony in Alliance, Nebraska, I hugged my wonderful mother and father and boarded a train headed for Oklahoma City, Oklahoma. I was off to college. I had $35—my entire net worth—in my billfold, and knew that my family, though they loved me very much, couldn't offer any further financial support. It was up to me to earn every nickel from that point forward. I was young, poor, and a little nervous. But I was also excited and full of ambition, eager to take on the world and make something of myself. As I sat in that loud, rattling train, leaning my head against the window, I could only guess at my future. I had no idea how important the next 10 years would be in shaping who I would become as a leader.

During college, in order to afford tuition and living expenses, I either found or created different jobs, including a paper route that ultimately became a 55-mile motor route that I traveled twice a day—starting at 3:30 am and 3:30 pm—six days a week and once on Sundays. I later became a spot welder on the graveyard shift at Western Electric, manufacturing coin telephones. I finished my college career as a classical and flamenco guitar teacher with seventy students per week. Suffice it to say, I was seemingly working, attending classes, or doing homework all hours of the day and night. It was tough, no doubt about it. It took me seven years to graduate from college because of all the work I was doing to support myself (and, by the time I graduated from college, a family of my own).

In the midst of these challenging, exhausting days, about halfway through my college career, a wonderful man and incredible leader came into my life and made a powerful impression on me that has never faded. He was kind, considerate, humble, thoughtful, and gracious. His name was Talmadge Johnson (now Dr. Talmadge Johnson), and for some reason he took an interest in me. Talmadge had just become the first pastor of a new little church near my college, and he and his lovely wife Genell not only welcomed me and my family into their church, but into their home as personal friends. Whether it was a friendly game of ping-pong, a shared family meal, or a serious conversation over coffee, Talmadge invested in my life and quickly became an invaluable mentor. The more I got to know Talmadge, the more I grew to trust and admire him. His superb leadership—within his church, his home, and his community—inspired me and impacted me in a way that has resonated throughout my life ever since.

After graduating from college I left Oklahoma City and moved to St. Louis, Missouri for grad school. As happens so often in life, distance and distraction caused Talmadge and I to lose touch with each other over time. But I never forgot him. His leadership in those few years we had together influenced me deeply.

A few short years later, when I was 28 years old, I met another gentleman and incredible leader who would dramatically help shape my future in ways I had never imagined. I had earned a degree in healthcare administration from Washington University School of Medicine, and was just completing my administrative residency at St. Luke's Methodist Hospital in Cedar Rapids, Iowa. I was sitting at my desk, which was literally in a hallway behind one of the hospital secretaries (yes, they were called secretaries back then), when I received a call from Max Coppom, the founding CEO of what was then known as West Nebraska General Hospital in Scottsbluff, Nebraska. Max was interested in interviewing me for the position of vice president, administration at his hospital. Impressed by my academic record and knowing I had grown up in Alliance, Nebraska—just 55 miles from Scottsbluff—Max hoped I would be interested in returning to the Sandhills of my home state. We arranged to meet during an upcoming American College of Healthcare Executives (ACHE) congress in Chicago, Illinois. I hung up the phone with my heart pounding, wondering excitedly if this was the opportunity I had been looking for.

I vividly remember the drive from Cedar Rapids to Chicago, extremely short on cash but very long on enthusiasm. I met Max in a restaurant in Chicago's famous Palmer House for the interview that would ultimately set the course of my career and my life. Max immediately made a great impression on me, and apparently the feeling was mutual, because within days of our conversation I received another call from Max—this time with a job offer, which I accepted.

I started my new position in June of 1972, and the positive first impression I had of Max quickly grew into a deep respect and appreciation. My office was little more than a converted storage closet, with just enough room for my small desk and a couple of chairs, but I didn't mind. My tiny office was positioned just outside of what you could call the "executive suite," where just inside the door sat the secretary's desk in a small alcove to the right, facing Max's office on the left. Between the secretary's desk and Max's office door was a small open area just big enough for a couple people to stand. It was in that nondescript space between desk and door that some of my fondest memories of Max were formed.

As it happened, on a number of occasions I stepped into that space in front of the secretary's desk for one reason or another, either looking for Max or intending to speak to the secretary, and Max would come out of his office and we'd stand there outside his office door and start talking. These impromptu conversations almost always turned to Max's incredible vision for the hospital and the community we served. Whether it was something he was working on right then or something he was dreaming of for the future, Max's passion poured out as we talked, and I just soaked it up. By the time we concluded whatever discussion we were having and I returned to my office, I would be so excited and inspired I could hardly contain myself! It was truly exhilarating. After those conversations it would take me a full hour or two to come back down from the clouds! I was completely engaged and inspired, ready and eager to help make Max's vision a reality.

It wasn't just those passionate conversations that impressed and inspired me. Like with Talmadge, every aspect of Max's leadership impacted me and led me to develop a deep and enduring respect for the man. He not only inspired those he led, he also excelled at engaging and empowering them. He had impeccable integrity, and absolutely led by example. He loved people and took the time to get to know them and their families; he seemed to know everyone's name, and even knew their children, brothers, aunts, and cousins! He was respected and beloved by his employees, the medical staff, and the community as a whole. In fact, Max had such a positive impact on the community that he was honored as the "Man of the Century" by the Scottsbluff Chamber of Commerce years after he had retired and moved elsewhere.

After only two short years working for Max, I was offered a career opportunity I couldn't refuse, and I left his hospital to go to Texas to start a new hospital. Looking back now, I don't regret my decision to leave and pursue that new opportunity, but I do regret that I didn't have more time to labor and learn under the unique and powerful leadership of Max Coppom.

In comparison to the rest of my life and career, the handful of years I spent with Talmadge Johnson and Max Coppom could seem insignificant. However, the few years I spent learning from those two leaders were absolutely, categorically foundational to who I've become as a leader and as a man. It was their world-class inspirational leadership—their talent and passion for engaging, inspiring, and empowering—that shaped me as a young leader and set me firmly on a course to personal, professional, and organizational success.

It has been five decades since I first walked in the doors of Talmadge's little church and he shook my hand and introduced himself after the service. And it has been more than four decades since I said "yes" to that job offer and showed up for my first day of work at Max's hospital. In both of those situations, I had no idea at the time that I had just hit the jackpot for leadership growth and direction. I didn't have a name for it back then, but what Talmadge Johnson and Max Coppom exemplified was nothing other than true inspirational leadership.

Since first meeting those two men, I have served in multiple senior leadership positions over the span of forty years, and thus have directly or indirectly influenced tens of thousands of people. Any and all positive impact I have had over the years I attribute to the leadership of Talmadge Johnson and Max Coppom. Their impact has resonated throughout my life, and I hope that I have managed to lead half as well as they have! Writing this book is a tribute to them. I am extremely blessed to have had the opportunity in recent years to get back in touch with both Talmadge and Max, and have been able to express—however inadequately—my enduring respect and gratitude for the investment they each made in my life so many years ago.

No matter where you are in life—whether just starting out or already years into your career—if you desire to achieve greater success and to be a positive influence on those whom you lead, you can do so through inspirational leadership. My hope is this book will equip you with the principles, strategies, and tactics you need to become a more effective, inspirational leader. May today be just the beginning of a beautiful adventure that will forever change your own life, and the lives of everyone you influence and lead!

– Dan Nielsen

PART I
THE CRITICAL NEED FOR INSPIRATIONAL LEADERSHIP

1

WHAT IT IS AND WHAT IT ISN'T

"You can't pay your people enough to give you their hearts. Nor can you frighten them into it. Instead, you and I must become inspirational leaders—leaders who can inspire others to give their best efforts for the sake of a great cause." – Michael Hyatt

WHAT DOES INSPIRATIONAL MEAN?

What does it mean to be an inspirational leader? What is it to inspire? Let me share with you a message written to one of my good friends and an incredible inspirational leader, Bob Furman. For nearly thirty years Bob inspired others through his role as executive director of YMCA Camp Kitaki in Nebraska. Years after retiring, he received this note from a young man who had worked at the camp under his leadership:

> I want you to know how sincere I am about you being one of the biggest influences in my life. Your mentoring, guidance, and friendship are responsible for allowing a shy boy with few friends, low confidence, and much self-doubt to mature into a young man with purpose, direction, and a firm moral foundation. You gave me an environment I thought I would never find: one where I could be myself and feel accepted. And it was full of good people who cared about the 'right stuff' in life. I know my feelings of gratitude are echoed by the countless others who likewise have

had the privilege of knowing you. Still, your spirit was able to make me feel special, unique, and individually valued. I cannot express enough the appreciation and respect I have for you. If I can but achieve a fraction of your good service to others, I will be a blessed man.

– Jonathan Camp[1]

That is what an inspirational leader looks like. That is what it means to inspire. My friend Bob never mentioned or shared this note with me, for he is far too humble to do so. But I had the good fortune to talk to Jonathan Camp, who did not want this truly inspirational leader to go unrecognized, and so passed a copy of this message on to me. Jonathan also had this to say about this highly esteemed leader:

Bob Furman is a truly unique inspirational leader. Bob does not inspire with motivational clichés, flattering words, or hollow rehearsed speeches. His leadership transcends those elementary forms. Bob has the gift of creating internal inspiration in others; the type of inspiration that motivates others from within. The result is long-lasting confidence and genuine personal change to the inspired.[2]

I spoke with others who served under Bob's leadership, and their comments indeed echoed those of Jonathan. "He has inspired me forever and has been a true leader in my life," said Jill Gable, "and I can speak too for others whom he has empowered."[3] Wayne and Gladys Peterson said they "could write a book about Bob Furman and what he did for others—he was and is a great guy."[4] I think there is no greater way to define "inspirational leader" than the picture these individuals have painted with their heartfelt words of appreciation. Like Bob Furman, inspirational leaders use their leadership roles to inspire, to change lives, and to leave beautiful and lasting legacies. I believe that's what *inspirational* means.

Without that context, the definition of *inspirational* varies, and means different things to different people. From inspirational music and quotes, to inspirational speakers and seminars, to the inspirational section in bookstores—there is a wide variety of what people consider "inspirational." For some, *inspirational* carries a connotation of frivolity. It's a term that brings to mind concepts that are overly idealistic or naïve, with not enough concrete application; there's nothing necessarily wrong with it, but it's not for everyday pursuit. So *inspirational* is considered "soft" or "spiritual," and regulated to Sunday mornings, airplane reading material, and mandatory seminars selected by the HR department.

But to me—and I hope to you—*inspirational* is so much more than that. Something inspirational is something that influences. Dictionary.com defines *influence* as "the capacity or power of persons or things to be a compelling force on or produce effects on the actions, behavior, opinions, etc., of others."[5] Put in those terms, rather than being whimsical and impractical, *inspirational* is something very powerful and compelling. And that is why inspirational leadership is incredibly important and remarkably effective.

You may be wondering if there is a difference between *inspirational* and *motivational*. Like *inspirational*, the word *motivational* sometimes brings to mind things like cheesy quotes plastered on posters in the break room, and hyped-up motivational events where an exuberant speaker brings the crowd to their feet in an emotional fervor. As with *inspirational*, I think *motivational* is more valuable than the frivolous reputation it's gained over time. However, I believe there is a fundamental difference between these two terms.

> Inspirational leaders use their leadership roles to inspire, to change lives, and to leave beautiful and lasting legacies.

Motivation and inspiration are different in a couple key ways. They both are compelling forces, but while motivation hinges on external outcomes—either trying to achieve a favorable one or avoid a bad one—inspiration springs from internal passion and a desire for fulfillment. Essentially, motivation is external, and inspiration is internal. Or, as someone once put it, "Motivation is the push. Inspiration is the pull." Anyone can motivate others by "pushing"—by offering or threatening the right thing. But to inspire someone, that takes "pulling"—tugging at the heart and igniting a passion within. Wayne Dyer puts it this way: "If motivation is when you get hold of an idea and carry it through to its conclusion, inspiration is the reverse. An idea gets hold of you and carries you where you are intended to go."[6]

Another key difference between *motivation* and *inspiration* is their duration and effectiveness. Motivation is great, but tends to be short lived. Renowned motivational speaker, the late Zig Ziglar, used to joke, "People often say that motivation doesn't last. Well, neither does bathing—that's why we recommend it daily." Motivation is based on a concrete motive or reason for doing something—such as your reason for exercising might be to lose weight, or your motive for working late might be to earn a raise. But those motives often change, or their influence on your behavior fades over time. True inspiration, on the other hand, is more enduring. My friend and colleague Alan Cherry, an editor and content creator for Share Moving Media, explained, "Motivational leaders, both good and bad, use external factors to elicit actions from their followers. Motivational leaders' ability to acquire and maintain both followers and results lasts only as long as they can continue to provide adequate rewards and/or meaningful consequences. In contrast, the power, efficacy, and influence of inspirational leaders extends far beyond the limits of what a leader can do for (or to) those who follow them."[7] Essentially, inspiration has deeper roots; its influence sticks with you and propels you further than mere motivation can.

People respond to inspirational leadership exponentially better than they do to compensation or coercion. In an interview for *Inc.* magazine, Tony Hseih, the CEO of the online shoe and clothing shop Zappos.com, talked about this concept and how it has affected his organization:

> While there are lots of ways to motivate employees—fear, recognition, incentives... what we stumbled into and figured out over the years is there's a huge difference between motivation and inspiration... If you can inspire employees through a higher purpose beyond profits, that you're doing something that can help change the world, you can accomplish so much more.[8]

Alan Cherry beautifully summed up the difference between motivational leaders and inspirational leaders like this:

> Ultimately, the only thing that separates inspirational leaders from all the rest is that at his or her core, inspiring leaders seek to inspire others just as they have been inspired. Inspiring leaders do not waste time or energy trying to pinpoint the optimal balance of rewards and consequences that an individual follower thinks they want. Inspirational leaders focus on finding ways to spread that

which inspires them to their followers. They find reasons to stir their followers to action because those followers have become inspired and can no longer abide inaction.⁹

WHICH LEADERS ARE INSPIRATIONAL?

If you were to plug "most inspirational leaders" into any online search engine, you would get pages and pages of results referencing well-known, inspiring, and influential leaders from around the world and throughout history. From Mother Teresa to Winston Churchill to Steve Jobs, many very different people have been labeled as inspirational leaders for a large variety of reasons. So obviously, the term "inspirational leader" is extremely subjective.

Some leaders, like Mother Teresa, are considered inspirational because of their kindness and generosity. Other leaders, such as Winston Churchill, are remembered as inspirational because of how they persevered to overcome great odds and achieve significant success. And then there are the visionary and innovative leaders of the world like Steve Jobs, who are also labeled as inspirational thanks to the way they've transformed some element of society.

So when I say, "Be an inspirational leader," to what type of leader am I referring? Leaders whose compassion and generosity impact thousands? Leaders who are elected to political office and help lead a nation? Leaders who beat the odds and rise to great heights of corporate success? The leaders to whom I'm referring could fit into all or none of those categories. Because I believe that true inspirational leadership is more a matter of character than achievement.

> **True inspirational leadership is more a matter of character than achievement.**

Inspirational leadership is less about world renown and more about individual impact. Many leaders are considered "inspirational" because of the remarkable things they appear to have accomplished and the success they've achieved. But offstage, behind-the-scenes and down in the trenches, their

Inspirational
LEADERSHIP

---

is less about
world renown

---

and more about
INDIVIDUAL
IMPACT

attitude and character may be anything but inspirational. Yes, they might be visionary, they might be innovative, they might make their shareholders rich, and they might even be motivating, but that doesn't mean they're inspirational leaders. The personal, professional, and organizational impact they have on those they lead—whether individuals, teams, or entire organizations—that's where true and lasting inspirational leadership is found.

COMMON MISCONCEPTIONS ABOUT INSPIRATIONAL LEADERSHIP

As already mentioned, there are countless leaders who have been regarded as "inspirational" based on their inspiring stories and accomplishments. But for some of those people, when you examine their leadership more closely—look under the hood, so to speak—what you see isn't what I would call inspirational leadership. Let me be clear: my purpose in this book is not to slander, discredit, or re-label anyone, or make arguments for why a particular person is *not* an inspirational leader. However, I do want to clarify what I see as true inspirational leadership. I believe there are five common myths about what constitutes an inspirational leader:

- **Celebrity status**. Just because a leader is famous doesn't mean he or she has an inspirational leadership style. Even the most unknown individuals can be inspirational leaders, no matter how large or small their circle of influence.
- **Rags to riches story**. While a leader's story of overcoming great odds to achieve great success may be inspiring, it doesn't necessarily translate into inspirational leadership. Inspirational leaders don't have to have a remarkable backstory to make a significant positive impact.
- **Big title and compensation**. The Forbes 400 may judge a leader by these standards, but an inspirational leader's success is not measured by their title or net worth.
- **Brilliant communicator**. While effective communication is a key component of all leadership, inspirational leaders are not necessarily great orators or bestselling authors who get quoted and tweeted by the masses.

- **Moves mountains**. Inspirational leaders don't have to achieve incredible, newsworthy accomplishments to be inspirational; their most significant impact is felt on a personal level by the individuals and teams they lead.

While none of these characteristics prohibit someone from being an inspirational leader, they also don't guarantee it. True inspirational leadership is more often experienced by individuals on a personal level than recognized by society on the world stage.

So What Does It Really Mean to be an Inspirational Leader?

There is no one right answer to this question. While conducting research for this book, I asked dozens of highly successful leaders—from non-profit volunteers to corporate CEOs and everything in between—how they would define or describe an inspirational leader. The responses I received were all across the board, yet had one common denominator: inspirational leaders focus on positively impacting others. Here are just a few comments from some of the leaders I interviewed:

- "Inspirational leadership is about inspiring people to achieve at their highest performance level." – *Sandy Morford, CEO, Renovo Solutions*
- "An inspirational leader is one who creates an environment where others want to work and excel in the role that they have as part of that team." – *Bruce Lawrence, President and CEO, INTEGRIS Health*
- "First and foremost, inspirational leaders make heartfelt connections with people. They constantly show that they're humanists, and they show their true, passionate, inner caring soul." – *Jim Wetrich, CEO, The Wetrich Group*
- "By definition, an inspirational leader inspires others across many dimensions, encouraging them to take action." – *Curtis Rooney, Founder & CEO, Glen Echo Strategies*

- "When I think of inspirational leadership, I think of a leader who's able to create great followership in the organization, and one who is fairly selfless... they're not doing it for their own careers or for their own wellbeing." – *Mark Dixon, President, The Mark Dixon Group*
- "Inspirational leaders really serve the people who are following them—their team, their customers—and people understand that this is much more than just about the leader's ego or ambition. It's really to serve others." – *Dan Neufelder, Founder and CEO, Neufelder Consulting Group*

I think Geoff Brenner, president and CEO of TPC, sums this up very well:

> We all have a deep sense of what good leadership looks like, but unfortunately we would probably agree it is rarely observed. In most cases it has less to do with a technical mastery and more to do with emotional intelligence, intellectual courage, and a deeply sacrificial posture that understands that true leadership is being an effective member of a team, sweating and bleeding along with everyone else, and not a captain in a nicely pressed uniform pointing to the horizon while others row.[10]

ARE YOU A LEADER?

Setting the term *inspirational* aside for a moment, let's look at leadership in general. There are many different opinions about who is considered to be a leader. The popular perception is that leaders have titles and direct reports. From high school principals, to grocery store managers, to corporate CEOs, to the President of the United States, leaders are those in obvious leadership roles, right?

> Leadership is not limited by titles or hierarchy... *everyone* is a leader.

Yes and no. Indeed, each of those people with a leader's title and direct reports is a leader, but leadership is not limited by titles or hierarchy. I firmly believe that absolutely *everyone* is a leader.

No matter your title or lack of title, no matter where you fall in the corporate food chain, no matter if you have a corner office or if you're a stay-at-home-parent—*you are a leader*. A leader is someone who influences others, and we all have influence on someone—in fact, virtually every person has influence on many other people. Whether you are a colleague, a parent, a spouse, a teacher, a coach, a coworker, a minister, a supervisor, a subordinate, a mentor, a friend—anyone—you influence those around you! Because of this, as I've said time and time again, "Leadership excellence is the ultimate strategy for success."

> "Everyone is a leader, whether they think they are or not. Someone is looking, watching, learning—both the good and bad. So you can choose to be a good and inspirational leader or you can choose to be a bad leader... I'll choose the good!"
>
> *– Harla Adams*

If you stop to think about the people who have most impacted your life and influenced your behavior and decisions—positively or negatively—who makes the list? Do they all have titles like "President," "CEO," "General Manager," or "Senior VP?" Probably not. While including some of those, your list likely also ranges from parents, to high school coaches, to college roommates, to your best friend at work, to your spouse and even your kids. Whether you've realized it or not, the leadership of each of those people has impacted every part of your life. Just as you exert some level of influence on every person around you, every person around you similarly influences you. We all, in some form or another, follow each other's lead.

So everyone is a leader. But not everyone is a *good* leader. I'm sure you've known or are familiar with plenty of leaders whose leadership leaves something to be desired. Unfortunately there are some leaders who have abused their position and influence and have had a very negative impact, but most poor leadership is not intentional. The good news is we all have the potential to become better leaders, but like anything else of excellence, leadership excellence requires discipline and intentionality. Improving your leadership and influence and becoming a truly inspirational leader is not something that will "just happen." So if you truly desire to be a better and more effective inspirational leader, I hope this book is a good place to start!

One more note before we continue: As I just explained, I know leadership roles come in all shapes and sizes and are not limited to paid positions or official titles. But for the sake of simplicity, throughout the book I commonly refer to leaders in the organizational workplace. Please understand that I am by no means trying to pigeonhole leadership into the corporate world, but continually attempting to reference a diverse array of leadership roles would be wearisome. No matter the organizational association—or lack thereof—the leadership principles discussed throughout the book are absolutely relevant for everyone desiring to be an inspirational leader.

KEY POINTS

- Inspirational leaders use their leadership roles to inspire, to change lives, and to leave beautiful and lasting legacies.
- True inspirational leadership is more a matter of character than achievement.
- Inspirational leadership does not require celebrity status, a "rags to riches" story, a big title or compensation, being a brilliant communicator, or incredible, newsworthy accomplishments.
- Leadership is not limited by titles or hierarchy. Leadership is influence, and everyone influences someone; therefore, absolutely everyone is a leader.
- The leadership principles discussed throughout this book are absolutely relevant for everyone desiring to be an inspirational leader!

2

WHY IT WORKS

"You get the best efforts from others not by lighting a fire beneath them, but by building a fire within." —Bob Nelson

The Ultimate Strategy for Success

If you agree that leadership is influence, and everyone has influence, then you probably realize how very important effective, inspirational leadership is for every person in every walk of life. As I've said, leadership excellence is the ultimate strategy for success! Why? Because leadership touches every facet of your life, and leadership done with excellence changes everything.

Just think about the leaders you personally know whom you most admire. What is it about them that stands out to you? What makes them different? It might be hard to pinpoint exactly what it is. Often it's not one big feature or obvious talent; leadership excellence is found down in the detail of personal character and everyday habits more than in any one trait or skill. But whatever "it" is, when a leader demonstrates excellence, the impact is big.

My friend and colleague Marc Gelinas described to me two different inspirational leaders whom he had the privilege of working with early in his career:

> Both leaders had several key characteristics in common... The way they both communicated, everyone felt like an integral and important part of the cultural fabric of the organization. Cohesiveness

and camaraderie seemed to come naturally because of the way these leaders communicated and interacted with all of their stakeholders, from the board down to the housekeeper. Trust and respect flowed easily both ways. While both men had different personal styles and followed very different paths growing up and in their early careers, they were excellent leaders who inspired and motivated us.[1]

When telling me the above story, Marc mentioned that neither of these leaders "asked for loyalty." They didn't ask for it, but because of their inspirational leadership, they earned the trust and loyalty of those whom they led. A similar story was told by Brent Leisure, who is the Director of the State Parks Division with the Texas Parks & Wildlife Department. In an interview for this book, Brent contrasted two different leaders—one who was not inspirational and one who was:

> The great value of inspirational leadership is sustainability. Leadership methods and techniques vary, but those that are most effective stand the test of time. I had a football coach as a child that for all intents and purposes was an intimidating bully. He motivated his team through fear and intimidation, and I did not respect him. There is no doubt that fear and intimidation can be effective in altering behavior or motivating action in others, but it does not build respect, and therefore the positive results will not be sustained. Most people will respond to that type of motivation for only a short time, and then they leave. Many years following this poor leadership example, I had the good fortune to play for a coach that did inspire me. He instilled a desire in me to reach my potential. He was supportive after first helping me to imagine the potential that I did not see. He built confidence. He built trust. He invested in me, and for this I was inspired to do more. This approach to leadership had a lasting impact on me as I reflect on my relationship with him from forty years ago.[2]

Leadership, good or bad, has a significant impact on our daily lives. Poor leadership results in discouragement, cynicism, resentment, or anger, and can negatively affect the rest of someone's life. On the other hand, leadership done with excellence leaves a lasting positive impression. Inspirational leaders earn trust, respect, and loyalty. You can go a long way in life with those three ingredients!

I firmly believe inspirational leadership is the highest form of leadership excellence. To be an inspirational leader—in any area of life—is one of the best success strategies there is. Inspirational leadership *works*. It works because it is people based, not outcome based. Interestingly, by making people more important than products, services, or financial outcomes, success in those areas almost always increases as a result.

According to a study conducted by Zenger Folkman, the foremost authority in strengths-based leadership development, the leadership competency rated as the most important by managers, peers, and subordinates is "Inspires and Motivates Others." At all organizational levels, this competency was consistently rated as the most important.[3]

> **Inspirational leadership works. It works because it is people based, not outcome based.**

> Our own extensive 360° feedback data, which we've gathered from just under 50,000 leaders who have been assessed by approximately a half-million colleagues, strongly confirms the importance of inspiring leadership. Of the 16 leadership competencies we most frequently measure, it is clearly the one that stands out. In our data, the ability to inspire creates the highest levels of employee engagement and commitment. It is what most powerfully separates the most effective leaders from the average and least-effective leaders. And it is the factor most subordinates identify when asked what they would most like to have in their leader.[4]

As you can see, inspirational leadership produces proven results. In an era where organizations are scrambling to achieve stronger commitment and better engagement among their employees, I believe the answer lies in leadership—*inspirational* leadership.

MOTIVE MATTERS

While inspirational leadership is an ideal to definitely strive for, I think it must be said that inspirational leaders are far from perfect. There is no such thing as a perfect leader. However, truly inspirational leaders do have one thing right: *their motives.* As John C. Maxwell writes,

> I believe that as a leader, I need to ask myself tough questions on a regular basis. One of those questions relates to my motives as a leader. There is a big difference between people who want to lead because they are genuinely interested in others and possess a desire to help them, and people who are in it to help only themselves… As a leader, it's important to question your motives often, because the temptation to lead for selfish reasons is strong.[5]

I'm sure you can think of several examples of leaders who inspired their followers, but led them down a path toward destruction. In addition to extreme examples like Adolf Hitler or Jim Jones, we've all seen plenty of "inspiring" leaders later exposed as manipulative and self-serving. Even leaders with solid character and good values can fall prey to bad motives, which is why it's important to frequently evaluate the motivation behind your leadership. There really is great truth in the line the movie *Spiderman* made famous: "With great power comes great responsibility." Leaders have power. Power to influence. That power to influence can very easily be twisted from something positive into something manipulative for personal gain. So regularly asking yourself *why* you desire to lead and influence others is an important habit for every leader to adopt.

> **Inspirational leaders' focus is on how they can most positively impact others, not on what they will gain themselves.**

I believe true inspirational leadership cannot exist without the right motives. No matter how talented you are as a leader, if your intentions are selfish, your words and actions will be contrived and your impact shallow. Again, inspirational leadership is people based, not outcome based. Inspirational leaders' focus is on how they can most positively impact others, not on what they will gain themselves. John C. Maxwell explains, "You only inspire people if you value people." Maxwell then goes on to say:

> You see, it's the value that brings value to inspiration. When I devalue a person, I won't inspire them—I'll talk down to them,

I'll be cynical. When I devalue a situation or experience, I won't get excited about it—I'll be bored with it. Inspiring people is very simple… it's the essence of valuing the people that you lead.[6]

Perhaps the most important aspect of a leader's motives is where they begin. Celina Caprio, an attorney and a volunteer and board member for MANA, A National Latina Organization® that serves Latina women, youth, and families, explains: "In order to inspire other people, you have to inspire yourself. You can't just sit in front of somebody and speak without you also having that passion and that vision and also being excited about things."[7] Several years ago I wrote about this same concept in an article for my weekly column, *Tips for Greater Success*:

> How can you expect to inspire someone—to plant a seed in them that grows into passion—if you lack passion and inspiration yourself? Just like a religious adherent won't meet much success in converting someone to their religion if they don't really believe in it themselves, if you lack inspiration, you cannot inspire someone else.[8]

KEY POINTS

- Leadership excellence is the ultimate strategy for success!
- Leadership touches every facet of your life, and leadership done with excellence changes everything.
- There is no such thing as a perfect leader. However, truly inspirational leaders do have one thing right: their motives.
- Inspirational leaders' focus is on how they can most positively impact others, not on what they will gain themselves.

3

WHAT IT MEANS FOR YOU

"You've got to decide as a leader that one of your primary roles is to be inspirational." – Michael Hyatt

Inspirational leadership isn't limited to extroverts, leadership gurus, senior executives, or people who seem to be "born leaders." *Everyone* has the potential to become a better, more inspirational leader. No matter who you are or what your leadership journey has been thus far, you can begin by taking small steps in the right direction to develop your skills and take your leadership to the next level.

Do you remember the funny DirecTV commercials that start with "When you have cable…" and end with something ridiculous? The premise is that cable TV is disappointing in some way, and that disappointment results in a crazy domino effect of events, like this:

> When you have cable and can't find something good to watch, you get depressed. When you get depressed, you attend seminars. When you attend seminars, you feel like a winner. When you feel like a winner, you go to Vegas. When you go to Vegas, you lose everything. And when you lose everything, you sell your hair to a wig shop. Don't sell your hair to a wig shop; get rid of cable, and upgrade to DirecTV! [1]

While purposefully ridiculous, these commercials make their point that one seemingly little thing can lead to something much more significant.

Now imagine that instead of television, the issue here is leadership. Unlike the illogical series of events in the DirecTV commercials, seemingly small leadership behaviors really can lead to very significant results. By identifying just a few areas to modify or improve over time, the outcomes may surprise you.

STRENGTH TRAINING

You may have already browsed the coming chapters of this book and be thinking, "I don't have all these characteristics… if that's what it takes, I have no hope of being an inspirational leader!" But being an inspirational leader isn't about checking off a long list of competencies. Yes, obviously there are certain traits and behaviors that mark the lives of most inspirational leaders, but there is no absolute list that precludes you if you're weak in a few areas. Without a doubt, we are all weak in many areas. While I've included a number of characteristics and habits in this book that I consider key elements of inspirational leadership, I by no means believe this is *the* perfect and complete list. I don't believe there is any such thing.

Inspirational leadership is as unique as the leaders who practice it. Every person has a unique personality and particular strengths and weaknesses. It may seem logical that in your study of inspirational leadership you will identify several areas in which you are weak, and then commit to focusing on improving in those areas. But that is not what I want you to do. In fact, with the exception of "fatal flaws," (which we'll discuss later), I don't want you to worry about your weaknesses at all.

> "Everybody has weaknesses. Weaknesses are part of being human. And if they're not interfering with your performance or working on a team, the worst thing to do is fixate on them." [2]
>
> – *Kathleen Gallo*

Unfortunately, it is a commonly accepted practice—especially during performance reviews—to identify weaknesses and mistakes and focus the most attention and energy on eliminating those flaws. Even 360° feedback

Inspirational
LEADERSHIP
is as
unique
as the
LEADERS
who practice it

often tends to direct focus to problem areas more than to the areas in which an individual excels. I think this is a terrible and destructive problem. My longtime friend and colleague Harla Adams, CEO of the National Institute for Healthcare Leadership, described an experience she had with one such performance review:

> I worked at an organization for eight years under the leadership of three different people. I had always done exceptionally well on my annual reviews, and even received a number of different awards and financial bonuses for work well done, on teams and individually. I always strove to do my best. After a significant layoff and reorganization, I fell under the leadership of a man whom I knew, but with whom I didn't feel I had a strong connection. Upon time for my annual review with my new boss, who had been in place for three months, I received a poor review. He never commented on anything positive I did, the excellent feedback I received from customers, or any of the things that I had been recognized for in the past. Instead he focused on trivial things that he perceived I'd done wrong. I came out of that meeting feeling totally beat up, devalued, worthless, and incompetent. This had nothing to do with my work performance and everything to do with a lack of connection with my new boss. It was within two months that I left that organization after eight great years.[3]

The above scenario is all too common. While constructive criticism has its place, the focus should never be on all of your shortcomings and failures rather than your strengths and successes. Yes, significant weaknesses should be identified, but with the possible exception of destructive fatal flaws, should not become the primary focus of a performance review or your own personal development. Instead, leaders and organizations should pay more attention to and focus on the areas in which individuals and teams are strongest.

> **The very best ROI comes from investing in and leveraging your *strengths*.**

Sadly, the general consensus seems to be if you're already doing something well, no need to further develop it. Instead, pick something you're not very good at and throw your energies into improving in that area. "Well rounded" is the prize to set your sights on. But I totally disagree with this outlook and strategy. I believe the very best return on investment comes from investing in and leveraging your *strengths*. As I wrote in my book *Presidential Leadership: Learning from United States Presidential Libraries & Museums*, "It's my firm belief that focusing on and improving your strengths will bring you far greater success than fixating on and worrying about your weaknesses."[4] So instead of worrying about your weaknesses, I want you to identify and focus on your strengths. That's right, determine what you already do well, and work on getting even better at those things. As Peter Drucker once said, "Strengths are the true opportunities."[5] Zenger Folkman further backs up this philosophy with their extensive research:

> Zenger Folkman's deep research shows very clearly and convincingly that it is the presence of strengths, not the lack of weaknesses that differentiates the best leaders. This is the only way to move from an average or ordinary leader to extraordinary or exceptional. And extraordinary leaders deliver exceptional and dramatically higher productivity, innovation, employee engagement, customer satisfaction, sales, and profits."[6]

When asked to comment on the concept that leveraging your strengths is far more effective than worrying about your weaknesses, Alan Cherry noted, "It seems only logical that one would want to devote the majority of their time, energy, and resources into improving those areas they consider to be their strengths since they have a better chance of actually ever getting anywhere—not to mention that they already have a head-start."[7]

You may be concerned about focusing on only a few core competencies and neglecting the rest. After all, the need to be "well rounded" has been pounded into our psyches for decades. But I think the demand on leaders to strive for a well-rounded set of competencies is off base. As Jim Clemmer explains,

> When we really analyze the outstanding leaders we've known, very few are well-rounded. All have flat spots or weaker areas. But their strengths were so towering they overshadowed these weaknesses. We were willing to 'cut them some slack' or accept—and even compensate for—their weaker areas in order to be elevated by their exceptional strengths.[8]

Marcus Buckingham puts it this way: "The best leaders are not well rounded, they're sharp. Their *teams* are well rounded. Precisely because they've figured out where they're sharp, and then surrounded themselves with people who are sharp where they are blunt."[9] Dan Teeters, VP of corporate development for Compass Group North America, echoed that concept when answering some questions for this book. He explained, "The essence of leadership is identifying talent and coalescing disparate skillsets into a team. The best, most successful teams emphasize the strengths of each member sufficiently so that weaknesses are minimized."[10] Obviously we aren't all in positions where we can carefully recruit and engage a team of people who are strong in areas where we are weak. But we can always be more intentional about the people with whom we surround ourselves. And it still pays to focus on improving and leveraging the areas where we are already "sharp"—our strengths—instead of fixating on our "blunt" or weak spots. While leveraging your strengths might not eliminate your weaknesses, it can make them irrelevant.

If you've ever engaged in any sort of strength-training regimen, then you know that resistance is slowly increased over time, and accordingly, strength increases as well. Conversely, if you stop exercising a strong part of your body, that area will weaken over time. As Kathleen Gallo, SVP and chief learning officer at Northwell Health, points out, "You always have to keep your eye on the ball in terms of your strengths. Never get content with your strengths, because they will diminish very quickly. Continue to make them stronger and stronger."[11]

Leaders who focus on improving their strengths are often surprised to find that, in the process, they improve in other areas as well. To return to the strength-training analogy, think about how muscles work together in groups. When you target a particular muscle to strengthen, you can't help but strengthen some of the surrounding muscles as well. The same is true with leadership. For example, if a leader is already a strong communicator, but wishes to improve in this area by becoming an even better listener, the leader may also become more empathetic and responsive because of his or her improved listening skills.

FATAL FLAWS

An exception to this approach of ignoring your weaknesses and focusing on your strengths is when you identify a "fatal flaw." Unlike other minor weak areas, these are glaring shortcomings that are damaging to your impact and reputation. Fatal flaws, which overshadow your strengths and undermine your effectiveness, should be addressed immediately. Some examples of potential fatal flaws might be lack of integrity, poor interpersonal skills, failure to collaborate, resistance to new ideas, or lack of energy and enthusiasm—to name a few. These may sound like obvious leadership flaws that anyone would try to fix, but according to a study conducted by Zenger Folkman, that is often not the case:

> The ineffective leaders we studied were often unaware that they exhibited these behaviors. In fact, those who were rated most negatively rated themselves substantially more positively. Leaders should take a very hard look at themselves and ask for candid feedback on performance in these specific areas.[12]

The key to identifying fatal flaws is honesty. First, be honest with yourself. Carefully examine your own leadership behaviors and take time for serious reflection. Are any of your weaknesses causing major damage to your impact and reputation as a leader? Are those weak areas actually fatal flaws that are holding you back and hindering your effectiveness? Don't make mountains out of molehills, but be honest with yourself when answering these questions. Second, invite honesty from others. Ask those who know you well and are familiar with your leadership to comment on major weaknesses of yours they've observed. It is critical that you remain receptive to their feedback, no matter how difficult it is to hear. Defensiveness or anger will quickly shutdown the opportunity to receive honest input, not to mention the risk of alienating that friend or colleague.

Hopefully through personal reflection and honest feedback from others you will determine that your weak areas are relatively minor or irrelevant and not considered "fatal flaws." But if you do identify a fatal flaw that is hindering your success and overshadowing your strengths, focus your immediate attention on overcoming that flaw. Carefully process the feedback you receive, commit to learning from your mistakes, study other leaders' success stories—do whatever you need to do to improve your performance in that particular area. Then, once your fatal flaw is under control, you should turn your attention to identifying, improving, and leveraging your strengths.

Call to Action

I hope by this point you are convinced that being an inspirational leader and pursuing leadership excellence is the ultimate strategy for success! I also hope you agree that focusing on your strengths instead of your weaknesses will bring the very best return on investment. So as you continue through this book and read the many stories and examples in each chapter, I urge you to do so through the lens of looking for your strengths. Whether you're already familiar with your strengths or if you're still unsure where they lie, you may be surprised by what you learn about yourself as you embark on this journey.

As you read through each chapter you will undoubtedly recognize areas in which you already excel, as well as areas in which you know you are not as strong. While it will be tempting to zero in on the areas in which you seem to need the most development, I encourage you to keep your focus on your strengths.

> **Focus on your strengths. The very best areas of opportunity are those in which you are already sharp.**

Certainly take note of the competencies where you are weak, and make adjustments where needed, but remember that the very best areas of opportunity are those in which you are already sharp. What can you do to leverage your strengths and become even more effective and successful as a leader?

When you reach the last section of the book you will find two chapters designed to help you implement and apply the principles and concepts throughout this book. In these chapters we will:

- Take a look at the incredible power of habits and how they can be leveraged to bring you greater success.
- Dive into the basics of creating a personal success system where you can put everything you've learned into action.

Make the commitment now to give serious consideration and application to the principles and concepts throughout this book. By carefully and proactively leveraging the strategies and tactics outlined here, you will have a clear advantage as you continue your journey to be an inspirational leader.

KEY POINTS

- Everyone has the potential to become a better, more inspirational leader.
- Every person has a unique personality and particular strengths and weaknesses.
- The very best return on investment comes from investing in and leveraging your strengths.
- "Fatal flaws," which overshadow your strengths and undermine your effectiveness, should be addressed immediately… Then, once your fatal flaw is under control, you should turn your attention to identifying, improving, and leveraging your strengths.
- Remember, the very best areas of opportunity are those in which you are already sharp!

PART II
ATTRIBUTES OF AN INSPIRATIONAL LEADER

9 KEY CHARACTERISTICS

What is it that distinguishes an inspirational leader from any other leader? What special attributes set them apart and make them more effective? While most leaders demonstrate many similar traits, I believe there are particular characteristics that inspirational leaders consistently demonstrate. As I mentioned earlier, I do not think there is one preeminent list of competencies that a leader *must* have in order to "qualify" as inspirational. But I do think there are some key attributes and principles that will serve as a good starting point for anyone on a journey to becoming a better, more effective inspirational leader.

In the following chapters we will discuss nine key characteristics that I believe describe the most effective, successful inspirational leaders:

- Accountable
- Authentic
- Teachable
- Approachable
- Responsive
- Flexible
- Engaging
- Inspiring
- Empowering

As I've already said, this is not an absolute list. Any number of leadership traits could be included here, and I'm sure very legitimate arguments for why certain traits should or should not be on this list could be presented. However, it is not my intention to win an argument here, or to present a theoretical and academic study of leadership filled with statistics and percentages and scientific facts. Even so, this list is not haphazardly thrown together. I've selected these nine characteristics based on years of leadership experience and observation, months of research, and dozens of interviews with highly successful leaders from all across America, as well as dozens of additional interviews with those they lead. Through extensive experience, research, observation, and conversation, I have identified these key areas that really seem to differentiate inspirational leaders from "ordinary" ones.

The first six attributes listed above will be addressed in the next six chapters. The last three attributes—engaging, inspiring, and empowering—are better described as intentional strategies, or *habits*. Part III of this book is dedicated to further exploring each of these critical habits and the particular behaviors, strategies, and tactics that make up each one.

4

BE ACCOUNTABLE

"The most important persuasion tool you have in your entire arsenal is integrity." – Zig Ziglar

When seeking input from friends, colleagues, and interviewees about what they think are the most important characteristics of an inspirational leader, over and over the number one response I received was "integrity." This is not surprising. Integrity is at the core of a person's character, and drives so much of his or her words, actions, and behaviors. It is no wonder most people place such a high premium on that quality.

I believe the word *integrity* carries a lot of weight and meaning beyond the dictionary definition of "adherence to moral and ethical principles; soundness of moral character; honesty."[1] I think the broad spectrum of meaning surrounding *integrity* can be pretty well captured in the directive to "be accountable." Leaders who are accountable:

- Take responsibility for their decisions and mistakes and for those of their direct reports and teams, regardless of the circumstances.
- Offer explanations, but not excuses.
- Show sincere remorse for mistakes, but don't wallow in self-pity.
- Quickly take action to correct problems.
- Follow through and deliver on promises.
- Build credibility and trust, and earn respect.
- Set a strong example, both personally and professionally.
- Use "we" or "they" when accepting credit, and use "I" when taking blame.

- Hold those they lead accountable with both grace and firmness.

Accountability is one of the hardest yet most critical aspects of inspirational leadership. It is easily the greatest challenge any leader will face. But words can't express how important it is for a leader to set a strong example by consistently following through, avoiding excuses, shouldering blame, taking prompt corrective action, giving and sharing credit, and holding others accountable. You could say inspirational, accountable leaders demonstrate "strength of character." In my book *Presidential Leadership*, I described strength of character like this:

> Leaders with strength of character act out of conviction and with a solid sense of purpose. Demonstrating integrity and courage, they do what they think is right because it is right, not because it's easy or convenient. Principled and steadfast, leaders who possess strength of character are trustworthy and loyal even in the most trying circumstances.[2]

Take Responsibility

When asked to think about and describe the impact of an inspirational leader in his life, my friend and colleague Ed Crane referenced Joan Katz, a civic leader whom Ed had the privilege of working with over the course of a decade relatively early in his career. Ed described Joan as a high-energy, fun-loving leader who exhibited great respect for others and "always, always, always showed tremendous attention to detail that she herself took responsibility for executing." That example of always taking responsibility for what needed to be done is a trait that stood out to Ed, and continues to impact him all these years later. "Joan's commitment never flagged… the bottom line: she was inspirational, the type of person everyone loves to be around."[3]

Are inspirational leaders infallible? Of course not. No matter how responsible and strong in character a leader is, he or she will inevitably come up short in some way. Eventually there will be a promise not delivered, a mistake not admitted, or a problem not addressed. Because when rubber meets the road and mistakes are made and problems pop up, it's not always our first instinct to take ownership of the outcome. It is natural to defend our actions and decisions and to deflect blame when something goes wrong or we fail to follow through on a promise.

But the true mark of an accountable leader is his or her willingness and capacity to "own it." As soon as truly accountable leaders realize (or are made aware) they have messed up, they own it. Michael Hyatt explains:

> As long as you are making excuses you will not grow as a leader. You will also not earn the respect of others, whether it's your boss, your peers, or your subordinates. Instead, you have to look in the mirror and say, "I own this. I don't like it. I wish it were different, but it is what it is. I take full responsibility for this outcome."[4]

Sometimes it takes a little time and reflection to realize we haven't owned something we should have. After an immediate reaction of "it's not my fault," or "it was unavoidable," or "there's a good reason why ____," an inspirational, accountable leader thinks on it for awhile and realizes he or she must take full responsibility for that outcome, no matter the extenuating circumstances.

> **The true mark of an accountable leader is his or her willingness and capacity to "own it."**

Executive leadership coach Ed Hansen tells the story of a family member who was scheduled to have a potentially life-changing surgery. Arrangements had been made, schedules adjusted, time-off secured, and anticipation was understandably high. Then just one day before the surgery was to take place, the medical office assistant called to announce the surgery was being cancelled, because the patient had not followed pre-surgery protocol of stopping a particular medication two weeks prior. The shocked woman, who had shared her complete list of current medications with the surgeon and medical office but never received instructions to cease taking any of them, could do nothing but explain, "I didn't know!"

The office assistant brusquely put the blame on the patient, citing her failure to thoroughly read the paperwork, and offered no consolation or empathy for the patient's anxiety or the family's upturned schedule. In the next forty-eight hours, the understandably upset patient and her family wearily went through the necessary adjustments to reschedule the surgery and once again coordinate various family schedules in order to handle the pre-op arrangements.

Then, late on the day the surgery was originally supposed to take place, the patient came home to a voice message from the surgeon who was leading the medical team. The surgeon took full responsibility for the error, admitting she and her team had dropped the ball, and that the patient was not at all at fault. She apologized sincerely for the distress and inconvenience that had been caused, and expressed sincere empathy and remorse for the situation.

As it turns out, it was the office assistant who was directly at fault for this critical lapse in information. She had neglected to provide the appropriate paperwork instructing the patient to stop taking the medication, and had also failed to put the corresponding form in the patient's file for the doctor and nurse to relate the information during the pre-surgery consultation. Whether she was aware of her mistake at the time or not, the office assistant had tersely deflected the blame onto the patient rather than taking any ownership in the situation. In stark contrast, the surgeon, upon being made aware of the situation, immediately took ownership and responsibility, and took steps to rectify the mistake.

What a difference that one phone call made to the patient and her family! Though the rescheduling couldn't be helped, their anger, confusion, anxiety, and disillusionment caused by the situation were dramatically lessened, and their confidence and respect for the surgeon were greatly increased. Ed Hansen explains:

> This situation caused me to reflect upon the power of a leader "owning" everything that comes with the role. As a leader, you are not just responsible for your own actions. You are responsible for the actions of every person who works on your behalf. No less, you are responsible for any inaction on the part of those you lead.[5]

What an impact this leader made by choosing to be accountable! No doubt that phone call wasn't easy or pleasant to make, but the lead surgeon put any pride or defensiveness aside and graciously accepted responsibility for the mistakes of her team. Not only did she make a positive impression on her patient in the midst of an unfortunate situation, she undoubtedly made a lasting impact on her team, and likely influenced their future actions in similar dilemmas.

Offer Explanations, Not Excuses

Have you ever wondered what the difference is between an excuse and an explanation? The line between the two can be blurred and nearly indistinguishable. Because the real difference comes down to motive:

- An excuse is a defensive reaction made in an attempt to deny some or all responsibility.
- An explanation is information intended to clarify the circumstances of an event.

It takes courage, self-discipline, and practice to resist the urge to give an excuse and not just an explanation. Excuses are simply a form of self-preservation—our natural instinct to avoid harm or pain, whether physical or emotional. Children instinctively sob out excuses in hopes of avoiding punishment for misbehavior, and adults naturally give excuses in order to avoid embarrassment, disappointment, or disciplinary action. It is especially difficult to avoid defensiveness and excuses when faced with a hostile accusation. People automatically make excuses when they feel attacked—it is a powerful emotional response to confrontation. It takes great equanimity to counter an attack with a calm explanation instead of an excuse or heated defense.

Excuses and explanations do go hand in hand; sometimes when we're under pressure to respond to a question or accusation, these two responses intermingle into a combination of helpful clarification and defensive self-preservation. We may *think* we're simply explaining the circumstances, but in reality we're also hoping to mitigate our responsibility. It can be hard to differentiate between the two. That's why it takes self-discipline and practice.

My friend and colleague Stephen Collins shared a story with me about when he was a young Medical Service Officer in the U.S. Air Force. His commanding officer, Colonel Funsch, called him in one day and asked him to do a certain project. Collins accepted the assignment and agreed to complete it in the given timeframe. He dutifully did all the work on the project, but somehow the deadline slipped his mind. When approached by Colonel Funsch, asking about the late assignment, Collins was embarrassed. But instead of offering an excuse, he immediately owned his mistake and simply explained, "Sir, I have done all the work on it, but have not finalized it… because I forgot about it. Sir, I will have it to you in 45 minutes—I am so sorry." Surprised, his commander responded, "Collins, how can I chew you out after you said what you said?" Looking back on that experience years later, my friend noted "That taught me a lesson that when I am wrong, offer no excuses and just admit it. That lesson has served me well throughout my career."[6]

While never easy, one critical aspect of being an inspirational leader is to be fully accountable, and refrain from giving excuses. If necessary or if questioned, explain the circumstances, but carefully avoid the temptation to deflect blame for the sake of pride or self-preservation. Ultimately, your commitment to accountability will reap far greater benefits and better guard your reputation than attempting to protect your ego and avoid blame by giving excuses.

Express Remorse, Not Self-Pity

Being accountable and taking responsibility for mistakes doesn't mean carrying a burden of guilt indefinitely. Accountable leaders admit mistakes, show genuine remorse for any harm done, and do what they can to make amends. They don't brood over mistakes or wallow in guilt. Similarly, when life throws a curveball or disaster strikes, accountable leaders avoid self-pity, and instead accept their responsibility for future success despite the circumstances. An example of this characteristic can be found in a story told by my friend and colleague Bill Brown:

> In the aftermath of World War II, the American economy experienced a many-faceted boom as GI's returned from the war and began to get on with their lives. Their demand for housing created a great demand for products related to housing construction. The Brown Manufacturing Company of Jacksonville, TX, founded and managed by W. H. Brown, was well positioned to capitalize on that demand. The company manufactured hardwood flooring from the abundant forests of East Texas. Since pier-and-beam construction was the predominant mode of home building in the post-war period, the company had great success and profitability for many years.
> However, time marches on and the prevailing mode of home

construction is constantly changing. The market for hardwood flooring began to falter in the early 1960s with the advent of inexpensive wall-to-wall carpet and the concrete slab foundation/floor. Brown recognized the fundamental change and undertook a series of actions that demonstrated great personal courage and accountability in difficult circumstances, all the more impressive as these factors were converging on a man approaching seventy years of age—a time when many are thinking of leisure and retirement. He immediately began a program to diversify his own holdings to provide a base of future income independent of the mature and shrinking hardwood-flooring business.

By the latter half of the '60s the flooring company was no longer profitable, so Brown carefully paid off all outstanding obligations and employees and closed the operation. Throughout that process, which must have been very painful, he never complained or attempted to tweak elements of the failing business in order to thwart the forces and realities of a fundamental change in the market. He simply closed that door and walked away, moving on to different ventures and a new phase of life—and he was past seventy!

W. H. Brown was my grandfather, and I was just out of my teenage years when all of this took place. Since embarking on my own career in management, I have reflected on this story many times and marveled at W. H.'s personal accountability when faced with difficult decisions late in life. He took the courageous steps necessary to deal with a failing market and enterprise without complaint or hesitation. That is one of the marks of a true leader.[7]

TAKE CORRECTIVE ACTION

Accepting responsibility for something is only lip service unless you also take action. Owning up to a mistake is important, but will ultimately have little impact if nothing is done to correct that mistake. To really be accountable, a leader must *do* something. I had to give an appreciative chuckle during an interview with Lorna Shaw, external affairs manager at Pogo Mine in Alaska. When explaining to Lorna that I wasn't looking to "dig up dirt" during the interview process, she immediately responded, "If you find dirt let me know what it is so I can fix it! I've got to clean it!"[8] We both laughed, but I could tell she was genuine in her comment and concern—if something was amiss, she wanted to know so she could fix it right away. It is exactly that kind of take-action attitude that defines an accountable leader.

Of course, taking immediate corrective action is nice in theory, but in practice, it's not always that easy. Sometimes it can be hard to know where to start. I believe the first step toward corrective action is always communication. You may not immediately know what to do to resolve a problem or make amends, but a good starting place is to talk about it. Let the people involved know that you are taking responsibility and looking for a solution. Don't just assume that they know you're working on it—miscommunication, or lack of communication, can very quickly escalate a minor issue into a huge conflict. Also, when appropriate, get their input on the best resolution to the problem.

> **Accepting responsibility for something is only lip service unless you also take action.**

Unfortunately, not all problems have resolutions; some mistakes cannot be fixed. But even so, accountable leaders still take action by proactively learning from their mistakes—or those of their team—and making adjustments so those mistakes will not be repeated. In an interview for this book, Harla Adams shared a story with me about an employee who sometimes struggled to perform to her organization's standards of quality. Harla explained that instead of offering additional support and facilitating that employee's growth, she was impatient and critical. "I was too hard on her... she probably was afraid to do anything for fear it would be the wrong thing." As a result, the employee never improved, and eventually made the decision to leave the organization in order to continue her education and pursue a different profession.

In the years that followed, Harla reflected on the experience and realized she had not handled the situation well as a leader. She took responsibility for the employee's failure to thrive at that organization, and though years had passed and the mistake obviously could not be undone, she sought a way to make amends with her former employee. She was able to connect with her online, and through a simple but heartfelt gesture of apology, set things right and restored their damaged relationship. Harla noted, "The moral to the story is it's never too late to make amends and set things straight… it's never too late to take accountability."⁹

Follow Through

We've all been on the wrong end of a broken promise at some point in our lives. Whether it was your mom's last-minute "no" to a childhood sleepover, your lab partner's failure to do their half of the project, your spouse canceling your dinner plans together, or your manager giving that "guaranteed" promotion to someone else—a broken promise hurts, every time. My friend and colleague Mike Dewey notes that when it comes to the actions of leaders, "The impact of broken promises is corrosive in the extreme."[10]

I have found this to be absolutely true. Some leaders mean well, but in the busyness of their many responsibilities forget about a promise they made, and never follow through—I've definitely been guilty of this myself. Other leaders enthusiastically make a promise with every intention of making it happen, but then reality sets in and they realize they cannot keep their word. Some leaders make grandiose pledges intended to impress, but their exaggerated declarations ultimately prove false. Other leaders haphazardly make statements or imply things they are going to do, but with no firm plans to carry those commitments to fruition. And unfortunately there are also leaders who make a promise with no intention of ever delivering on that commitment, or who later make a deliberate "slap-in-the-face" decision not to follow through.

Whatever the reason, or however good (or bad) the intentions may have been, every broken promise and forgotten commitment corrodes a leader's reputation and influence. Even if it's "little stuff," colleagues, employees, and customers alike quickly lose confidence in leaders who over-promise and under-deliver. Colleagues stop relying on leaders who can't be trusted to keep their word. Employees lose motivation to do their jobs well when they discover they cannot depend on their leader. And when customers don't get the service or product they expected, they very quickly take their business elsewhere.

The corrosive effect of broken promises is evident everywhere—not just the workplace. Think about any relationship and the damage that is done when people don't keep their word. Students disillusioned with a fickle teacher, bonds broken because of a disloyal friend, or marriages disintegrating due to lack of trust. It can start small—a special project that gets reassigned, a favor from a friend that gets put off, a household chore that never gets done—but no matter how small the commitment, lack of follow through slowly erodes trust.

On the other hand, think about the immeasurable value of trustworthiness and dependability. My friend and colleague Hays Waldrop told me the story of two leaders—colleagues of his—who were men of their word and really came through for him. He explained, "They clearly delivered on what they told me they would do, and the impact it made on me was tremendous."[11] Being able to always take somebody at their word, knowing that they will follow through on what they've said—there's nothing else like it. Leaders who can consistently be relied upon are the leaders who gain the confidence and loyalty of others, and that kind of respect translates into greater opportunities and greater success for all concerned, including the leader.

Before moving on, I think it's important to note that "following through" doesn't always mean doing exactly what you promised. While accountable leaders don't often over-promise or make impossible commitments, at some point every leader will encounter a situation in which he or she is unable to deliver 100 percent. But leaders who are accountable don't just throw up their hands and say, "oh well." They address the issue, apologize, and press on—following through by finding an acceptable alternative outcome.

Earn Trust

Each facet of accountability we've looked at thus far goes a long way toward earning trust. People tend to trust leaders who take responsibility, avoid excuses, show appropriate remorse, quickly take corrective action, and consistently follow through on their word. Through their actions, accountable leaders gain credibility, build trust, and earn respect. Sometimes the words *credibility*, *trust*, and *respect* are thrown around casually. But these are very weighty words. None of these elements should be taken for granted. With them, a leader has great opportunity for success, but without them, success is nearly impossible. The late Stephen R. Covey, author of the famous book *7 Habits of Highly Effective People*, once said, "Trust is the

Accountable **LEADERS** gain credibility, *build trust,* **AND** earn respect.

glue of life. It's the most essential ingredient in effective communication. It's the foundational principle that holds all relationships." Covey's son, Stephen M. R. Covey, echoed that sentiment in his own book, *The SPEED of Trust*:

> Nothing is as fulfilling as a relationship of trust. Nothing is as inspiring as an offering of trust. Nothing is as profitable as the economics of trust. Nothing has more influence than a reputation of trust.[12]

Integrity and trustworthiness are invaluable. Amy Rees Anderson, a highly successful entrepreneur and investor, wrote a great article for *Forbes* magazine a few years ago about integrity. In it she says "the value of the trust others have in you is far beyond anything that can be measured... because it brings along with it limitless opportunities and endless possibilities."[13] This is absolutely true. Leaders who have the trust and respect of others have virtually unlimited opportunities, because, as they say, their reputation precedes them.

Of course, earning that trust is not something that happens overnight. While there may be a few big moments in which a leader proves him or herself credible and trustworthy, it takes time and consistency to really lay that foundation. Conversely, it may take only one misstep for that foundation to crumble. As my friend and colleague Dr. Keith Lepak, a board certified emergency room physician, says, "The cultivation of respect, like a field of growing wheat, is slow in the growing... and a single lapse is as damaging as a hailstorm or blight."[14]

Unfortunately, most of us have experienced—or caused—broken trust at some point in our lives. Whether in a work relationship or a personal relationship, that loss of trust can do great damage. And like Keith said, it often only takes a single lapse to destroy what has taken months or years to cultivate. So what do you do if you mess up and lose someone's trust? Depending on the situation and circumstances, rebuilding that trust may be as simple as owning your mistake, apologizing, and moving forward. But on the other end of the spectrum, for grievous mistakes, it could take years to make amends, repair your reputation, and regain the confidence of others.

Just as cultivating trust takes intentional focus and consistency over a long period of time, there is no "quick fix" for rebuilding trust. While small blunders can sometimes be smoothed over with an honest and sincere apology, the best way to rebuild trust is to practice the same habits that helped build it in the first place: be accountable, be honest, and keep your word. Only by "putting in the hours" and slowly building or rebuilding trust will a leader gain the credibility and respect so crucial for success and for effective inspirational leadership. John C. Maxwell makes this point beautifully when he writes, "Credibility is a leader's currency. With it, he or she is solvent; without it, he or she is bankrupt."[15]

Share Credit, Shoulder Blame

Inspirational, accountable leaders understand the importance of sharing credit with others when things go well. This may be a less obvious element of accountability, but an extremely important one. Leaders who practice accountability and demonstrate integrity avoid the spotlight and recognize positive accomplishments as a team effort. Even achievements that outwardly appear to be a direct result of a leader's decisions or actions almost always are made possible because of the support of a good team, and an accountable leader credits his or her team accordingly.

Leaders who easily share credit and cede glory to others are recognizable by their use of the pronoun "we" instead of "I." Throughout my career I have been privileged to speak with and interview hundreds of highly successful leaders all across America. Within a minute or two of starting a conversation with someone, I can tell a lot about that leader by his or her choice of pronouns. It may be a subtle difference, but truly accountable leaders use "we" or "they" to deflect praise and shift focus from themselves onto their team. Just as accountability as a leader means taking responsibility for the bad, it means sharing responsibility and praise for the good.

In my book *Presidential Leadership*, I wrote about the accountability and humility of Abraham Lincoln and how it allowed him to set aside his ego and share the spotlight with others. This was most evident in President Lincoln's diverse cabinet selection, which—contrary to popular practice—included many of his former political rivals. When questioned about this extraordinary decision, Lincoln made it clear that he had no hesitations about sharing the spotlight:

> "I need them all. They enjoy the confidence of their several states and sections, and they will strengthen the administration. The times are too grave and perilous for ambitious schemes and rivalries."

Lincoln went on to say, "Let us forget ourselves and join hands, like brothers, to save the republic. If we succeed, there will be glory enough for us all." While Lincoln firmly established his authority and leadership as president, he did not hesitate to take the council of his former rivals and to share credit with every member of his administration.[16]

Like the example of one of America's most beloved presidents, accountable leaders openly and intentionally acknowledge their need for the unique skills and support of others, and publicly share or defer credit to them.

As we discussed earlier in this chapter, accountable leaders also accept responsibility for their team's mistakes and take the blame for things that go wrong, no matter who appears to be at fault. In an article for *Inc.* magazine, author Bill Murphy, Jr. wrote, "A true leader... recognizes that no matter why the team falls short, he or she is to blame. Even if he or she believes that a specific team member might have been the cause, the true leader shoulders the blame and spurs the team to do better."[17]

My friend and colleague Mark Dixon, president of The Mark Dixon Group, LLC, notes that "So often leaders over-delegate some levels of accountability and don't take it on personally to say 'yes, the buck does stop here.'" He explains, when there's an issue or problem in an organization, it is up to the leader to own that and take accountability for it. "They have to lead. That's what leadership is."[18] Or as John C. Maxwell puts it, "A good leader is a person who takes a little more than his share of the blame and a little less than his share of the credit."

Just as I can usually identify accountable leaders by their use of "we" or "they" when accepting credit, I can also recognize them by their use of "I" when taking blame. It's a distinction as remarkable as it is subtle. One minute a leader will be talking about his or her team and how *they* really are going above and beyond to exceed this quarter's goals, and the next minute he or she will be mulling over how the team missed the mark last quarter because "*I* fell short in such and such way," or "*My* leadership didn't make that possible." That kind of transparency and accountability is rare and refreshing.

Hold Others Accountable

While it is an essential characteristic of accountable leaders to ultimately take responsibility for the shortcomings of their team or organization, that doesn't preclude the leaders' responsibility to also hold the individual members of their team accountable. It is impossible to practice personal, professional, and organizational accountability unless you as a leader also commit to holding those whom you lead accountable.

In the interview he did for this book, my colleague Mark Dixon spoke about the ramifications a lack of accountability in leadership has:

> I've entered many different roles where I've seen what I call a culture of "diffuse accountability." Where everybody and nobody was responsible for certain things, and you were operating in these heavily matrixed environments. "Who's in charge of this?" "Well, everybody is. That's everybody's job in the organization." "But who's really driving it?"… You ended up with this culture where you really didn't accomplish anything. When something went wrong all the fingers were pointed away from yourself and toward everybody else. And so now as a consultant I always like to talk about trying to align authority, accountability, and responsibility inside of an organization, and being very clear and descriptive about what that looks like for each person.[19]

While ultimate responsibility always lies at the top, there should be a clear structure of accountability throughout every level of an organization. As Michael Hyatt notes, "If a leader avoids responsibility and won't hold their team accountable, they'll shipwreck the organization. Accountability is essential."[20]

I think it's important to note that holding others accountable is not the same as pointing fingers or placing blame. Inspirational, accountable leaders always assume responsibility and shoulder the blame for problems, but they also give honest and direct feedback, holding those they lead accountable for what is expected of them. Bob Furman, a retired YMCA camp director and a lifelong friend of mine, explains the practice of accountability in this way:

> As a leader, you accept the responsibility. You demand high standards, you teach, you train, and then you expect and monitor. When

it occasionally doesn't produce the desired effect, you question, examine, and forgive (yourself too, if needed). Then you correct and move on.[21]

I really like what Bob says about questioning, examining, forgiving, correcting, and moving on. Holding those you lead accountable doesn't mean making assumptions about why an expectation wasn't met, or dictating a course of action without first asking questions and listening to the responses. Accountability involves authority, but it also requires collaboration, and demands excellent communication.

In the interview I did with Celina Caprio, an attorney who volunteers with a mentorship program for girls and young women, I asked Celina how she handles situations where a young lady becomes inconsistent in her commitment to the program or backs out altogether. Celina explained that she always starts by asking questions, not making accusations:

> My first question to her is "what's going on at home?" because that is one of the main reasons I observe for why a girl is absent or not completely committed. Maybe because her parents work on the weekends and she has to take care of her younger siblings, so she cannot attend the weekend sessions. So I approach that first.

Celina went on to say that the second most common reason girls become inconsistent is that they lose interest; as she says, "Teenagers will be teenagers." When this is the case, Celina questions what it is they want out of the mentoring program, and offers solutions and alternatives. But ultimately, she holds them accountable to their decision.

> I guess I don't want girls that are not there for the right reasons either, because I have a waiting list of girls that want to be in the program. And so I tell them that—I say, "I have a waiting list. Are you sure you want to make this choice?" I make them be accountable to their own decisions, and I give them enough information for them to make that choice.[22]

Whether you're leading a small non-profit organization, a huge international corporation, a high-school football team, or your family of four, establishing a consistent structure of accountability among those you lead is key to accomplishing goals and achieving success. As much as the ideas of "freedom," "free reign," and "no rules" are popularized in today's culture, most people thrive better in a structured, stable atmosphere than one lacking rules and accountability. Author Jeff Haden explains that great leaders provide reliable consistency:

> Most people don't mind a boss who is strict, demanding, and quick to offer (not always positive) feedback, as long as he or she treats every employee fairly. (Great bosses treat each employee *differently* but they also treat every employee *fairly*. There's a big difference.)[23]

Accountability is a basic tenet of leadership, and an essential characteristic of inspirational leaders. Without it, trust is not established, problems are not addressed, results are not achieved, and a leader's overall impact suffers severely. Accountability is essential for success. Michael Hyatt tells a story of how his executive coach, Ilene Muething, helped him learn the importance of always taking accountability for the performance of his team, and not making excuses. She said, "Look, if it's someone else's fault, then you are just a victim. But if you accept responsibility, you can change your behavior. And if you can change your behavior, you change the outcome next time around."[24]

KEY POINTS

To be a more accountable leader:

- Take responsibility for your decisions and mistakes and for those of your direct reports and teams—regardless of the circumstances.
- Offer explanations, but not excuses.
- Show sincere remorse for mistakes, but don't wallow in self-pity.
- Quickly take action to correct problems.
- Follow through and deliver on promises.
- Build credibility and trust, and earn respect.
- Set a strong example, both personally and professionally.
- Use "we" or "they" when accepting credit, and use "I" when taking blame.
- Hold those you lead accountable with both grace and firmness.

5

BE AUTHENTIC

"To be inspirational, you have to be believable. In order to be believable, you have to be authentic."[1] – Lisa Hill

We all value authenticity. No one likes a fake. Whether we're talking about antiques, handbags, friends, or leaders, authenticity is a coveted quality. We all want the real thing. We want to know that what we're getting is what we're seeing, with no unpleasant surprises lurking beneath the surface. To be authentic is to be real, genuine, and transparent—without any pretense. We desire authenticity and seek genuine interactions in relationships of all sorts, but authenticity is particularly important in leadership. My colleague Kelly Breazeale, a retired healthcare executive and former hospital CEO, notes that inspirational leadership absolutely requires authenticity, explaining, "Duplicity and insincerity are toxic to effective leadership."[2] Marcus Buckingham put it simply when he said, "Authenticity is more important than perfection as a leader."[3] There's no such thing as the perfect leader. But people easily forgive the imperfections of leaders who instead of trying to assume a guise of perfection, choose to be open, honest, and authentic.

One reason authenticity is so important for inspirational leadership is because being authentic is key to making genuine connections and building trust. Christine Márquez-Hudson, president and CEO of The Denver Foundation, told me in an interview that she consciously tries to be authentic all the time, in every situation. "I think that is so key to your ability to connect with others. Because when other people sense that you're being really down-to-earth and authentic, you break down a lot of barriers to connection."[4]

Inspirational leaders must be authentic in order to earn trust, and must earn trust in order to inspire others. Authentic, inspirational leaders:

- Avoid compartmentalizing themselves into separate personas for different situations and environments.
- Are careful to not merely imitate the leadership and behavior of others instead of leveraging their own strengths and nurturing personal, authentic leadership.
- Strive to be self-aware, familiar with their passions, personality, strengths, and weaknesses.
- Refrain from the extremes of acting too "buddy-buddy" with their direct reports, or asserting themselves as the overbearing "big boss."
- Recognize the need to lead with a balance of both humility and confidence.

In the interview he did for this book, Brent Leisure said, "I have found that most people are intuitive, and generally good at detecting authenticity. Leaders must be genuine. They must speak from the heart to reach the heart." He went on to explain that authenticity is foundational to an inspirational leader's character, impact, and influence:

> To me, inspiring leaders are first authentic. Their authenticity establishes them as credible and worthy of consideration. They are of good character. They model integrity consistently. They are confident but not self-centered. They have genuine concern for the colleagues they lead. Their passion is evident; they could not disguise it if they tried, but they would never try because sincerity is important to them.[5]

DON'T COMPARTMENTALIZE YOURSELF

As a kid, did you ever run into any of your teachers while out at a restaurant or in the grocery store with your parents? Do you remember how weird it was to see them in an environment other than school? Maybe they were wearing much more casual clothing or had their hair down, or they were there with their family, talking and laughing. Whatever it was about them, they probably seemed different somehow. Outside of their authoritative role and the rigor and structure of the classroom, your teachers were suddenly just ordinary people, like your next-door neighbor or your mom's best friend.

For good reason, most teachers have two different personas—one for at school, and one for everywhere else. There is a distinct and carefully defined teacher-student relationship that dictates this necessity. But the transformation of a teacher coming or going to work is a unique phenomenon that shouldn't apply to most other leaders, who aren't governed by those same rules. However, this transformation phenomenon is all too common, no matter the industry. Have you ever run into a leader or colleague outside of the workplace and wondered at how mysteriously different they seemed? Or have you made this transformation yourself, using one persona at work, and another everywhere else? This dichotomy between work and home is a symptom of a bigger problem: lack of *authenticity*.

> **Authenticity is foundational to an inspirational leader's character, impact, and influence.**

While there is an expectation of professionalism in the workplace, and organizational hierarchy does naturally create some detachment, that doesn't mean leaders should be completely different people depending on where they are or who they are around. No matter the environment or place in the organizational food chain, leaders' interactions with those around them should be genuine. Inspirational leaders know that truly authentic leadership is holistic, not compartmentalized. Inspirational leadership is a smooth composite of an individual's character, personality, values, habits, and unique skillset. So while dress, speech, and behavior may vary depending on the situation and environment, these core components should remain the same whether a leader is at work, at home, or out with friends. In an article for *Forbes* magazine, contributor Kevin Cashman wrote about lessons he learned from the late Warren Bennis. One such lesson was how in order to live and lead authentically, one must do so as an integrated, whole person: "We can't take out a knife and carve out one belief or another to suit the situation. We can't leave our values, character, even our deep sense of purpose behind, then pack it up again like baggage as we move through our lives and our leadership. To be truly effective and transformative, we must be whole, authentic... fully integrated."[6]

BEWARE OF ACCIDENTAL INAUTHENTICITY

In striving to become better, more inspirational leaders, we might read books and articles, seek trusted advice from mentors, and attempt to imitate highly successful leaders whom we admire. Unfortunately, in doing so we sometimes sabotage our own efforts by losing our authenticity. In our effort to improve our leadership, we start changing our behaviors to mirror those of a mentor, or try to follow a list of prescribed actions we read in a book. But instead of discovering the magic formula for leadership excellence, we just end up looking inauthentic, like we're trying to be something we're not. It's not purposeful dishonesty or deceptiveness, but even accidental inauthenticity can be destructive to a leader's impact and reputation.

> "Always be a first-rate version of yourself, instead of a second-rate version of somebody else."
> – Judy Garland

Though it can affect every leader at every level, I think this temptation to counterfeit leadership excellence is most common for leaders in a new role. Whether you just landed a new job or finally got a promotion, when you find yourself trying to fill big shoes, you sometimes attempt to fill that extra space with unfamiliar habits and borrowed behaviors. Of course, there's nothing wrong with trying to change your behaviors and become a better, more inspirational leader—I wouldn't be writing this book if I thought it wasn't possible! But a key element of successful self-development is staying true to yourself and to your unique personality, talents, and strengths. While there are obvious benefits to emulating highly successful leaders, one must remember there's no such thing as a prepackaged leadership kit or magic formula; you can't borrow someone else's excellence, you have to develop it yourself.

It is for this very reason that I emphasize the importance of focusing on improving and leveraging your strengths instead of fixating on your weaknesses. Channeling your energy and attention into areas where you are weakest is ineffective at best, and most likely will cause you to come across as inauthentic. So instead of awkwardly attempting to wield leadership traits that don't come naturally to you, identify areas in which you are already strong, and build upon those. Not only will you be more authentic, you'll very often find that as you improve in those areas of strength, your areas of weakness will naturally begin to diminish or become irrelevant.

Know Yourself

Obviously, in order to act and speak authentically, you must first develop a clear picture of who you are and what your strengths are. According to an article in the *Harvard Business Review*, "When the 75 members of Stanford Graduate School of Business's Advisory Council were asked to recommend the most important capability for leaders to develop, their answer was nearly unanimous: *self-awareness*."[7] So what does it mean to be self-aware? Lisa Hill, the executive director of Invest in Kids, a Colorado-based non-profit, says that knowing who you are means "knowing what motivates you and what drives you, and what causes you to stumble."[8] Intentional self-awareness is a leadership journey Lisa has been on for the last several years. In the interview she did for this book, she explained that for a long time she didn't really know who she was as a leader. She thought she was being real, but came to find out that she didn't know enough about herself, didn't have enough insight into her strengths and weaknesses and what was driving her.

> It took me a long time to realize that there was as much deep and thoughtful work that needed to occur from the inside out as on the outside. I really had to go in and re-work and re-wire and better understand myself. Now I do things, and I'm like, "Wow, I really understand why I just made that choice, and where that came from." Or I can stop myself before, realizing "Wow, that is an old story for me. That is an old belief about how I need to operate. That is not how I need to show up in this situation."[9]

So how do you become more self-aware? Similar to the process of identifying "fatal flaws" (addressed in Chapter 3), the key is a combination of personal reflection and honest feedback. Take the time to seriously reflect on what makes you "you." Think about your core values and your biggest goals. Consider what's important to you, what you dream about, what you fear, what you enjoy, and what inspires you. Be careful not to construct an image of what you *wish* were true of you. Be as honest and realistic as possible. Also acknowledge that you have blind spots (we all do) and seek out the perspective of people you trust and who know you well. These blind spots aren't necessarily negative—often someone looking in from the outside can see strengths and abilities you haven't yet recognized in yourself. You may also consider utilizing one or more of the many assessment tools available, such as the Myers-Briggs Type Indicator® instrument, DiSC® assessment, or Gallup's Clifton StrengthsFinder® assessment.[*]

Take sufficient time to examine and evaluate what you learn as a result of personal reflection, professional assessment tools, and candid discussion with others. Take any test results and outside feedback seriously, but also be careful to not let those perspectives define you; those perspectives are by definition merely points of view, and only represent a glimpse of who you are—not the whole picture. Like the famous lines William Shakespeare penned in *Hamlet*, "This above all: to thine own self be true,/ And it must follow, as the night the day,/ Thou canst not then be false to any man."[10] Know yourself, and be true to yourself. Once you really know yourself and what drives you, you can begin to leverage your strengths and truly lead from a place of authenticity.

> **Once you really know yourself and what drives you, you can begin to leverage your strengths and truly lead from a place of authenticity.**

---

[*] All registered trademarks are the property of their respective owners. I am listing these assessment tools for reference only. I am not endorsing or otherwise promoting any particular assessment tool, and have no connection or affiliation with any of the tools mentioned above.

Avoid "Buddy-Buddy" and "Big Boss" Syndromes

Making connections and building trust is a critical aspect of inspirational leadership, and is very dependent on a leader's commitment to being authentic. However, there can be a fine line between being an authentic, personable leader, and being overly "buddy-buddy." Leaders can also swing too far in the other direction, assuming a stern authoritative exterior and acting like the "big boss." Neither scenario reflects true inspirational leadership.

A potential danger of becoming overly "buddy-buddy" with colleagues and direct reports is loss of authenticity. In their attempt to build connections with those they lead, some leaders may say and do things not in line with their character, personality, or values. They try too hard to be liked, and their attempts to connect come across as contrived and inauthentic. Instead of building trust and genuine connections, "buddy-buddy" behavior may do the opposite—alienating colleagues and causing loss of respect. As Greg Schinkel puts it, "Having too strong a desire to be everyone's buddy creates weak leadership."[11]

Unlike inauthentic attempts at being buddy-buddy with those you lead, there's nothing wrong with developing deep and sincere friendships with professional colleagues—in fact, most of my closest friendships began as work connections. But a degree of professionalism must still be retained. Brent Leisure says it well: "There must be a mutual understanding and respect for the professional roles you each maintain."[12] One potential risk of close friendships in the work setting—especially with direct reports—is the impression of favoritism. Whether true or merely imagined, perceived favoritism can be very damaging to a leader's reputation and overall effectiveness. For this reason inspirational leaders must be very careful to maintain a respectful degree of professionalism, yet not compromise their authenticity by completely separating their personal and professional lives. Sincere friendships between leaders and direct reports are definitely possible, but must be pursued and handled with great care and discretion—a challenging but important balance.

On the other end of the spectrum, sometimes leaders fear crossing that line between authority figure and friend, and err on the side of caution—

choosing aloof authority over gracious and collaborative leadership. This "big boss syndrome" and its ramifications are completely contrary to true inspirational leadership. While inspirational leaders do not sacrifice their authority in order to be liked, they also do not wield their authority as a weapon or as a prize they've won.

My friend and colleague Eric Kugler shared an example with me from the experience of one of his good friends, Bob. Eric described and contrasted two of Bob's leaders. One leader, Bob's direct supervisor, tends to micromanage and assign mundane tasks, exhibit passive-aggressive behavior, and in general lord his authority over Bob and his coworkers—which is frustrating and demoralizing. In contrast, the second leader, a senior manager who is based in another town but occasionally interacts with Bob's team, leads much differently. Eric explained, "This leader is truly an inspirational leader. When he comes to town he fires up the team. He tells jokes and stories and uses colorful language. He infrequently sees my friend Bob, but already knows him on a personal level much more than Bob's direct supervisor, who sees him almost daily." Eric went on to note that the behavior of the first leader zaps Bob's drive for doing the great work he once enjoyed, while the other leader's actions truly inspire him. Eric explained,

> The second leader is authentic. He doesn't talk down to the team or use office jargon. The team feels he is one of them. He is fun-loving and shares personal stories, and he truly listens when his team members speak. He is humble, as he does not portray an aura of superiority to the team—again, his team feels he is one of them. He is without a doubt an inspirational leader, as my friend trusts and respects him, and wants to follow his lead.[13]

There is a distinct difference between just being "the boss," and being a truly inspirational leader. Inspirational leaders never lord their authority and position over their subordinates or anyone they lead. Instead they collaborate and connect authentically "with a quiet confidence," as my friend Anne Pogson says, "that encourages others to achieve."[14] So to be inspirational as a leader, don't try too hard to be liked, but also don't demand obedience with an iron fist—earn respect and credibility by remaining authentic and vulnerable as a leader. It's not easy, but inspirational leaders recognize the incredible value of leading with sincerity, not casual chumminess or aloof superiority.

Lead with Humility and Confidence

I remember the first time I watched a live online broadcast hosted by internet entrepreneur Jeff Walker. I wasn't very familiar with Walker before tuning into the live video, but I knew he was wildly successful, and I was interested in what he had to say. As the event got underway, I was struck by his on-air personality. I'm not sure what I was expecting, but I was surprised by his very relaxed, casual demeanor. The broadcast experienced a few technical difficulties at first, but he appeared completely unfazed and unhurried. As he talked and answered questions, I noted how he occasionally stumbled over words, interrupted his own sentences, and allowed long silences while he read viewers' questions or formulated responses. At first I was a little put off by his unpolished presentation, but as time went on, I found myself drawn in by his transparency and unfiltered authenticity. He never got flustered trying to pull off a smooth performance; he just went with the flow and simply enjoyed being himself, without any pretense or affectation. I came to realize he had worked his way toward great success by being genuine and passionate, and achieving that success didn't alter his authentic behavior.

Like Jeff Walker, inspirational leaders are comfortable in their own skin. They demonstrate confidence, yet are not prideful, and don't put on airs to impress people. They understand and accept the fact that they can't make everyone happy, so instead of trying to be people pleasers, they choose to follow their instincts, leverage their strengths, and be transparent. Obviously they won't always be liked and not everyone will appreciate their unfiltered personality. But they will ultimately garner more respect for being real and authentic than for trying to fit into an unnatural mold to make others happy.

> **Being truly humble is not just about being modest or self-deprecating, but about being grounded and realistic.**

Confidence and humility are two traits that some people find hard to reconcile. But having confidence does not have to equal being prideful, and being humble is not the same as having low self-esteem. Confidence and humility are key to being authentic, and both are essential qualities of inspirational leaders. It should go without saying that confidence is an absolutely critical element of leadership. Without healthy self-confidence leaders cannot and will not cast a vision, set goals, make decisions, or stay the course. In an article for *Inc.* magazine, columnist Francisco Dao wrote:

> At the end of the day, leadership is about having the confidence to make decisions. If someone is afraid to make and commit to decisions, all of the communication and empowerment in the world won't make [any] difference... Passion? No one will be passionate if you can't set a course for the future with confidence. Communication? People don't listen to those who are unsure of themselves. Empowerment? If you don't have the internal fortitude to make decisions and commitments, then empowerment is just an empty word. Confidence is the foundation, and if you want to be a strong leader then you must pour a foundation of stone.[15]

Less obvious, but equally important to inspirational leadership and true authenticity is humility. As mentioned earlier, humility does not equal meekness or low self-esteem. Being truly humble is not just about being modest or self-deprecating, but about being grounded and realistic. Genuine humility and self-confidence can and do coexist in inspirational leadership. "Humble confidence" *is* possible. To lead with authentic, humble confidence:

- **Create a passionate vision**. "Inspiring others is really about modeling and creating vision. Modeling what you want to see by showing up authentically with confidence, passion, and commitment."[16] – *Lisa Hill*
- **Recognize your need for team support**. "It's important that an authentic leader recognizes that it's not a one-man show. Nothing significant is done by a single individual."[17] – *Lorna Shaw*
- **Share and learn from your mistakes**. "Everybody makes mistakes. You learn from them. When you share about your own mistakes with those you lead, you're saying, 'Let me tell you my story. I've been there.' You have to be willing to share. That's part of authentic leadership."[18] – *Kathleen Gallo*

- **Admit you don't have all the answers**. "The most important thing is that authentic leaders know what they don't know and aren't afraid to admit it."[19] – *Jim Wetrich*
- **Seek out and consider the input of others**. "Take everyone's input into consideration. You may not always agree with each other, but nine times out of ten, you reach a resolution that everyone can live with and support. As a leader you can't be dictatorial in how you treat coworkers, employees, and clients. You have to reach that middle ground where at the end of the day, everyone can say, 'I can live with that, I can support that, let's go on.'"[20] – *Sandy Morford*

Without humility, leaders will lack authenticity, and without confidence, leaders will lack authority. So without a good balance of both, leaders are really leaders in title only. Don't sell yourself short as a leader by being overly modest or self-deprecating. Also don't puff up your reputation with a façade of leadership bravado. These are both inauthentic ways to lead, and will reduce your effectiveness and sabotage your ability to connect with and inspire those you lead.

KEY POINTS

To be a more authentic leader:

- Avoid compartmentalizing yourself into separate personas for different situations and environments.
- Be careful to not merely imitate the leadership and behavior of others instead of leveraging your own strengths and nurturing personal, authentic leadership.
- Be self-aware, familiar with your passions, personality, strengths, and weaknesses.
- Refrain from the extremes of acting too "buddy-buddy" with your direct reports, or asserting yourself as the overbearing "big boss."
- Lead with a balance of both humility and confidence.

6

BE TEACHABLE

"Great leaders are lifetime learners. They turn every success, setback and failure into a lesson that will guide them in the future."[1] *– Michael Josephson*

No matter their title, position, experience, education, or expertise, inspirational leaders know that they don't know it all, and they remain open to learning new, different, and potentially better methods and information. They realize that without an attitude of teachability, leaders plateau, sabotaging their own success and that of those they lead. In contrast, teachable leaders:

- Retain the open and eager mindset of a beginner, no matter their level of experience.
- Are expectant and ready to learn from every situation and every person.
- Make every mistake or failure a learning experience.
- Are committed to a lifelong journey of learning.

To be an inspirational leader and to achieve greater success, it is absolutely critical that you be teachable—always willing to learn and eager to grow.

Retain the Mindset of a Beginner

Most leaders are in their positions of influence and authority because they've attained some level of experience and expertise that warrants it. Unfortunately, the more experienced and successful a leader becomes, the more difficult it is for that leader to remain teachable. To overcome this "expertise barrier," inspirational leaders must intentionally pursue and retain the mindset of a beginner.

This beginner's mindset is relatively easy in the beginning, when you're just starting your training or education in a particular field or subject. But as time goes on and you gain more and more knowledge and experience, it can be difficult to keep that mindset. And as budding leaders become seasoned leaders and receive more and more recognition and respect for their expertise and accomplishments, that mindset is very often all but lost. So the beginner's mindset must be a conscious, intentional choice, chosen again and again throughout a leader's career. Sandy Morford, the CEO of Renovo Solutions, noted in an interview, "You have to continue to always be open-minded, no matter how many years of experience you have in your field, how old you are, or how much of a veteran you are in your industry." He went on to say:

> People at my level have been in this business for a long time. But that doesn't mean we know everything about every client, every business model, or any other aspect of the business. So I continually seek out feedback from clients—prospective clients, established clients, and even lost clients. I also leave myself open to input from our entire organization; not just from the management team, but from every level of the organization. If there are ways we can do things better or more cost effectively, I want to know about it. I want to keep learning.[2]

When first hired for a new job or promoted to a new, more senior position, leaders are put into a unique situation. On the one hand, they are expected to take the lead (quite literally), and be change agents—assertive, decisive, and visionary. On the other hand, they are very often expected to defer to established methods and provide some measure of continuity for the individuals who have been there awhile and are used to doing things a certain way. So it is common for leaders who find themselves in a new position to struggle with finding the right balance between these two directions. This is where teachability is crucial. Bruce Lawrence, president and CEO at INTEGRIS Health, explained how he handled such a situation as a young leader fresh out of graduate school:

When I came out of my residency program I was hired as the assistant vice president at a hospital, and I was put in a position where I was managing departments with department heads that were old enough to be my parents. They had been there for many years and had always done things a certain way, and here I was, a new kid coming in fresh out of grad school, with all these ideas and ideals. That was a really tough job. So I approached it by saying, "Hey, teach me. I'm here to learn. I don't know everything there is to know about the lab or radiology or materials management or pharmacy. Teach me what I need to know. Use this as an opportunity to mold the guy that you report to." I went in saying "Teach me," as opposed to going in and saying, "Okay, I've got a graduate degree from a great school, so this is how we're going to do it here." That wasn't my approach, and that wouldn't have been successful.[3]

Decades later, Bruce Lawrence continues to retain that same beginner's mindset. He has been in major executive leadership roles for many years, including president and CEO of Oklahoma's largest healthcare system since 2010. Yet he still knows he doesn't know it all, and he remains teachable and open to new ideas. Marshall Snipes, who serves as chairman of the board of directors for INTEGRIS, had this to say about Bruce Lawrence's teachability: "Bruce receives others' thoughts and ideas with respect. He has been open to being proven wrong, and will gladly change his mind when others present their case. Bruce attends conferences and meetings and talks with his colleagues in other organizations for guidance and ideas. When the board has made suggestions, Bruce has always been willing to listen, think through the comment or recommendation, and take action with a well-thought-out decision."[4] Bruce's colleague Beth Pauchnik, who serves as the health system's general counsel and chief administrative officer, made a similar observation: "Despite his years of experience and high level of expertise, Bruce is still very open to constructive feedback. In fact, very often he asks our opinion on his performance or on how he handled a situation and what he could have done differently. While confident, he is also teachable."[5] That mindset of a beginner and attitude of continued teachability no doubt has helped Bruce achieve significant success throughout his life and career as an inspirational leader.

Just as Bruce Lawrence is willing and eager to listen to and learn from others, inspirational leaders recognize the value in proactively seeking input from their colleagues and direct reports. While there is certainly a need for leaders to be assertive and decisive, there is still room for collaboration in many areas. Christine Márquez-Hudson explained how important this kind of collaboration and feedback is to her as the CEO of an organization:

> I think it's always important to ask others around you, "What do you think? What do you see as a fallacy with this idea? Push back. Tell me what isn't going to work, and then tell me what will work." I think gathering input like that from all different levels of your staff, your executive leadership, and your board is important—even though it's time consuming. Sometimes you might be perceived as being a weak leader because you're not just using your authority to make a decision, but I think when you get those varied perspectives you're not being a weak leader, you're being a wise leader. By seeking out that input you will really think differently and more carefully about an issue. I believe in going slow so that you can go fast later on.[6]

By retaining the mindset of a beginner, even the most senior leaders can learn and benefit from the perspectives and ideas of others. This mindset also helps leaders become more comfortable with asking for help. When you foster an attitude of teachability and frequently and easily say the words "teach me," it's not very hard to go one step further and also use the words "help me." Being comfortable and willing to ask for help is an important characteristic of the beginner's mindset. By asking for help, leaders set aside their egos and admit that they don't know everything and they don't have all the answers. Humbly and sincerely asking for help demonstrates an attitude of teachability and an openness to learning from others.

My colleague Marc Gelinas told me about an experience from early in his career, while serving at the then relatively new healthcare organization Voluntary Hospitals of America, Inc. (now Vizient):

> One of the best examples of a teachable leader comes from those formative years at VHA. The organization had come a long way. It had grown to a larger size than anyone had predicted, and was continuing to grow so much that no one was quite sure how we could or should manage it. CEO Don Arnwine told his senior management team that he didn't know either—that he didn't have all the answers. So he decided to invite the leading thought leaders,

innovators, and most forward-thinking people he could find to come teach, discuss, and collaborate with us. Then he made it an annual exercise, with Don always leading each series of sessions as the most eager student and with the most open mind. For as often as Don was featured on the cover of various magazines as a thought leader himself, and as often as he had been asked to present to large audiences of hospital leaders from around the country, Don still retained that mindset of a beginner, and knew that he had to learn from everyone who had something to offer him. The example he set gave all of us the stimulus to do the same, during those times and ever since.[7]

No matter your experience or level of expertise, no matter your age or number of years in your industry, no matter your education or the letters following your name, you can always learn something new. So approach the world with a beginner's mindset, and see every situation as an opportunity to learn and to grow. I am a prime example... you *can* teach an old dog new tricks! Be humble, be willing to be taught by others, be willing to be a student, and you will be a far more effective, inspirational leader. Be teachable—and model that teachability for those you lead—by retaining the mindset of a beginner.

BE EXPECTANT AND EAGER TO LEARN

An important key to being teachable is to always be expectant and eager to learn. Teachability is an attitude, and your attitude—how you approach every situation—is always a choice. In his book *Life's Greatest Lessons: 20 Things That Matter*, author Hal Urban wrote, "The right approach to anything sets the stage for creating the results we hope for. In essence, our attitudes are the way we approach life. And the way we approach it will determine our success or failure."[8] This is so very true. Our attitudes and expectations have an incredible impact on our actual experiences. If you start out with a sour attitude about something, or go in expecting something to be boring or irrelevant, nine times out of ten you will get that expected result. And the opposite is true as well—if you enter a situation with a positive attitude and an eager expectation to learn something, you almost always will do just that! Inspirational, teachable leaders approach each day and each

Expect **TO LEARN** something, *and you* **WILL!**

situation—no matter how good or bad it may seem—with an expectant attitude. They are alert and ready to learn in every situation. *Expect* to learn something, and you will!

I have learned this firsthand from years of experience. After more than three decades serving in numerous leadership roles, I tried out retirement back in 2003. I knew from the beginning that I wouldn't be able to sit still and do nothing, so I bought a small motorhome, packed up my camera gear, and set out to travel, explore, discover, and photograph all that I could all across America. Now more than a decade later, I still have that motorhome—which I've dubbed my "Inspirational Vehicle" because I am so inspired when I'm traveling in it—and I still travel all over the nation on a regular basis. I have visited virtually every area and every corner of the United States, and have taken more than 250,000 photographs along the way. Why do I continue to travel and photograph America? Because I am eager to learn! And I *expect* to learn. I go into every trip and every new destination with a positive and expectant attitude, knowing that each day and each experience is what I choose to make of it. People often ask me what my favorite place is, assuming I have discovered a favorite city, national park, beach, or something. I always tell them I don't have a true favorite; I find uniqueness and things to love about every place I visit. As I like to say, there is life in Death Valley. Throughout my travels I've discovered if you look for it, if you expect to find something beautiful and unique and interesting, you will find it!

My colleague Jim Wettich—affectionately known as "Big Red" by those who know him well—is a perfect example of an inspirational leader and eager and expectant learner. Twenty-five years after receiving his master's degree from Tulane University, Jim decided to go back to school for a second master's degree, which he earned in 2009 from Emory University. Did Jim need a second degree? No. But the point wasn't to get another degree, it was to *learn*. By choosing to go back to school, Jim was acknowledging that the world had changed dramatically since he earned his first master's in 1983. So he intentionally and eagerly sought new knowledge. In his application to Emory he wrote in part, "…I expect to learn many new things, to challenge some of my current assumptions, to correct misunderstandings, and frankly to relearn things that I have long since forgotten."[9] One of Jim's former colleagues, Sanchia Patrick Rasul, described Jim as having "sensational curiosity" and noted that he is "always asking questions and eager to hear and learn from diverse perspectives."[10] Another colleague, Michael Britton, said this about Big Red: "Not only does Jim possess an intentional attitude toward learning, but he has the proven ability to remain humble and receptive and to model a teachable spirit. It all begins at the top with Mr. Wetrich."[11]

Being expectant and eager to learn also means being ready to learn from *anyone*. Whether we admit it or not, we all have subconscious biases and assumptions about who we can and cannot learn from. My old friend Bob Furman told me the following story from when he was the executive director of YMCA Camp Kitaki in Nebraska:

> One day early in my career after I dismissed the kids from the dining hall, I noticed an 11-year-old playing in the dirt under the steps. Wanting to engage the young man, I joined him, sitting in the shade in the dirt under the porch, and asked him how and what he was doing. He matter-of-factly informed me that he was "waiting for lions." Marveling at the great imagination kids have, I inquired how he was doing that. He responded, "You see these little holes?" (We had a very fine clay soil at camp, and it looked like he had taken a stick and poked a few holes in the dirt, making cone shaped divots.) The boy continued, "Well, when an ant walks into one and tries to get out, the sides cave in and he's trapped. Then a lion comes out and grabs the ant and eats him!" Indulging the boy and his imagination, I remarked on how neat that was. About the same time, an ant ambled into a divot and started frantically trying to climb out. Momentarily, a pair of tiny pincers appeared from the bottom of the hole, grabbing the ant and pulling it under the dirt in an instantly-quick disappearing act. Utterly stupefied and with my mouth wide open, I was unable to say anything intelligent. Later I learned about the insect known as the ant lion, and gained a huge respect for 11-year-olds that I never forgot. Relaying this story each year during staff training taught us never to underestimate kids, and that you can always learn something from everyone.[12]

No matter whether it's a child, a stranger, a direct report, a coffee barista, a homeless man, an annoying coworker, or someone far below you on the corporate ladder, everyone has something to offer, and everyone can teach you something new. Make a point to be open and eager to learn from *anyone* and *everyone*. You might be surprised at what you can learn!

In addition to being eager and willing to learn from everyone, also be open to learning from ideas and perspectives that differ from your own. You may not agree with a particular method or point of view, but you can strive to learn something from it regardless. Don't put up your defenses or shy away from things that challenge your outlook or way of doing things. Instead, welcome different perspectives and friendly debate. This is important not only in conversation, but also in what you choose to read or watch. I am an avid reader, news junkie, and lifelong learner. I have learned over the years how crucial it is not to limit my information intake because of political, religious, or other preferences. For example, I frequently record and later watch or listen to programs like the Charlie Rose show or TED talks, which feature an extremely diverse roster of interviews and presentations. I began this habit years ago, often listening while I get ready in the morning, eat a meal, walk around my neighborhood, or exercise at the gym, and it is amazing the breadth and depth of information that I've learned over the years. No matter my own opinions, I can always learn something from the perspectives, ideas, and experiences of others.

> Everyone has something to offer, and everyone can teach you something new. Make a point to be open and eager to learn from *anyone* and *everyone*.

Dr. Mark Kehrberg, who served for many years in the Affinity Health System, described to me the teachable attitude of his colleague Dan Neufelder, former president and CEO of Ministry Health Care, which sponsors the Affinity Health System:

> Not only is Dan teachable, I would also say he is challengeable. That's important, because it's when you're challenged—when your basic tenets, your basis for your decision-making, your thoughts and your beliefs are challenged—that we really find out what sort of a person you are. Dan is very comfortable with that. He doesn't take those sorts of confrontations as a personal affront, he takes them as an opportunity to learn and make a right decision. He's an incredible leader and an incredible man.[13]

Teachable, inspirational leaders are not only willing and eager to learn from others, they are open about their teachability. To be a more teachable, inspirational leader, set your ego aside and don't let pride or embarrassment prevent you from learning. Make it clear that you are ready to learn, and when you do learn something from someone, acknowledge it—don't try to hide it or pretend you already knew something you didn't. Be expectant and eager to learn, be willing to be challenged, and openly acknowledge your desire and need to learn from others. Do this, and you will gain greater credibility and respect, and truly be a more teachable, inspirational leader!

Learn from Your Mistakes

As already mentioned, teachability requires humility. My friend and colleague Dan Neufelder defines humility as "being grounded," and agrees it is essential to being teachable.[14] An attitude of humble teachability not only means you're open and seeking to learn from others, it means you're also willing to acknowledge and learn from your own mistakes. In 2013 I wrote an article that was featured on *The Journal of Healthcare Contracting* blog, where I submit a regular column on leadership. In the article I asked readers to consider the question, "What is your greatest failure?" In essence, I was pointing out the critical importance of learning from your mistakes and failures. I went on to say:

> When you stop to think about it... our "greatest" failures shape us as much or more than what we perceive to be our greatest successes. Our greatest failures force us to reevaluate our methods and strategies, goals and priorities, and even our passion and direction in life. Our greatest failures challenge us to fix our mistakes, address our weaknesses, focus on our strengths, and try again.[15]

While you should never fixate on your weaknesses, you also shouldn't avoid looking at your mistakes or facing your failures. Be intentional about seeking out answers—even when it's uncomfortable—so you can learn how you can do better next time. Sandy Morford shared with me an example of how he makes a habit of doing just that:

> From a sales perspective, we don't always win every deal that we try to go after. We have a very high success rate, but of course there

are times that we don't win a deal. Recently we competed with nine different companies for an opportunity to serve a new client, and they narrowed it down to two finalists—us and someone else. But at the end of it, they awarded that contract to our competitor. So I sent an email to the leadership of that decision-making team—respecting the fact that they've made the decision, and not trying to get them to change their mind, but wanting to know if we could have a brief conversation about what our organization could have done differently to better win their business. When we're given those opportunities, it allows us to learn things that we could have done differently to maybe achieve greater success in similar situations. Every time a situation like that occurs in the organization, I want to know the answer to the question, "What could we have done better to gain your confidence that we were the company that you should have selected?" Not only does learning from those perceived mistakes benefit our organization, it benefits me personally as a leader.[16]

When faced with a mistake or a complaint of something done poorly, don't get defensive or refuse to learn from the situation. Seeking answers and input regarding a mistake, while excellent, is only the first step. Upon receiving that feedback, avoid the temptation to defend, excuse, or justify your actions. To truly learn from your mistakes, you must graciously accept whatever feedback you receive, and then carefully and honestly reflect on that input and determine if and how it will affect your decisions and actions in the future. My colleague Kelly Breazeale related to me one experience where he received some negative feedback. It was understandably hard to not make excuses, but by being open to that individual's input, Kelly ended up learning an important lesson from a unique perspective:

> I recall an incident in my consulting days when my client was my teacher—a rather upside down relationship. For a host of reasons (mostly out of our control) my firm's contract with a particular client organization was canceled. I had significant sales responsibility for the firm, so I was tasked with debriefing the client to determine what had gone wrong and what we could do better. Among the issues he shared with me, the representative from the client organization noted:
> "I always felt like you had other clients."

"Of course we have other clients," I replied, "you knew that when you selected us."

"Sure," he said, "but I should not have felt it."

That was a big lesson for me. Hopefully, no subsequent client ever felt like they weren't our only client.[17]

An important aspect to remember when learning from mistakes is to not let those failures define you. Yes, learn from them, and let what you learn help shape your future decisions and actions. But do not focus or dwell on past mistakes. And be aware that not every failure is a signal that you must change your course of action. Sometimes the most important thing you learn from a failure or mistake is that you just have to keep trying. So be open, be ready and willing to learn, but also remain grounded and steadfast despite challenges and setbacks. Colleen Collarelli, a former colleague of Christine Márquez-Hudson's, shared with me a little bit about Christine's leadership style and how she handles failure:

> Christine transparently shares both the wins and the losses from a balanced, wholesome, and appreciative perspective. I got the sense that she embraces failure for the opportunities to learn and deepen her and the organization's perspective and knowledge. But I also got the sense that she does not allow the losses to define her, her leadership, or her organization. She is very grounded. She possesses clear-thinking and certainty that the situation can and will be resolved.[18]

When you make a mistake, experience a failure, or something doesn't quite go the way you had hoped, don't give in to feelings of anger or embarrassment. Don't ignore, deny, or avoid facing mistakes. Instead, make the most of the situation by *learning* from the situation. Embrace the lessons that invariably are found within every failure. Seek honest feedback, and don't make excuses or put up your defenses when you receive that input. Be open, be teachable, and learn from every mistake.

> **Be open, be teachable, and learn from every mistake.**

BE A LIFELONG LEARNER

I am a firm believer in lifelong learning. I believe sustaining a lifelong curiosity and desire to learn is a critical element of inspirational leadership. While I may have never gone back for a second master's degree like my friend and colleague Jim Wetrich, I have been an eager, relentless student my entire life. Not only have I carefully and intentionally studied and learned from thousands of world-class leaders, books, institutions, presentations, and articles, but I have also learned so much from just interacting with ordinary people on a day-to-day basis. Everywhere I go and everything I do, I try to learn something new. Of course I am far from perfect, and I don't always succeed in being open and teachable. But I've made it a habit to try to consciously and intentionally choose an attitude of teachability every single day.

In addition to approaching every situation with an eager expectation that I can and will learn something from it, I have found that one of the very best ways to really learn something is to teach it. And to be a teacher, you really have to be teachable. I have been honored to have the opportunity to teach at four different universities, as well as teach, present, and facilitate at hundreds of corporate meetings and conferences all across America. Without exception, I have learned more from being a teacher than I could have ever imagined. To truly and sufficiently prepare to speak and teach on a particular subject, I must study more than I ever did as a student in school! And teaching has a way of making the content stick in your brain far better and far longer than any test ever could. So if you really want to learn something, I highly recommend pursuing opportunities to teach about it!

Another way I believe inspirational leaders pursue lifelong learning is to be adventurous, and to frequently put themselves in positions where they will be challenged to learn something new. They don't just accept it when it comes their way—they actively seek out new experiences and different perspectives. Inspirational leaders realize the value in trying new things, whether it's a new physical learning experience like training for a marathon, trying out yoga, or learning to water ski, or a more creative or intellectual pursuit, like studying a language, taking an art class, or starting piano lessons. Going through the process of learning by starting as a true novice at something is a very healthy and valuable exercise for every leader. Not only does it help leaders continue to broaden their horizons, but it also gives them more empathy for novices in their own areas of expertise. It reminds leaders what it was like when they were first starting out, and helps enforce the importance of retaining the mindset of a beginner.

Georgetown University has a leadership coaching program where they require their students to do exactly that. Kate Ebner, who is the director of Georgetown's Institute for Transformational Leadership, wrote about the coaching program in an article titled "Embracing the Beginner's Mindset." She explained that they require the students to engage in one new "body practice" throughout the six-month program. This can by anything physical—sports, music, dance, etc.—as long as it is brand-new to them:

> This requirement surprises and startles our students. Sometimes there is resistance. ("I thought this was a coaching program! What does this have to do with coaching?") We respond by explaining the enormous value of being a beginner and experiencing the discomfort, awkwardness and self-consciousness of asking one's body to do something new. As we ask ourselves to learn, we let go of resistance, we drop self-consciousness and devote attention to doing just the basics and then, slowly, reaching new levels of mastery. We remember how to laugh at ourselves, how to connect with others in moments of not knowing, rather than trying to assert our expertise and mastery as daily life teaches us to do. We make new friends. We become reacquainted with our bodies again, feeling muscles we've forgotten about. Being a beginner in the domain of body, as we say at Georgetown, awakens us to the joy of learning and trying on new ideas. We discover again the gains made by a good effort as well as the benefits of practicing. From this open stance, we are ready to grow, change and step into the great possibilities of our lives. Perhaps best of all, as beginners, we feel great empathy for other beginners. As beginners, we are vulnerable and open. We are open once again to helping and being helped.[19]

By intentionally challenging themselves and regularly stepping outside of their comfort zones, inspirational leaders stay curious and teachable, open to new experiences, and more empathetic toward beginners and others who do not share their expertise.

Similar to venturing outside of their comfort zones to try new things, inspirational leaders intentionally seek out knowledge, information, and ideas outside of their industry. In this regard, they are "well rounded" (this is different than the dangerous goal of well-rounded leadership competencies we discussed in Chapter 3). While they may have particular expertise in a certain area (and focus on leveraging their strengths in that area), inspirational leaders also are familiar with a large variety of topics, and learn for the sake of learning. In 2014 I wrote about this for another article published on *The Journal of Healthcare Contracting* blog. While acknowledging the vast and excellent resources available within the healthcare field (or any industry), I encouraged readers to "actively and consistently engage in some of the many excellent developmental resources outside of [your] field. Broaden your horizons and perspectives. Broaden your understanding and experience…" I went on to explain, "Although your intentions may be good, by limiting and restricting your developmental time and energy to only [your] field, you are significantly limiting your personal, professional, and organizational potential, impact, and legacy."[20]

Effective, inspirational leaders recognize the value in being well rounded in regard to knowledge and personal enrichment. They intentionally pursue knowledge and education outside of their field, industry, or area of expertise. And in that pursuit, very often they discover that subjects seemingly unrelated to their given field will reap unexpected benefits. Maybe familiarity with a unique topic leads to a great conversation that results in an important and instrumental connection. Or perhaps knowledge of a certain subject gives you an edge when negotiating with a prospective client. Or maybe a breakthrough idea or innovation in another industry can be applied to your own area of expertise. Whatever it may be, learning from other people, other fields, and other industries never fails to enrich your life—personally, professionally, and organizationally.

Attorney Celina Caprio, who volunteers as a mentor for girls and young women, is a great example of a lifelong learner with a lot of curiosity. "I'm constantly seeking knowledge, wanting to learn things. I'll read random articles on science, biology—things completely unrelated to my field—because it's knowledge." During our interview Celina mentioned that she was currently taking a creative writing class for personal enrichment. While it was mostly just for fun, Celina also noted that the class would likely help her in her mentoring roll, as it was geared for young adults. She explained, "I want to know what gets to them, what they think about, and what engages them in writing, so I can use my work more efficiently when I need to make a point."[21] Celina is an example of an inspirational leader who recognizes excellent opportunities to not only learn for the sake of learning, but to add value to herself and those she serves in her own area of expertise.

Another key to lifelong learning is to recognize that the world is a rapidly changing place, and you must be proactive and intentional in order to keep up. This is especially true in the area of technology. It seems like every day a new innovation is discovered, a fancier gadget invented, or a better version released. There's *always* something new to learn. How well do I know this! Just when I think I've gotten the hang of the latest updates to my computer or mobile devices, they change again. With every improvement and upgrade comes a whole new batch of tricks to learn, and if we're not careful, we'll be left in the dust. My friend and colleague Cathy Eddy, president of Health Plan Alliance, echoes this concern, and shared with me an example of one senior leader she knows who is seeking and graciously accepting help in the realm of technology:

> The rapid development of technology has left many senior executives behind the curve on new forms of communication. But one of my colleagues has been able to find ways to "reverse mentor"— he has some of his younger employees pushing his knowledge and use of apps and social media. It is nice to see someone in a leadership role showing he can learn from some of the newest employees.[22]

Whether it's technology or something else entirely, everything changes with time, and as I said, there is *always* something new to learn. So don't get too comfortable! Be a proactive, intentional learner. Be curious and seek out new experiences. Read widely, and regularly socialize and engage in conversations with people outside of your industry. Be willing to admit when you need help, and accept it when it's offered. I guarantee, when you choose to be a more teachable leader, you will become a much more effective, inspirational leader!

KEY POINTS

To be a more teachable leader:

- Retain the open and eager mindset of a beginner, no matter your level of experience.
- Be expectant and ready to learn from every situation and every person.
- Make every mistake or failure a learning experience.
- Remain committed to a lifelong journey of learning.

7

BE APPROACHABLE

"Employees, at all levels, have a hunger for leaders who are approachable and candid in their communications." [1] – *Mark J. Campbell*

Approachability is not something you can just claim. Some leaders might consider themselves approachable, but approachability is defined more by the perceptions of others than anything else. If your colleagues and employees do not feel you are approachable, then by virtue of the definition, they're right! Too often there exists in leadership an invisible barrier separating leaders from the people they lead. This detachment, whether intentional or not, results in far less employee engagement, trust, commitment, effectiveness, and overall success. This in turn significantly impacts the success of the leader and the organization as a whole.

Inspirational leaders break this unfortunate pattern by being genuinely approachable. They realize that no matter their industry, as leaders, they are in the "people business." And in order to thrive, people need the kind of connection and communication approachable leaders have to offer. Approachable, inspirational leaders:

- Know that being approachable is more than being accessible, and they rethink and redefine the trite term, "open door."
- Show genuine concern and respect for everyone, regardless of status or title.
- Welcome input and put people at ease by demonstrating an open and inviting demeanor.

- Are committed to being fully present and focused on individual conversations and tasks.

Only through genuine approachability can leaders overcome the invisible barrier between themselves and those they lead. And when that barrier is breached, people—and organizations—truly begin to flourish.

REDEFINE "OPEN DOOR"

I'm sure you're familiar with the term "open door policy," usually found buried somewhere in an organization's employee handbook or vaguely verbalized during new-hire orientation. The "open door" concept, as the term implies, is for leaders to leave their office doors open (literally or figuratively) to allow anyone in the organization to come in and voice concerns, ask questions, discuss issues, or offer suggestions. The idea is to promote greater accessibility, transparency, collaboration, and mutual respect between management and employees at every level. While nice in theory, official open door policies are often ineffective in practice—for a host of reasons. In an online article for *Inc.* magazine, entrepreneur Logan Chierotti said of the open door policy, "In the eyes of your employees, it's one of those throwaway buzzwords that management uses all the time, but never means."[2]

While I'm sure there are many organizations that have implemented excellent, effective open door policies, for the most part I believe Chierotti is exactly right. Many executives and senior leaders who claim to have an "open door" rarely see anyone outside of the C-suite walk through that door—literally or figuratively. Why? Because people in the organization don't feel as though the door is really open. No matter the official corporate policy or what was said during their orientation, countless employees perceive their most senior leaders as inaccessible, unavailable, and unapproachable.

> Approachability requires more than merely being present and expecting people to come to you.

Inspirational leaders recognize that approachability requires more than merely being present and expecting people to come to them. They take intentional steps to ensure they are truly accessible and available to people at every level of their organization. Curtis Rooney, founder and CEO of Glen Echo Strategies, notes that, "Approachable leaders break down the barriers that separate them from others. They have open doors and open routes to direct dialogue and communication. They answer their own phones or return calls themselves when they can. In little but significant ways they reinforce openness through their actions."[3] To put it simply, inspirational leaders don't just verbalize an open door policy, they demonstrate it. They typically don't even bother to say the words "open door policy." Instead, whether through an intentional conversation or simply by practicing consistent habits, they make it clear that they welcome interaction and encourage input from everyone in the organization.

One of the most obvious and key components of being truly approachable is to be physically accessible and available. But beyond having an open door and regular office hours, inspirational leaders make themselves even more accessible and available by purposefully leaving their office and interacting with employees throughout the organization. Cathy Eddy, president of Health Plan Alliance, explained that she's had a lot of executives tell her they have an open door policy. "But," she said, "I always thought that implicit in that statement is 'you come to me.'"[4] This version of an open door policy is stale and ineffective. Inspirational leaders use a different approach. As Logan Chierotti urges leaders in his *Inc.* magazine article, "Don't tell employees to feel free to walk into your office. Instead, free yourself to walk out of it."[5]

While doing the interview for this book, Christine Márquez-Hudson noted, "If you're going to be an approachable leader, you can't wait until people come to you. You have to go out and connect with people proactively." Those connections can be made in small, daily ways. It may be as simple as walking down the hall and saying good morning to people, asking them how their weekend was, how their kids are doing, or remembering to ask if their sick dog is getting better. It's those little things that help you come across as more approachable, and building that foundation makes a huge difference when it's time to really talk about something difficult. Christine, who at the time of our interview was the CEO and executive director of Mi Casa Resource Center in Denver, Colorado, went on to explain,

> We have four different sites here in Denver. So it's important for

me to get out to those different locations periodically. I have a regular schedule of visiting each site on a monthly basis just to stop in and chat with the staff and ask, "How's it going?" "What challenges are you confronting?" and just observe what's going on and talk to a few of the participants. I don't need to stay long, but it means a lot to my staff that I make the effort to see what they're doing, appreciate what they're doing, offer my support, connect with them—things like that. So I hope that when the going gets tough and they have an issue, they will feel they have a relationship with me and that they can come in and talk to me about it.[6]

When I asked him for his perspective on approachability in leadership, my good friend Jim "Big Red" Wetrich echoed Christine's thoughts on the importance of visibility and interaction with those you lead. He explained, "I truly believe, Dan, that inspirational leaders make their presence known throughout the organization. They're open, they're available, they're accessible, and they walk around and interact with everyone. It's an important truth that familiarity truly does build trust."[7] Jim definitely practices what he preaches. His former colleague Sanchia Patrick Rasul had this to say about Big Red's leadership:

> When I worked with Big Red, he was the highest ranking officer in the U.S. in our company. In my previous experience, it was commonplace not to see or interact with executives for months. But this all too common "Ivory Tower" never existed with Big Red. If he was in the office, you could expect to see him, hear his laughter, and benefit from a story, a new book, or a *Harvard Business Review* article he wanted to share. Big Red was and is not only fully present and approachable—he has the type of influence to cause others to fully engage.[8]

Like Jim Wetrich, my colleague Bruce Lawrence also agrees that familiarity builds trust, and "One's accessibility adds to one's credibility." Bruce explains, "The more that people see you, know you, and are comfortable around you, the more trust is established. And it gives you an opportunity to show a true interest in others, both on a work level and on a personal level... simple things like knowing someone's child has graduated from high school, or knowing that there's been a milestone in their life or their family's life that you can acknowledge. Not that you have to be intimately involved, but by acknowledging those things you can show them you care."⁹

A critical element of having a truly "open door" is to be genuine in your interactions with those you lead and everyone with whom you speak. Don't interact with people just because you're "supposed to," or grudgingly strike up conversations you don't actually want to have. As a leader, it is crucial that you develop sincere interest and concern for those you lead, and that you genuinely *engage* people, not just offer polite conversation, shallow pleasantries, or feigned attentiveness. My friend and colleague Sam Breneiser shared with me the following story and his candid observations about leaders with various levels of approachability:

> I once had the opportunity to meet a number of famous politicians here in California with one of my colleagues. His wife was busy and he had to attend a fundraiser for a state assemblyman, so he asked me to join him. It was a fascinating experience. I met city, county, state, and federal elected officials who I saw on television constantly. They were all gracious and polite, but varied widely in sincerity and warmth. All checked me out—some like a scanning machine, measuring me, assessing my value and relevance. Some obviously only greeted me because of my companion, while a very few others genuinely engaged me as a person. They were all elected leaders, and yet their ability to connect seemed to vary considerably.

Sam went on to say, "Merely meeting and acknowledging someone is not the same as actively engaging them. I think a leader who is genuinely approachable is one who is simply honest and brave enough to open themselves a little to each person they engage."¹⁰ Sam is exactly right. To be a genuinely approachable, inspirational leader, don't merely acknowledge and converse with others, truly engage others with openness and honesty. So get out of your office, avoid the "Ivory Tower," and redefine your open door policy. Remember, to be approachable, don't merely open your *door* to those whom you lead, open *yourself*.

> To be approachable, don't merely open your *door* to those whom you lead, open *yourself*.

Treat Everyone with Respect

Sam Breneiser's story about the polite politicians with thinly veiled indifference is a perfect example of leaders who failed to treat everyone with respect, no matter title or level of perceived importance. Many of the elected officials Sam met that night immediately wrote him off as someone of little worth to them and their own agendas. While they may not have treated him with obvious disdain, they also did not truly engage him or show any genuine interest in him as a person. They were all polite, and some may have even been charming and gracious, but courtesy does not equal respect, and charisma does not equal approachability.

In contrast, inspirational leaders are approachable by anyone, regardless of status or title. They show genuine interest and concern for everyone, and do their best to make time for each person with whom they interact. They show respect and appreciation for individuals' opinions, ideas, work, families, and time.

> "Most of the leaders I know who are really approachable have a genuine interest in others, get to know the people they work with, and pick up a lot from the conversations they have. It isn't hard to approach them with an issue when there is an established relationship... An approachable leader spends time with the team, collaborates with others, is out with customers, and has the capacity to listen." [11]
>
> – *Cathy Eddy*

Of course even the most inspirational leaders are still only human. They do have limited time and resources to engage every person and address every problem, and they do encounter people who are difficult to connect with, or who are downright unpleasant. Nonetheless, they see every person as innately valuable and worthy of their time, attention, and respect, and they do what they can to show interest and concern and to be responsive. It is this attitude of genuine respect and consideration that forms the foundation of true approachability.

In his book *The Mentor Leader*, author and former NFL coach Tony Dungy wrote: "Being available and approachable isn't always as easy as it might sound... Being available—available to teach, available to interact, available to care—also means being involved." It's a sad truth that some leaders actively avoid "getting involved" in the lives of those they lead. Yes, there are definitely lines that shouldn't be crossed, and there is wisdom in maintaining a certain level of professional distance, "But," Dungy went on to say, "by allowing others to approach you, and by being open to and sincerely welcoming interaction in your leadership role, you'll have the opportunity to relate to people on a much more meaningful basis. It will pay enormous dividends for you and your organization in both the short and long term."[12]

As Dungy implied, "being involved" is not simple or easy. The more you get to know people, the more of their burdens you begin to share. The more available and approachable you strive to be, the more your time and energy will be drained away by the needs of others. It's no wonder so many leaders choose stiff professionalism and cool detachment over the messy, exhausting work of being available and approachable by anyone and everyone! But Dungy is also completely correct when he states that being approachable will ultimately "pay enormous dividends for you and your organization in both the short and long term." And Dungy also writes, "Being available and approachable is necessary for effective leadership."[13] I absolutely agree. Being available and approachable really is necessary for effective and successful leadership, and really will result in a huge return on investment. When you are willing to get involved as a leader, and when you are committed to treating everyone with respect and consideration, you make huge strides toward establishing trust

> Leaders who are available, accessible, and approachable are the ones who truly inspire people.

and loyalty. And when trust and loyalty exist within an organization, commitment grows, energy rises, and productivity, profitability, and sustainability increase exponentially.

It is not surprising that throughout the many months of interviews and research I conducted for this book, when I asked people to define or describe an inspirational leader, one trait referenced over and over was "approachability." Though described using various terms, approachability really stood out as being a definitive characteristic of inspirational leaders. Leaders who are available, accessible, and approachable are the ones who truly inspire people. To put it simply, people want to follow and work for leaders who genuinely care, respect, and make time for them as individuals.

Curtis Rooney, who has long worked in the arena of public policy and is the former president of HSCA, has been repeatedly described as a leader who excels in the area of approachability. As I interviewed his colleagues, I noticed a reoccurring theme throughout their comments: Curtis treats everyone with equal respect, regardless of title or position. Jennifer Bell described Curtis as "an innately approachable person." She explained, "He is genuinely interested in the people he meets, and they respond to that. Whether someone is the CEO of a company or an assistant, Curtis treats everyone with the same level of respect and consideration."[14] Michael Payne described Curtis' leadership style and demeanor as one that "encourages and welcomes staff and others to engage, no matter their level. It's the consummate open door policy."[15] Fred Pane said of Curtis, "He is there for people. He's always been approachable, and he's very accessible—from the high end, the senators and congressmen, down to any member of an association. He understands the needs of others and really tries to meet as many needs as he can."[16] Bob Van Heuvelen noted that, "Curtis has a very natural conversational style with which he engages others, routinely and disarmingly connecting with his own organization's members and staff, as well as colleagues outside of his organization… Without question, Curtis is very approachable."[17]

When I asked my good friend and colleague Jack Lawless for his thoughts on approachable leaders, he responded, "The best leaders I ever worked for always made people feel like they were the priority, no matter who they were talking to—whether it was a senior executive, an hourly associate, or someone in the street. Whoever it was, they showed them respect and were completely involved with that person while they were having a conversation with them."[18] Jack himself has been described in those same terms by many of his colleagues. Michael Svagdis described Jack as having a "mindset of putting people first," and recalled how while Jack was division president at Morrison Management Specialists (a food service and hospitality company) any and all levels of associates could approach him to discuss their concerns without hesitation.[19] Ed Clark echoed that observation, noting how Jack always made himself available for discussion and kept an open mind. "If I had an issue, I felt very comfortable about approaching him."[20]

In addition to reducing the perceived "title gap" that so often deters people from approaching their senior leaders, Jack Lawless has also excelled in demonstrating his respect and appreciation for individual employees by intentionally making time to interact with them. Arthur Sparks recounted how, back when they worked together, Jack would spend the majority of his time "on the floor" of the business so he could interact and have face-to-face communication with everyone in the organization—not in a micro-managing sort of way, but in a genuine way that showed he valued each person. Arthur said of Jack, "Not only is he approachable by his team, but he encourages them to approach him, to reach out and communicate with him about whatever is on their minds."[21] Jay Niner adamantly agreed that Jack is "very approachable," and recalled how when checking in on regional offices Jack would always begin the day by just visiting with staff and employees. "He knew how important it was to ensure everyone felt comfortable with him and knew how much the company valued them. Half the time the conversation involved their families, such as kids and grandkids."[22] Scott Lewis said of Jack: "Those who know Jack know that he is highly approachable. He lives for interaction and engagement with his team." Scott went on to give an example of how Jack demonstrated his care and consideration for individuals:

> In providing food service and hospitality for healthcare facilities, the most important part of our business here at Morrison is our patients. To set the example, Jack would always ask the patient services managers to go rounding with him to check in on patients. This conveyed to those managers that 1) It's important for all leaders to make the patients their priority (i.e. walk the talk), and 2) Jack wanted to personally spend time with each manager.[23]

Another excellent example of an approachable, inspirational leader is my friend and colleague Traci Bernard, president of Texas Health Harris Methodist Hospital in Southlake, Texas. When answering the interview questions, Traci's colleagues simply couldn't say enough positive things about this remarkable leader. Laura Wahl described Traci as "the most inspirational leader I have ever had the pleasure of working for."[24] Jessica Hill said, "Traci inspires through the way she treats others. She shows respect and compassion to all she encounters every time, all the time. She is consistent, and that is so important as a leader."[25] Karen Adams noted that Traci leads by example, and is "positive, caring, and genuine."[26] Anthony Romero said of Traci, "She is absolutely an inspirational leader, and does a phenomenal job engaging, inspiring, and empowering those whom she leads… She makes time to interact with employees, and communicates with them on a regular basis."[27] Laura Redman eloquently summed up the general consensus regarding Traci's leadership by describing her own daily experience working with this remarkable leader:

> She is beyond what the typical definition would be for an inspirational leader. In my entire career, I have never had such a privilege, as I do now, to come to work each day and work for such a fantastic role model and leader. Traci always exudes positivity and leads with an uplifting calm that permeates through the halls of the hospital and influences everyone she comes into contact with. She knows every single person's name. She remembers stories staff and physicians share with her, and she follows up on them when she sees them. Her door is always open and she will stop whatever she is doing to talk with anyone who comes by her office. Everyone feels valued here. We all feel special. We all feel at home. We are family. And it starts with Traci.[28]

From the testimony of their colleagues and direct reports, it is obvious that these three inspirational leaders—Curtis Rooney, Jack Lawless, and Traci Bernard—treat all whom they lead and all with whom they interact with a great level of genuine respect and consideration. In turn, they have earned their colleagues' respect, appreciation, and loyalty. Like these leaders, you also can demonstrate to those you lead that you respect and value each of them through small but significant gestures and everyday actions, such as knowing individuals' names, verbalizing appreciation for their work, intentionally making time to speak with them, and following up on stories they've shared.

DEMONSTRATE AN APPROACHABLE DEMEANOR

Beyond making themselves accessible and available to those they lead, inspirational leaders also demonstrate an approachable demeanor. This means that their behavior and attitude is open and inviting toward others, welcoming input and putting people at ease. Approachable, inspirational leaders are intentional and very aware of how they come across to others, and they continually strive to make people feel comfortable and relaxed in their presence.

One of the simplest but most important ways you can improve your approachability is to be more conscious of your body language and the nonverbal messages you send. Leaders are taught to exude confidence—to sit or stand up straight, square their shoulders, make eye contact, and speak with a powerful, resonant voice. This is good advice, but not necessarily good for every situation. If you want those you lead to approach and open up to you with confidence, then you may need to temper your own confident behavior in order not to intimidate. *Forbes* magazine contributor Stephen J. Meyer wrote an article about how leaders' confident behavior can actually hamper their effectiveness by stifling communication and preventing honest feedback. Meyer noted that by employing behavioral cues that make you look smart and competent, you might cause others to clam up. "So what's this mean to you as a team leader, or a senior executive?" he asks, "It means that if you want your team to 'dial up' its participation and feedback, you need to 'dial back' on the behavioral cues that make you seem confident."[29]

Of course, dialing back your confident posture doesn't mean you should swing to the other extreme and slouch down in your chair, hunch your shoulders, avoid eye contact, or quietly mumble your words. That extreme does not communicate approachability either. But you can strive to be more aware of the effect your body language has on others, and start with the most basic nonverbal cue: *smile*. While this should be obvious, it's astounding how many leaders unconsciously neglect this basic tenet of approachability. Some people seem to be blessed with a per-

> **Start with the most basic nonverbal cue: *smile*.**

petual, genuine smile on their faces. But for many people, smiling is something they have to consciously make an effort to do. It's not that they are unhappy or unpleasant people, but for whatever reason, their faces tend to settle into expressions a little south of smiling. I happen to be one of those people. When my mind is elsewhere or I am focusing on something, I can often look serious, stern, or even somber. So I know firsthand how important it is to make a point to smile—throughout a conversation, not just in greeting. Smiling not only makes you look friendlier and more relaxed, it immediately puts others at ease. So to appear more approachable and open, start by smiling. Also avoid signals that can make you look closed off, distracted, or bored, such as tightly crossing your arms, looking down, or glancing at your watch or mobile phone.

Peter Fine, president and CEO of Banner Health, is a very confident leader who realizes the importance of being aware of how others perceive him. Peter explained, "I consider myself an approachable leader, but I'm not sure everybody considers me approachable. I realize I'm a big guy with a hard voice, and I can be intimidating to people before they get to know me." Peter went on to say that he consciously strives to come across as more approachable, noting that, "The ability to demonstrate being approachable is, in my mind, the ability to allow yourself to be vulnerable. You have to open yourself up, be vulnerable, and be responsive. I try to give that impression of approachability by encouraging a lot of interactions, getting out in front of people, and being willing to answer any and all questions."[30]

As Peter noted, being vulnerable, open, and willing to answer any question, is an important aspect of approachability. Approachable leaders should make it clear that no topic is off limits. Bruce Lawrence, president and CEO of INTEGRIS Health, was described by his colleague Beth Pauchnik as a leader who "actively communicates and behaves in a way that demonstrates no subject is off limits for discussion."[31] Chris Hammes echoed that observation, saying, "Bruce has an open door, is always available when needed, and creates a safe environment to ask questions and discuss any topic, no matter how difficult the subject matter may be."[32] This is a critical element of being truly approachable. Those you lead need to know they can broach any topic, and that you will welcome and answer their questions, listen and respond to their concerns, and respect and consider their input. They should not only feel as though they have permission to approach you with anything, but that they can do so without judgment or repercussions, and that they can walk away comfortably and return confidently. As Christine Márquez-Hudson explained, "Your team needs to know that when something goes wrong, or they're struggling, or they're confronting a significant challenge, that you're there to support them, not to criticize them."[33]

Be Fully Present

Closely related to the practice of demonstrating an approachable demeanor is another key aspect of approachability: being "fully present." With increasingly hectic and demanding schedules, leaders tend to function in a state of perpetual distraction. Whether it's due to physical distractions caused by people, technology, or environment, or due to a mind full of priorities and concerns, many people—and leaders in particular—struggle with being fully present and focused on individual conversations and tasks.

To this day multitasking is still considered by most people to be a beneficial and coveted skill. The more things you can do at once the more productive and efficient you are, right? While that sounds nice, the reality is that multitasking is essentially a myth. With the exception of "autopilot" behaviors, like walking or chewing gum, most of what we consider to be multitasking is really just task *switching*; and switching your focus and attention back and forth between tasks or other stimuli is inefficient at best. The more tasks you attempt to juggle, the more your productivity goes *down*, not up.

Common examples of "multitasking" include reading and sending emails while in a meeting, talking on the phone while holding a child and cooking dinner, watching television while texting a friend and doing homework, or checking social media on your phone while having dinner and holding a conversation with your spouse. No matter how skilled you believe you are at simultaneously juggling these kinds of physical or mental activities, the reality is that no one does this well. And unfortunately, many tasks that people and leaders attempt to juggle include interactions and conversations with other people. The impression this leaves isn't one of efficiency, but of distraction. Beyond inefficient, the results and consequences of this kind of "multitasking" are often negative or even disastrous.

Inspirational leaders are by no means immune to the temptation to "multitask." With so much needing to be done, it may seem impossible (and even irresponsible) to direct energy and attention to only *one* thing at a time. But that ability to be fully present and give your undivided attention—especially when interacting with others—is critically important for true approachability. It takes great discipline and intentionality as a leader to be mindful and fully engaged in the present moment, but the consequences of not being fully present can be extremely destructive to your impact and credibility and the relationships you have with employees, colleagues, and customers.

Cathy Eddy told me a story about a particular company president. Whenever she happened to pass by him she always offered a friendly greeting, but he rarely ever acknowledged her. After this happened a few times, she mentioned it to a colleague, who offered this analogy: "This leader is like a person with a pen light in a dark stadium full of people. When he focuses the light on someone, he can see that person clearly, but doesn't see anyone else around him." While this analogy helped Cathy realize that she shouldn't take the lack of acknowledgment as a personal affront, it was also a sad assessment of a leader who failed to be fully present within the halls of his organization. He apparently had great focus, but at the cost of not noticing what was going on right in front of him.[34]

We all have had interactions with distracted leaders at some point. Whether it was a greeting in the hallway that went unnoticed, a conversation in their office where they appeared to be talking to their computer screen instead of you, or a meeting in which they paid more attention to their smartphone than to whoever was speaking, it is all too common to observe leaders who appear distracted and disconnected from what is happening in the present moment. While moments of distraction are inevitable, those moments shouldn't become the norm for anyone, and especially not for leaders. To be a leader who truly inspires others, you must give people priority, respecting their time and contributions by disconnecting from distractions and committing to be fully present whenever with them.

Probably the most important way in which inspirational leaders practice being fully present is by being patient and attentive listeners, both one-on-one and in group settings. In response to a question about how leaders demonstrate being fully present, Sam Breneiser told me a story from his own experience:

> My own lesson in this regard was provided by a very bright and kind physician who I was negotiating with early in my career. After about thirty minutes of talking we were getting to the meat of the conversation. After I explained some terms in the contract I was presenting, he began to speak for a minute, then stopped and looked at me for a second and said, 'Are you listening to me, or thinking about what you are going to say next?' It took me completely by surprise that he could read my mind like that, but he really wanted to make a point and it really mattered to him that I actually heard him. And I did.

Sam went on to say that ever since he received that gentle but direct admonition from his colleague, he has strived to always fully listen to the person speaking, and not let his own thoughts distract him. He also is very intentional about not interrupting, cutting off, or otherwise disrupting the other speaker's train of thought. "I once had someone tell me that they feel smarter after talking to me because I let them finish speaking," Sam said. "I think they meant I respect their own intelligence because I don't presume to cut them off and finish their thought for them in my own manner. It's sort of a version of the old adage that the best salesman is the one who knows when to shut up."[35]

Lisa Hill, the executive director of Invest in Kids, shared a similar learning experience about the importance of listening:

> For me, being fully present has been about learning how to listen. I have a staff member who reminded me at one point that I have two ears and one mouth, so I need to be listening twice as much as I'm talking—which was not my M.O. before. That has been a really powerful lesson for me. Because I'm going a million miles an hour, and I'm always sort of anticipating what's next—strategizing and analyzing and thinking. I still struggle with it, because my mind struggles to slow. It takes discipline, and it takes practice.

Lisa went on to explain that she has always been rewarded for being "quick on her feet," for having quick answers, getting things done, and being responsive. "Quite frankly, until recent years I had not really felt rewarded by just being and hearing and listening, so I didn't always prioritize that," Lisa said. "It has been a challenge for me, but it's important, because that's what I think it means to be fully present."[36]

Like Sam and Lisa, approachable, fully present leaders strive to listen fully, with patience and understanding. Thoughtful and deliberate in their responses, they show genuine interest and concern for the person with whom they are speaking. They do not patronize or act superior or condescending. While maintaining authority and demonstrating prudence and honesty, inspirational leaders also speak with optimism, striving to encourage and provide hope, kindness, and understanding to those they lead.

Listening, of course, isn't limited only to one-on-one conversations. In the business world, group meetings are a fact of life. They happen every week or even every day, and they can often be tedious—to put it mildly. Some people call meetings a "necessary evil." Evil or not, they *are* necessary, and leaders more than anyone must attend them. Due to the frequency and tedium of meetings, the temptation to check email on your phone or simply let your mind wander is quite high. But inspirational leaders realize the importance of remaining fully present in meetings, paying attention and showing respect for the time and contributions of others. When a leader fails to do this, the negative impact reverberates around the room and throughout the organization.

> Give people priority, respecting their time and contributions by disconnecting from distractions and committing to be fully present whenever with them.

Jack Lawless told me a story about a meeting with a particular client organization whose leader had insisted on being there, since the meeting included a big presentation. To begin with, the leader came in about thirty minutes late. He then proceeded to spend almost the entire time on his phone responding to emails. "My thought at the time was it's almost like walking in with your physical in-basket in front of you, dropping it down and working through your correspondence. Or walking in and opening up a newspaper and reading the news of the day," Jack said. "You would never do that because it's rude; but a lot of people don't think twice about using their mobile device throughout a meeting." Jack went on to note,

> He wasn't only disrespectful to us as an organization trying to partner with him, he was disrespectful to his entire team who had to wait for him, giving their time to this meeting. He allowed

whatever was going on in his life to distract him so much that he didn't hear anything. Even if he did somehow take in the essence of the presentation, his behavior left us with a feeling that if we went forward and partnered with this guy we were going to have a challenge, because he didn't value us the same as he did everyone else, and he didn't value his team the same way he valued himself.

The negative impression and lasting consequences of that leader's behavior is an all too common scenario. But often leaders don't feel as though they have a choice, circumstances seem to demand that they give their attention to multiple people or activities at once. After telling the above story, Jack Lawless related another story, about the regional managers within his organization. Many of these managers were chastised for spending too much time on the phone or computer when out visiting the locations within their areas of responsibility, instead of spending quality time with that local team. "What we found though, in many cases we were creating the circumstances that caused those managers to spend so much time on the phone and computer," Jack said. "We were setting up conference calls, and giving deadlines for reporting that basically meant they had to take that time away from their visits." That realization triggered an organizational shift that resulted in extended deadlines for reporting, and mandated time each day free from conference calls. "Because if you travel two, three, four hours to get somewhere and then you don't spend any time with that team, A), it's a wasted trip and wasted dollars, and B), it sends a message to every hourly associate, every supervisor, every manager in that organization—as well as the clients—that you're not really concerned about them."[37]

Bruce Lawrence, the president and CEO of INTEGRIS Health, echoed Jack's sentiments, adding, "I can't tell you how easy it is to get distracted as a leader, especially when you're in a meeting… staying fully engaged and focused, looking around the room, etc." Similar to Jack's organization, INTEGRIS recognized the importance of facilitating more "fully-present" moments for their teams and leaders. They have a policy that unless it's an absolute emergency, mobile phones are not to be used in meetings—so no checking emails or answering text messages. "And as the leader, it has to start with me," Bruce said, "If they see me on mine, I've blown that rule, and everybody's going to do what I do. I think that's really important."[38]

Limiting distractions and giving your undivided attention to those around you is difficult, requiring great discipline and intentionality. But when leaders do focus their attention on those they lead, they demonstrate that they respect the time and contributions of each individual, making them feel they are valued and important. The resulting return on investment is incredible.

KEY POINTS

To be a more approachable leader:

- Be more than just accessible; rethink and redefine your "open door policy."
- Show genuine concern and respect for everyone, regardless of their status or title.
- Welcome input and put people at ease by demonstrating an open and inviting demeanor.
- Commit to being fully present and focused on individual conversations and tasks.

8

BE RESPONSIVE

"Effective leadership isn't about having power over people, it's about doing good for people."[1] — *Bill Treasurer*

If you were to look up synonyms for the word *responsive*, you would find a list that includes terms like *active, aware, compassionate, conscious, receptive,* and *sympathetic*. Inspirational leaders truly embody this. They recognize that responsiveness takes courage and determination, and it also takes compassion and discretion. To be responsive means to be decisive, assertive, and not afraid to take action and get things done. But it also means to be compassionate, sympathetic, and willing to make sacrifices. Responsive leaders:

- Stay alert, recognizing and quickly responding to needs.
- Follow through on their commitments, communicating throughout the process about what's going on.
- Do what they can to prevent conflict from happening, but when it does happen, they address it quickly and ensure it is resolved appropriately.
- "Look outside the box," recognizing that true responsiveness encompasses organizational as well as individual needs, and the long term as much as the urgent.
- Are careful to maintain their own energy and passion in order to be ready and able to respond to the needs of others.

In short, responsive leaders are dynamic—characterized by energy and effective action that not only achieves results but also inspires and energizes those they lead.

Be Alert, Available, and Proactive

As indicated by the list above, responsiveness is about *awareness* and *action*, and leaders who are aware and active—first recognizing need, then readily taking action to respond to that need—are the ones who are truly inspirational. The first step toward responsiveness is being alert and able to recognize need. One way in which responsive leaders do this is by being intent and observant listeners. Inspirational leaders not only listen well, they learn to hear what's not being said, to interpret body language, and to pick up on subtle indicators of need. They are active and engaged listeners, consciously avoiding distractions and the temptation to let their thoughts wander. Jack Lawless describes responsive listening like this:

> It's making sure that you fully listen to that individual, whether it be an associate, a peer, or a customer. So that means not just sitting passively in the conversation or on the call, but being engaged and fully understanding their challenges, being able to verbalize what their challenges are, and even repeating what they said back to them, making sure you're on the same page.[2]

Responsive, inspirational leaders are also careful to avoid only hearing what they want to hear, making sure to seek out varied perspectives, opinions, ideas, and feedback. Jennifer Bell, who worked with Curtis Rooney when he was president of HSCA, described him as just such a leader, noting, "He really thrives in situations where everyone is contributing their ideas and thoughts." She explains, "He does not want to be surrounded by 'yes men,' and instead prefers to hold discussions with team members who hold a variety of opinions."[3] My friend and colleague Joel Allison, CEO of Baylor Scott & White Health, agrees with this perspective, noting, "Responsive leaders are inclusive; they value others' thoughts and opinions."[4]

Another aspect of responsiveness and being alert and tuned in to the needs of others is to be proactive in seeking out those needs. Dr. Mark Kehrberg, former CMO at Ministry Health Care, told me that former president and CEO Dan Neufelder made a habit of closing one-on-one meetings with his direct reports with the question, "What do you need, and what can I do for you?" Mark explained, "There wasn't a meeting where that didn't happen. Dan is clearly invested in each of his direct reports and what they need to be successful. He certainly is a leader who serves others and always leads by example."[5] Another leader well known for her commitment to meeting the needs of her team and her organization is hospital president Traci Bernard. Traci's colleague Laura Wahl told me that when Traci rounds the hospital, she calls everyone by name, and if she sees anyone in need of assistance, whether an individual or a department, she is the first person to ask, "What can I do to help you?" Laura explained, "Traci leads by example, always. There is never a moment that she asks of you something that she would not do herself. Traci has stood beside me many times stuffing binders, folding letters, or getting gifts ready during National Hospital Week. And she breeds this culture throughout the hospital."[6]

As we discussed in the previous chapter, one key element of being an approachable leader is being available to those you lead. The same is true of responsiveness. To be a responsive leader, you must make yourself available for people to bring questions, concerns, suggestions, and various needs to you. Joel Allison is a great example of a leader who excels in this way, continually seeking out needs and making himself available to everyone within his organization. Baylor's chief legal officer Steve Boyd noted that Joel is available to his coworkers on a 24/7 basis, and that he finds time to meet and truly listen to all with whom he works. "He is very organized, and always follows up with everyone who has a need."[7] Gary Brock, executive vice president at Baylor Scott & White, described Joel in a similar way, and explained that he has an internal website called "Ask Joel," where any employee in the organization can send him questions, complaints, suggestions, etc.

> Joel personally reviews every message and personally responds back to the sender in writing on a timely basis. This disciplined response also applies to all his internal and external letters, emails, telephone calls, as well as any comments or questions that he receives during meetings or while rounding. Furthermore, when others express an unpleasant comment or complaint, Joel doesn't reprimand or correct them or otherwise react in an emotional manner. Instead, he listens to their perspective, calmly explains the situation, and explains why their perceptions are not in alignment

with what he believes the situation to be and what he expects will be the situation going forward.[8]

Of course, as mentioned in the previous chapter, it's not reasonable or realistic to believe that every leader can be available to everyone all of the time, or that every leader can respond to every need all of the time. That's simply not possible. However, responsive, inspirational leaders do make a conscious effort to be available and aware, proactively anticipating and readily responding to needs to the best of their ability. As a leader, are you being alert to, available for, and ready to meet needs? Be proactive, and be responsive!

Follow Up and Follow Through

Dealing with customer service or tech support can sometimes be a nightmare. Whether in person, over the phone, or online, once you've submitted your question, complaint, or plea for help, it's usually a long waiting game and often convoluted process to get a response or solution. You might be drumming your fingers on the customer service counter while waiting for the manager to finally materialize, or sitting at your desk listening to obnoxious hold music and advertisements, or anxiously checking and rechecking your email for that long-awaited message that hopefully contains the response you're seeking. None of us like that kind of waiting game. I think the worst part of that kind of waiting is that you're almost always waiting on additional communication. You're not just waiting for the answer or solution. Yes, that's the ultimate goal, but you're also stuck in the dark, so to speak, not knowing what—if anything—is being done to address your problem. That kind of waiting is very frustrating.

If you've ever been in one of those situations—and I'm sure you have—then you know how much of a game changer communication can be. There is a huge difference between "please hold," and "I'm sorry for the wait, but can you please hold for about five minutes while I find your file in the system and get that discount applied to your account?" The behind-the-scenes effort and eventual resolution in those two scenarios may be identical, but the experience is drastically different. The difference? Communication. Simply by letting you know they're working on it and by giving a basic explanation of what they're doing, customer service reps can significantly change your perspective and overall satisfaction with the experience—almost regardless of the outcome.

The same holds true in leadership. Every day leaders are faced with new challenges, questions, problems, and needs. And attached to nearly every one of those issues are people who are waiting on a response. Leaders are daily tasked with this prioritizing and delegating and problem solving, all while balancing the expectations and desires of the people whom those decisions affect. So communication is critical. There are of course entire books—thousands of them—dedicated to the topic of communication. In fact, at the time of this writing, you can search the key word *communication* in the "books" department of Amazon, and get over 350,000 results. So it is not my intent to delve deeply into this enormous topic here. However, I want to stress the importance of communication as part of being a responsive, inspirational leader.

To begin with, responsive leaders promptly acknowledge a need or request, ensuring that those involved know that their need has been recognized and something is being done about it. If you've ever sent an email or left a voice message and waited hours, days, or even weeks to receive a reply, you understand the value of a prompt response. Even if an immediate resolution is not possible, that basic acknowledgement of the need is an important first step. After that initial contact, another key component of being responsive is to follow up regularly. Just as lack of communication can sour an otherwise positive customer service outcome, lack of communication can diminish a leader's efforts in responding to a need. By failing to communicate about what they are doing to address a problem, leaders risk losing the confidence of those depending on them to help. No matter how quickly and appropriately you begin working on resolving a need, if those involved don't know how or if you're doing something about it, then you will not be perceived as responsive, which can have major ramifications to your influence and effectiveness. Likewise, just as good communication can soften a less than ideal customer service outcome, it can also help in leadership situations where you cannot deliver the preferred solution or response. Either way, following up and communicating regularly throughout the process is an essential part of responsive leadership.

As my friend Jack Lawless noted, even leaders with great intentions can still drop the ball when it comes to communicating, so it's important to be specific and set a time for follow up. "Always set a specific time for follow up; say, 'I'll get back to you by next Tuesday,' or 'I'll get back to you this afternoon,' or whatever the timeframe is, and make certain that you're doing that. Set an alarm, put it on your calendar; make it happen." Jack went on to say that even if you delegate tasks to someone else, it is still important that you as the leader check back in and make sure the issue has been or is being resolved—not just for the sake of ensuring a resolution, but also for the sake of communicating with anyone involved. He explained,

> At times early on in my career I would take care of a problem or need but not necessarily follow back up to say I took care of it, and the individual would miss it. I may have truly resolved it, but without closing the loop they didn't know I did it, so it was essentially wasted effort. Later I learned to always follow up, multiple times if needed. I might have resolved the issue the day that they asked for it, but the next time I saw them I would make sure it was still resolved. Even a year later, depending on what the issue was, I'd again ask if it was still resolved, making sure they knew it was still on the top of my mind, and that when I thought of them I tried to make sure I was taking care of whatever their issues or concerns were.[9]

As Jack implies, following up is as much about building trust and developing a cooperative relationship as it is about achieving tangible results. And Jack is a man who knows what he is talking about; he excels in building connections and earning the respect of those he leads. Every one of his colleagues I interviewed had nothing but praise for Jack and his passionate and responsive leadership. Scott Lewis described Jack as the most responsive leader he has ever known, saying he could always expect immediate responses to emails, even at night, and calls always returned within a few hours. "And most importantly, Jack always followed up on a timely basis on those items he could not resolve immediately."[10] Arthur Sparks described Jack in the same way, telling me he didn't recall a single time when he had a question or concern and Jack did not either immediately make himself available, or ensure that they scheduled a time to talk soon.[11] I also learned that in addition to consistent emails and phone calls, Jack also makes a habit of periodically checking in with people by sending personal handwritten notes. It's that kind of simple but significant gesture that makes a leader stand out as responsive and invested in the lives and needs of those he or she leads.

Hand in hand with regular communication and follow-up is the commitment to consistently follow through on whatever actions you have promised to take. This is critical. Without follow-through, true responsiveness is impossible. There are far too many leaders who publicly "respond" to a need, make big promises, and then fail to deliver on those promises. That's not responsiveness, and that is most definitely not inspirational leadership. In discussing responsive leadership during our interview, Bruce Lawrence said, "You really have to do what you say you're going to do, and in a timely manner. If you tell someone that you're going to do something by Friday morning at 8:00, do it by Friday morning at 8:00. Be consistent, and be dependable."[12]

> Without follow-through, true responsiveness is impossible.

Of course not every resolution works out perfectly, and there are times when leaders simply aren't able to follow through on what they said they would do. In situations like those, communication and follow-up are absolutely vital. Lorna Shaw also emphasized the importance of fulfilling the expectations that you set, saying, "Not doing so is not okay." But she quickly followed that by saying, "Oh my goodness, things change all the time! If you're not able to deliver on what you originally said you were going to do, that's okay—as long as you're communicating along the way why or why not."[13] She's right—things do change, and no matter your intentions and efforts, you will not be able to follow through exactly as promised in every situation. But by regularly following up and consistently communicating throughout the process as you find another resolution, you will still set an example and make an impression as a responsive and dependable leader.

Prevent and Resolve Conflict

Another component of responsive, inspirational leadership is actively preventing and resolving conflict. Responsive leaders take intentional steps to help avoid conflict from ever happening. They also learn to recognize the signs when conflict is brewing, and proactively respond to those indicators before the conflict really erupts. And when conflict does happen, they respond quickly and appropriately—acting with decisive authority when needed, but also respecting the ability and responsibility of direct reports to handle some areas of conflict themselves.

One key way in which responsive leaders prevent conflict is by doing their part to not cause it. They realize the significance of seemingly small details and how a careless statement, critical comment, misdirected praise, overlooked indiscretion, or forgotten thank you can get under someone's skin and begin to chafe and cause friction. As a leader, it is critical that you respond quickly and appropriately to the variety of situations and events that come across your desk—literally or figuratively. Not doing so can cause unnecessary discord, which is distracting and often damaging. Here are a few examples of responsive actions you can take as a leader to help prevent conflict:

- **Give credit where credit is due**. As a leader, you should not only give credit whenever it is warranted, but should also pay careful attention to where that credit is going; when showing appreciation or rewarding work well done, be mindful and careful to direct appropriate credit to the right individuals. Misplaced credit can quickly stir up resentment and discord among coworkers.
- **Give private criticism and public praise**. Constructive criticism is a necessary part of growth, and giving it is an important responsibility of every leader. But in almost every scenario—with the exception of certain team settings—negative feedback is better delivered one-on-one. On the flipside, praise and appreciation should be given openly; public recognition not only honors individuals, it reinforces work well done for everyone in the organization and reinforces your credibility as a leader who is engaged and aware of what's going on in the organization.
- **Provide help whenever asked**. Whether you involve yourself directly, delegate to someone else, or find an alternative resolution, always respond promptly to requests for assistance. Delaying or neglecting to respond to an email, return a phone call, or schedule a meeting is an invitation for misunderstanding and discontent.

- **Don't make snap judgments.** As a leader you must be quick on your feet and able to quickly assess situations. However, you should avoid making snap judgments—good or bad—regarding people's behavior. Hold your tongue, check your emotions, and get the facts first. A critical comment or careless statement can fester and cause more damage than you might think.
- **Don't overlook misconduct.** While you shouldn't "rule with an iron fist," you should also be cautious about letting too many things slide. Seemingly minor indiscretions can soon add up to substantial grievances within your organization, creating big headaches for you as the leader. Avoid this by dealing with misconduct promptly and tactfully on a case-by-case basis. Use discretion, understanding that your actions will have ramifications not only for the individual(s) involved, but also for your organization as a whole.
- **Communicate, communicate, communicate.** Jeff Haden said it well: "Exceptional bosses know the key to showing employees they are consistent and fair is communication: The more employees understand why a decision was made, the less likely they are to assume unfair treatment or favoritism."[14] Perceived "unfairness" is probably the number one catalyst for conflict, so clearly communicating the rationale behind your decisions and actions will help keep the peace.

As much as I'd like to say that following the above advice is the key to leading a conflict-free life, it's not that simple. No matter how hard you work to prevent conflict, inevitably it will still happen. Whether caused inadvertently by something you did or did not do, or caused by something out of your control, conflict is a fact of every leader's life. No matter the source, when discord does happen, or someone brings a conflict to your attention, it falls to you as the leader to manage, resolve, and transform it. How you do that has the potential to set you apart as a responsive, inspirational leader.

I recall a situation early in my career as the CEO of a new, rapidly growing hospital. Like most hospitals, we had a substantial body of volunteers, mostly made up of kindhearted retirees who generously and faithfully gave of their time and energy to fill in the gaps and keep the hospital running smoothly. But as is the case with any group of people—no matter how sweet—conflict still happens. One day a few concerned volunteers asked to meet with me to discuss a particular situation. Upon having a seat in my office, they launched into an explanation of what was going on, laying it all out before me and seeking advice for handling the delicate situation. I patiently and attentively listened to their story, and then talked through some possible resolutions, helping them come to a decision as to how to proceed. My response was not remarkable. I didn't give any earth-shattering insights, nor assert my authority to take matters into my own hands. Yet my sincere interest, willingness to listen, and thoughtful advice made all the difference in the world to those volunteers and the others involved in the situation. Had I declined to meet with them, passed their problem off for someone else to deal with, or made a quick assessment and cursory diagnosis of the issue, the results and lasting impact of that conflict would have been completely different.

Traci Bernard shared a story with me that demonstrates another important element of responsive leadership and conflict transformation—especially when you are directly involved in the conflict: approaching conflict from the other side's perspective. She explained how her administration had been struggling with getting routine documents signed by some of the hospital's physicians. The process was ineffective and frustrating for the administration, as that paperwork simply must be done. However, instead of putting her foot down and demanding the physicians sign the documents on the administration's timetable, Traci realized she needed to see it from the physicians' perspective as well. In order to better understand the situation, she asked one of the key physicians to describe his schedule and talk her through his day, so they could determine when the documents should be made available to make it work best for him—and ultimately for everyone. As it turned out, people had been stopping the physicians between cases to have them sign the documents, and Traci quickly realized that interruption was an unnecessary irritant and distraction. Because of that realization, a more effective and mutually beneficial method for dealing with the paperwork was soon agreed

> "To inspire people... you've got to live in their world, put their shoes on, and understand where they're coming from."
> – Traci Bernard

upon, virtually eliminating the conflict. Traci noted, "To inspire people to do the right thing and to get things done, you've got to live in their world, put their shoes on, and understand where they're coming from. That's the only way to make that process successful."[15]

Effective conflict resolution requires alertness, patience, careful consideration of the details, and sensitivity to the needs of everyone involved. It is impossible to be a responsive leader without carefully handling and ultimately transforming conflict, both internally within your organization as well as externally with clients or customers. As a leader, you must address conflict quickly before it causes lasting damage to relationships, morale, and organizational success. As Harla Adams put it, "Positive responsiveness takes effort, takes time, takes being willing to stop what you are doing and respond positively and quickly to those around you."[16]

Look Outside the Box

It's important to realize that responsive leadership is not limited only to individuals' needs or to urgent responses. While that is certainly a large part of the daily leadership experience, there are subtler, growing needs throughout an organization that require responsiveness as well. Responsive, inspirational leaders must "look outside the box," staying alert and tuned in to the life of their organization as a whole, and looking for and responding to needs at every level—both inside and outside the walls of their organization.

When things seem to be going well, it is easy to accept the status quo and become complacent and less alert. But as I like to say, "The one guarantee in life is this: 'things change!'" Change is not only guaranteed, but also necessary. Without change, growth and improvement is virtually impossible. So to be a responsive leader, you must be vigilant, looking for needed change and opportunities for improvement—personally, professionally, and organizationally.

Marc Gelinas shared a story with me about how Don Arnwine, former chairman and CEO of VHA (now Vizient), recognized and responded to the gradual changes happening within his growing organization:

> Don recognized that we had grown from a management team of
> five people to a management group of nearly fifty in a very short

time, and there were obvious elements of fragmentation in the cultural fabric. We had felt like a very cohesive group in the first few years, but the sudden and rapid growth of the organization made us worry that we were losing that cohesiveness and sense of camaraderie. With some people scattered around the country in regional offices, we weren't sure what to do about it. Don shared his senior management's concern, so he initiated a three-day planning retreat for the entire management group at a resort location. He had the meeting organizers plan a series of team-building exercises that led to people getting to know each other in different ways. The appreciation we gained for each other generated a remarkable boost in morale, trust, and eagerness to work more closely together.[17]

In addition to recognizing and responding to emerging and growing needs within their organizations, responsive leaders also act on things they learn and discover through books, podcasts, media outlets, conversations, and various other channels. While at Mölnlycke Health Care as president and general manager over the Americas, Jim "Big Red" Wetrich served on the board of The White House Project, a nonprofit organization designed to help advance women's leadership in communities, business, and politics. Inspired by his experience on that board, as well as by an article in the *McKinsey Quarterly* addressing the slow progress of gender diversity and equality in the workplace, Jim decided to do something tangible to help support and advance the careers and leadership of the women within his organization. So he created an annual event, called the Women at Mölnlycke Summit.

The first Summit took place in May 2013, with Mölnlycke paying all expenses to fly in every female employee in the U.S. organization to the two-day conference held in Dallas, Texas. The event featured nationally renowned female speakers as well as some of Mölnlycke's own, and addressed a diverse array of topics, including external and internal barriers women face in the workplace, strategies for career development, the unique ways in which men and women communicate, and the importance and impact of mentors. Sanchia Patrick Rasul, a speaker at the event, and senior project manager at Mölnlycke at the time, said of the Summit, "I watched hundreds of women connect, network, and gain critical knowledge to support their careers. We will all remember that event—it was life-giving."[18] Jim himself said,

The event engaged our female colleagues in topics of communication, networking, and personal life stories of other successful women. After the two-day event, the ladies walked away feeling empowered, and many stepped forward afterwards seeking promotions or other opportunities that they had thought were not within their capabilities before. It was an unbelievable meeting, and the results have been just dramatic.[19]

Another way in which responsive, inspirational leaders "look outside the box," is by finding ways to respond to needs in their communities and beyond. They do this personally as well as professionally and organizationally, modeling responsiveness for those they lead. Dan Neufelder, founder and CEO of The Neufelder Consulting Group and former president and CEO of Ministry Health Care, was described by his colleague Tom Veeser as being very active in the community: "Whether it's through United Way, by serving on agency boards, or serving people directly through the emergency shelter, his church, or other organizations, at every level Dan is very active and responsive to the needs around him."[20]

Curtis Rooney is another leader described by his colleagues as responsive—not only within his own organization and among the clients he serves, but also in charitable pursuits. His colleague Michael Payne described Curtis as having "boundless energy," marveling at his work ethic and commitment both in and outside his organization.[21] In 2007 Curtis and his wife helped found the Children of Kibera Foundation, which has since provided hundreds of educational scholarships for impoverished children living in one of the largest slums in Africa. The foundation merged with The Kenya Education Fund in late 2013, but the Rooneys continue to be very involved. Curtis' colleague Bob Van Heuvelen noted, "Curtis embraces challenges in the work environment and in his outside life, always motivated by his fervent desire to prompt positive change in our world."[22] I believe this "desire to prompt positive change" is a hallmark of truly responsive, inspirational leaders.

Maintain Your Energy

My friend Dr. Keith Lepak, a board certified emergency room physician, explained how in the medical field the most urgent and stressful events doctors and nurses must respond to are the hospital emergency codes, such as "Code Blue," which generally indicates respiratory or cardiac arrest. Keith said, "There's an old saying: 'during a code check your own pulse first; if you find it, then everything else is easy.' This sounds glib, but sometimes the best thing we can do to lead the resuscitation team is to stay calm."[23] As Keith noted, while the saying is facetious, its premise holds some truth: to be able to respond well to the needs of others, you must first make sure you are functioning well yourself.

The same is true of leadership in all areas. Being alert, available, and proactive, following up and following through, preventing and resolving conflict, and looking outside the box all sound like excellent and ideal elements of responsive leadership. That's all great in theory, but what about in practice? How do inspirational leaders actually accomplish all of that? The more leaders I spoke to about responsiveness, the more I heard the reoccurring theme: in order to consistently and readily respond to others, inspirational leaders must be sure to maintain their own energy and passion.

Curtis Rooney explained, "It is important to maintain your energy as a leader. Responsiveness and problem solving take work, and can be either energizing or depleting."[24] Personally, Curtis usually finds problem solving—especially when it helps other people—to be energizing, but he recognizes it can also be taxing. He went on to suggest developing and practicing daily habits that will help you create perspective and maintain balance. He gave the example of physical activity, describing how his daily commute via bicycle helps him arrive at work energized and relaxed, ready to respond to the needs of others.

A few years ago I wrote an article for my weekly column, *Tips for Greater Success*, about some of the things that energize me. Like all leaders, I have a lot of things I want and need to accomplish each day, so it's essential that I remain productive and effective. Like Curtis, I have discovered a handful of personal habits that energize me and help "keep the juices flowing" throughout the day:

1. **Eat Brain Food**. While I'm the first to admit that what I'm really craving is a big juicy burger from Five Guys Burgers and Fries, I've lived long enough to know that what I eat significantly impacts how I feel and how my body and brain perform. So a lunch of

leafy greens, walnuts, avocado and fruit it is. My brain—and my waistline—thank me!

2. **Exercise Daily**. I've heard that starting your day with a good workout will pump you up for the rest of the day, but for me personally, my sweet spot is early afternoon. Right when that after-lunch energy lull is threatening to hit, I head to the gym. While I realize not everyone's schedule is as accommodating as mine, I strongly recommend getting active for at least fifteen or thirty minutes in those early afternoon hours—the energy boost is absolutely worth it!

3. **Brainstorm New Ideas**. Nothing gets me going better than a creative discussion with a colleague or a personal brainstorming session where I take lots of notes (usually as voice memos) about a new idea. If my brain is struggling to get into creative mode, I go for a brisk walk. As soon as my blood gets moving, so do the creative juices. I am a big fan of walking meetings for just this reason (plus the added health benefits)!

4. **Reach Out to Someone**. One of the simplest and most effective ways I've found to raise my energy levels is to do something nice in word or deed for someone else. Something as simple as complimenting a stranger, thanking a colleague, or giving a friend a gift never fails to lift my spirits, refuel my mind, and inspire me for the rest of the day.[25]

As with everything, there is a balance; some of the very things that normally boost your energy, increase your passion, and bring you focus, can also drain and deplete you if overdone. While I try to eat healthy most of the time, I know that treating myself to that occasional cheeseburger is a good thing—for my soul, at least! I also realize that there is such a thing as too much exercise, that quiet reflection needs to balance out brainstorming, and that if I give too much of myself, I will burn out. So the key is balance, and finding what works for *you*. Also, as Celina Caprio pointed

> To be a responsive, inspirational leader, you must first pour into yourself in order to pour into others.

out, "You have to create a schedule and prioritize. It may not be perfect, yet it helps in getting the most out of the day… and yes, you have to learn to delegate."[26]

Ultimately, to be a responsive, inspirational leader, you must first pour into yourself in order to pour into others. Only when you have responded to your own needs will you be ready and able to respond to the needs of those you lead and serve. So find that balance, create a schedule, determine priorities, and don't be afraid to delegate. Remember, responsive, inspirational leadership is extremely challenging, but also incredibly rewarding.

KEY POINTS

To be a more responsive leader:

- Be alert, recognizing and quickly responding to needs.
- Follow through on your commitments, communicating throughout the process about what's going on.
- Do what you can to prevent conflict, but when it does happen, address it quickly and ensure it is resolved appropriately.
- "Look outside the box," responding to both organizational and individual needs, and the long term as much as the urgent.
- Be careful to maintain your own energy and passion in order to be ready and able to respond to the needs of others.

9

BE FLEXIBLE

"Change in this world is constant… in a culture that seems to be shifting beneath our feet, a leader must grow."[1] — *Steve Strang*

Decades have passed since I first became a leader. Over the years, many things have changed. From years before fax machines and pagers, to present-day computers and smart phones, technology is advancing quickly, and our world is being transformed. Technology isn't the only thing changing; but no matter the changes, they demand flexibility. Countless examples exist of leaders and organizations whose inflexibility and failure to embrace change ultimately led to their downfall (think Kodak, Blockbuster, and RadioShack). In contrast, flexible leaders and organizations:

- Seek innovation and remain open to beneficial change, no matter how difficult.
- Gracefully adapt to disrupted plans and unexpected circumstances.
- Appropriately adapt their style and policies to fit individual situations, realizing that not everything fits neatly into the parameters of corporate policy.

Inspirational leaders understand that in order to lead well, they must be continuously growing and looking for better and more efficient methods and strategies, remaining flexible and open to important and beneficial changes for themselves, their direct reports, and their organizations.

BE INNOVATIVE AND OPEN TO CHANGE

My longtime friend and colleague Jane Shlaes shared a story about an inspirational, innovative leader and physician by the name of Dr. Arnold "Ned" Wagner, Jr., a board certified OB-GYN at NorthShore University HealthSystem (formerly Evanston Northwestern Healthcare). "Dr. Ned is a man with a vision," Jane said. "In the late nineties he approached the administrative leadership to propose they be one of the first healthcare systems in the country to adopt a fully electronic medical record (EMR)." At the time, though most healthcare professionals agreed EMR was an important goal, no large healthcare system had successfully navigated that transition; of the few systems that had tried, some had experienced the backlash of disgruntled physicians who chose to split from the health system rather than make the proposed changes.

> As you can imagine, throughout the process Dr. Ned took a great deal of grief from his fellow physicians, not to mention thousands of other caregivers who had to change the way they work, take the time to be trained, and tolerate lower productivity (translating to lower pay) when working their way through the learning curve. But Dr. Ned was able to clearly paint a picture of the benefits of the change for the physicians, nurses, and leaders. Under his leadership and persistence, NorthShore became one of the very first fully integrated healthcare systems to achieve full EMR implementation, and they did it in record time. It wasn't easy, but they have made the change and are living the benefits of the new way—including better clinical data, improved service, improved financials, and increased quality of care.

Jane went on to share how she too played a role during the transition. As the chief learning officer for NorthShore during that time, Jane was tasked with leading the EMR training and communications throughout the organization.

> We required a minimum of two days of training for all physicians, and in some cases they had to complete three or four days of training to be fully prepared to use this robust tool. As you might imagine, this requirement did not go over well with many. There was no similar precedent, and most of these physicians did not

even work directly for the health system, but rather held admitting privileges. There was much at stake and many resisted participating. My role was not an easy one to play, but Dr. Ned made the role much easier for me. He had my back. If I encountered a particularly resistant physician or clinician, Dr. Ned would say, 'Let me deal with it.' And deal with it he did.

Like Dr. Ned Wagner, inspirational leaders have the vision and courage to enact difficult but important changes, accepting full responsibility for the outcome and taking the heat from those who disagree with their decision. They also are committed to supporting and assisting the individuals tasked with making the transition happen. "I had the privilege of working side-by-side with Dr. Ned for twelve years," Jane said, "and I've never been so proud as to work with and for one of the best, most inspirational leaders in healthcare."[2]

That willingness to push the envelope and advocate for important changes is a critical element of inspirational leadership. But while flexibility and willingness to change are certainly crucial leadership characteristics, leaders should also be wary of changing just for the sake of change. Inspirational leaders are careful to avoid hasty decisions, and refrain from impulsively jumping on the bandwagon anytime a new and exciting innovation or opportunity arises. Their decisions are well thought out, striking a balance between sticking with "tried and true" or taking a calculated risk with "new and groundbreaking." And no matter how attractive a new innovation or opportunity appears, inspirational leaders never compromise their personal, professional, or organizational core values to pursue it.

> Be wary of changing just for the sake of change.

John Hensing, executive vice president and chief medical officer at Banner Health, described president & CEO Peter Fine as a courageous yet cautious leader: "Peter has definitely demonstrated a willingness to shift organizational direction when the external environment requires it, but only after he has dedicated very significant effort to analyze the consequences—both intended and unintended—of his decisions."[3] Ron Bunnell, executive vice president and chief administrative officer at Banner, agreed that Peter is strategically cautious, but is definitely not afraid of change: "Peter is courageous and makes bold moves... he makes great strategic decisions and then leads the organization unwaveringly down the path of successful execution."[4]

Like Peter Fine, the leadership of my friend and colleague Mark Dixon reflects courageous flexibility. Mark, a former hospital CEO, is now the president of his own organization, The Mark Dixon Group, LLC. Mark's colleague Brad Beard described Mark as "a risk-taker who is willing to try new ideas and processes. He does not stay in the status quo and is willing to think out of the box."[5] Baylor Scott & White Health CEO Joel Allison is another excellent example of an inspirational leader who is not only flexible, but is continuously looking for better and more efficient methods and strategies for success. Joel's colleague Gary Brock explained,

> Joel is extremely flexible and always on the lookout for new ideas, insights, and information; he understands that innovation can come from many places. He is an avid reader, and a leader who is constantly scanning the national market in an effort to provide our organization an advantage.[6]

Each of these leaders understands the importance of remaining flexible and open to new ideas and different ways of doing things. But they also know that too much flexibility can be a bad thing for leaders and organizations. There are definitely situations and areas where steadfast commitment is absolutely essential; so flexibility and tenacity are two characteristics of inspirational leadership that must be carefully balanced. Bruce Lawrence, president and CEO of INTEGRIS Health, shared a great example of that balance:

> Since I moved into the CEO role back in 2001, a lot has changed. We've had the economic downturn, we've had the Affordable Care Act; we have all this unrest in our industry. The question is, 'How are we going to work through all of these changes?' The message I've tried to communicate throughout our organization is, "We can't depend upon what's going to happen in Washington, or even our own state capitol. They're not going to solve our problems there. At the end of the day, we have to be true to our patients, because we are the ones our patients depend upon to be there in their greatest time of need. It's not Washington that they depend upon, it's

Flexibility *and* tenacity *must be* CAREFULLY BALANCED

not 23rd and Lincoln [the state capitol] here in Oklahoma City that they depend upon. It's us. Regardless of what happens, regardless of what changes we must enact, we're going to be asked to take care of more people, and we're going to be paid less to do that. So let's get that, let's acknowledge it, and then let's get to work." And that message from me has been consistent—to our board, to our leadership team, and throughout our organization.

As the leader of a health system during a period of significant change, Bruce recognizes that there are some things his organization needs to be very flexible about, and some things they need to remain very steadfast on—namely their responsibility to their patients to continue providing high quality care, no matter the changes and challenges. Bruce went on to explain that by taking that approach, they've been able to accomplish a lot in the years since the Affordable Care Act first came on scene. "I think we're in really great shape today because of that. We weren't waiting on a new president to be elected and the ACA to be repealed. We weren't waiting on the Supreme Court to rule it unconstitutional. We weren't waiting on all this other stuff," Bruce said. "We just went about the work of taking care of patients, getting our cost structure in place, and providing the best quality and most efficient care that we can provide. And at the end of the day, I can feel really good about that."[7]

BE ADAPTIVE

Just as Bruce Lawrence and INTEGRIS Health have had to adapt to the myriad of changes taking place in the healthcare industry in America today, leaders and organizations in every industry in every corner of the world must be ready to adapt to changes outside their control. Whether foreseen or not, changes are inevitable, and inspirational leaders have the readiness and flexibility to acknowledge, accept, and adapt to those changes as they come.

Lorna Shaw is the external affairs manager at Pogo Mine in Alaska. Lorna has been in the mining industry for more than fifteen years, and it is obvious when talking to her that she loves what she does. Over the years, Lorna has had to adapt her role to accommodate the whims of the industry and to fit the needs and expectations of her employers. Lorna explained that when she first started in the industry, she was hired to build and coordinate a tourism operation for Kinross Gold Corporation. But just six months after she came on board, the nation was hit with the tragedy of the September 11 terrorist attacks, and suddenly the bottom fell out of the tourism market.

So over the next eleven years Lorna's role at the company was reinvented several times. During her twelve-year tenure at Kinross, the Fort Knox operation where Lorna worked experienced a parade of general managers come and go. "We had twelve general managers in twelve years. So I sort of had to re-create my position under every general manager. My job was to make myself useful, and explain to the GM why I deserved to be there and how I was going to assist him and assist the company." At that time, public relations was not very prevalent in the mining industry. "Historically," Lorna explained, "marketing and PR have always been the first things cut when mineral prices fall. I joined the mining industry when gold was at a very low $250/ounce. Nobody had public relations. So I've had to be very inventive and flexible in my role, and as a result have done all kinds of things in my career… and I think in the end all of the general managers that I worked for were very happy with the work I did." Lorna noted that she has been very fortunate in her career. Though she's always reported to someone else, she has had the freedom to essentially figure out what needs to be done and then set about doing it. Her work ethic and positive, flexible attitude have distinguished her as a respected, inspirational leader in her organization, state, and industry, and she has been the recipient of numerous honors and awards.[8]

In addition to adapting to natural and gradual changes over time, leaders must also be ready to adapt to sudden, unexpected, or undesirable changes outside their control. While derailed plans are never ideal, flexible leaders understand the importance of remaining positive and playing the best hand they can with the cards they're dealt—personally, professionally, and organizationally.

My good friend Buddy White told me a story about a friend and inspirational leader who was faced with unexpected and very undesirable circumstances. As the owner of a small business that did government contracts, this leader was held liable for the criminal actions of some of his employees, and as a result served a prison sentence for several years. When he got to prison, he decided that he couldn't just sit around and feel sorry for himself. A man of faith, he looked around and discovered that the

Sunday services at the prison could use some help. So this former business leader began volunteering, and soon became a leader in the prison ministry. Not a role he ever expected to play, but as a flexible, inspirational leader, he adapted his goals and expectations to fit his circumstances, determining to make something positive come out of this unexpected experience. Because of that mindset, he ended up experiencing what he describes as the highlight of his life. The prison ministry grew, at one time drawing in over 300 men for one service. Through that ministry, this leader got to make an impact in the lives of hundreds of men, and personally saw dozens of inmates turn their lives around in response to the Christian message of hope, forgiveness, and reconciliation.

While a very unusual and unique situation, this is definitely an excellent example of an inspirational leader who chose to be positive and adaptive in the face of unimaginably difficult circumstances. After telling me this story, Buddy said, "I have to wonder, if I was knocked down that hard in life, would I look around to see how I could adapt to my circumstances and how I could continue to help others? My hope is that I could be as strong as this man!"[9]

While very flexible, positive, and ready to adapt and adjust as needed, inspirational leaders also know there are some areas where adjustments shouldn't be made. In an interview for this book, one of my good friends and colleagues explained how when faced with a choice that would have required him to compromise some firmly held values, he chose instead to walk away from his executive position and twenty-eight-year career. Obviously that was not an easy decision, but one that he felt had to be made. "There are some things that aren't that flexible," he explained. Joel Allison agrees: "Successful leaders have to be flexible, certainly, but without compromising a set of values and principles."[10] No matter the perceived benefits and advantages to certain changes and opportunities, inspirational leaders do not compromise their core values for the sake of flexibility.

Choose People Over Policy

A very key way in which inspirational leaders demonstrate flexibility is in how they treat those whom they lead, and how they respond to and handle individual situations. They realize that not every situation fits neatly into the parameters of corporate policy. Rather than assume their leadership style and corporate policies should be "one-size-fits-all" for every person whom they lead, inspirational leaders have the wisdom and flexibility to appropriately adapt their style and policies to better engage, inspire, and empower each unique individual on their team.

When I asked Lisa Hill, executive director of Invest in Kids, how flexibility is modeled in her organization, she noted that flexibility is actually named as one of their company values, and is a very important part of their company culture. "We live in a very innovative environment, where even though we're advocating for evidence-based programs that have very specific rigor and model elements associated with their fidelity, we have to be very flexible in how we respond to a unique community's needs." Lisa went on to explain that when first considering the question, she initially thought about flexibility in terms of how her organization relates to their clients and client needs. But she also thought about how her organization embodies flexibility internally. "What I thought of as an example is more about our work schedules, and being responsive to people's whole selves and whole lives." Lisa went on to explain,

> Our staff demographic is mostly made up of very strong, committed, competent women who also value their home life. We have very few staff members who are actually full time, in order to accommodate their family obligations. One particular example comes to mind. There is a woman on staff who, upon becoming pregnant with her first child, came and told me she was going from five days a week to three days a week after she came back. Well, at first that threw me off a little bit. I was thinking, "You know, you have to actually ask, not just tell me that's what you're going to do." But the more I thought about it, the more I realized she was right to assume. Because that is always how we've responded to those requests—within reason. I thought to myself, "you know what Lisa? That is a true testament to the culture that you've created, which says that 'we value your whole self and we invest in you and expect a lot of you. For all that you give us, we are going to give it back.'" As much as I wasn't thrilled with her approach, I thought it was a nice commentary on the environment that we have here.[11]

Unfortunately, there are countless examples of leaders and organizations that are not flexible or open to change. Sadly, some have chosen legalistic adherence to corporate policy over careful consideration of individual personalities, circumstances, and situations. While there's no doubt that most organizational policies and processes are important and in place for a reason, inspirational leaders should have the discernment and courage to make changes or allow appropriate exceptions. Above all, they should treat everyone with respect and understanding, and always be willing to consider change.

One of my friends and colleagues told me about an experience she had with an inflexible leader, and the negative impact of that experience. She described it as "soul-draining," explaining how the CEO of a very large corporation ran the company using bullying tactics, ignoring input and quickly removing anyone who dared challenge her. "So obviously everyone just kept their heads down," she said. "This created such an unhealthy culture throughout the organization. It was a combination of fear, frustration, and mostly resignation to the situation." The negative and inflexible leadership modeled in that organization was not the kind that my friend wanted to emulate, so she soon left. She later learned that the CEO left as well—no reason given.

Another friend and colleague, Sharla Jones, told me a similar story about a manager in one organization where she worked who was neither open to change nor flexible in how he engaged his direct reports: "He was stubborn and unyielding, and only considered the options through his own perspective," Sharla explained. "Even if he received feedback and information that was valuable and relevant to the situation and presented in a non-defensive way, he was still unwilling to make changes or listen to the opinions of others… Eventually, that manager was asked to change his behavior or leave the organization, and he chose to leave."[12]

> Above all, flexible leaders put people first, understanding that true concern for those they lead and serve demands flexibility.

As is apparent in the above examples, that kind of inflexibility simply isn't compatible with true inspirational leadership. Flexible leaders are willing to change their methods—and their minds—when given good reason. They seek out other perspectives and opinions, always receptive to suggestions and to appropriate "give and take." Above all, flexible leaders put people first, understanding that true concern for those they lead and serve demands flexibility. Tim Orellano, president of The Human Resources Team, said it well: "How do I personally model flexibility? By listening and observing, and being flexible enough to put someone else's needs before mine."[13]

Anne Granum, vice president of strategic business development for RENOVO Solutions, shared a unique story and excellent example of this kind of flexible, inspirational leadership. I first spoke with Anne following the publication of my book *Presidential Leadership*, when she submitted a comment on my blog as her entry for a drawing I was doing for free copies of the book. Anne ended up not being one of the randomly selected winners, but her submission—a comment about the best leader she had ever had—stood out to me. I ended up following up with Anne and eventually interviewing that leader, Sandy Morford, whose comments appear in several chapters of this book. Here is an excerpt from the blog comment that first caught my attention:

> The best leader I ever had is the leader I have now… He doesn't ask anyone to do what he's not willing to do, is always looking out for the best interests of his internal and external clients, [and] is a wonderful husband, father and friend… I've had my share of bosses and I'm extremely grateful for this one. He embodies everything that I try to be.[14]

A year and a half after Anne posted that comment, I was communicating with her about my progress on this book, and she sent me an email relating an incredible personal story that beautifully highlighted the flexible, caring leadership of Sandy and the other leaders and co-owners of RENOVO. Anne graciously gave me permission to share her story and remarkable personal experience. The email began this way:

> Hi Dan, Thanks so much for reaching out to me. I have another story to tell you about the leadership of RENOVO Solutions that brings me to tears. On Friday, April 10th I was diagnosed with Stage 3 Ovarian Cancer…

As I read on, I learned that Anne's devastating news came just two months after being told during a check-up that she was in excellent health.

In the weeks following that shocking diagnosis, she was hospitalized multiple times, underwent major surgery to remove affected organs, began preparing for chemo treatments, and of course missed a great amount of work. While in the hospital for the fourth or fifth time, Anne received a call from her leaders Sandy and Haresh, who had met with the other two owners of the company, Don and Joe, to discuss the issue of Anne's health and what to do about all the work she was missing. Continuing the email, Anne described that call:

> Sandy and Haresh informed me that the owners of the company wanted me to take all the time that I needed to focus completely on my health and not worry about RENOVO. They are going to make sure that I am kept whole with my income while I'm healing. Dan, I burst into tears. They are going to make sure that I continue to be paid my total income during this process and didn't want me to worry about anything. This isn't a loan, this is how they treat their family. In my entire career working for other companies that I valued I never imagined anyone willing to do this for me and my family. Practically speaking, most companies would figure out how to cut their losses knowing that I will be unable to work potentially for the next five months plus the two weeks that I've already had to take off. This leadership team is amazing. The reason for our incredible growth with loyal employees and clients is because of this type of action.[15]

Anne's story about the very impactful decision and actions of her leaders is a perfect example of how flexible, inspirational leaders handle difficult and unusual circumstances, and how they choose people over policy. Anne's story gets even better. Three months after she received that life-changing diagnosis, the cancer went into remission. As of the writing of this book, the cancer had returned once, but proved very responsive to chemo, and Anne continues to be joyful and optimistic, declaring, "I'm going to live a long, long life."[16] What a beautiful ending to an incredible story about the impact of truly flexible, inspirational leadership!

KEY POINTS

To be a more flexible leader:

- Seek innovation and remain open to beneficial change, no matter how difficult.
- Gracefully adapt to disrupted plans and unexpected circumstances.
- Acknowledge that not everything fits neatly into the parameters of corporate policy, and be willing to appropriately adapt your style and policies to fit individual situations.

PART III
THE STRATEGIES & TACTICS OF AN INSPIRATIONAL LEADER

3 CRITICAL HABITS

"A good leader leads the people from above them. A great leader leads the people from within them." – M.D. Arnold

As explained in the introduction to Part Two, there are three key characteristics of inspirational leaders that are best described as critical and intentional *habits*. These three habits, which encompass a multitude of very important leadership behaviors, strategies, and tactics, can be summed up as an inspirational leader's ability to *engage*, *inspire*, and *empower* others.

In the next six chapters we will explore each of these critical habits in depth, looking at specific leadership strategies and tactics such as:

- Building genuine connections with the individuals you lead and influence.
- Investing your time, attention, and resources in those you lead.
- Providing opportunities for your direct reports to use their unique skillsets and achieve greater success—within your organization and beyond.
- Creating a clear vision for your teams and direct reports to work toward.
- Demonstrating—not just articulating—strong core values.
- Building and nurturing excitement for the work and mission of your team or organization.
- Facilitating the personal and professional growth of those you lead.
- Giving appropriate authority to your direct reports—along with plenty of encouragement and support.

While there is no secret or magic formula for effective inspirational leadership, I sincerely believe the habits of actively and intentionally *engaging*, *inspiring*, and *empowering* those you lead will pay huge dividends toward your personal, professional, and organizational success—as well as the success of those you lead! I believe if you begin with a foundation built on the six key characteristics outlined in the previous section—accountability, authenticity, teachability, approachability, responsiveness, and flexibility—and practice these three habits, you will have a guaranteed road map to success. So let's get started!

ENGAGE

"Management is about arranging and telling. Leadership is about nurturing and enhancing." – Tom Peters

10

BUILD CONNECTIONS

"People will not follow you if they do not trust you, and before someone will lend you a hand, you must first touch their heart." – Robin Sharma

In a 2012 article for CNN, author Dov Seidman wrote about how leaders should inspire others. The first step, he said, is to "connect and collaborate," rather than "command and control." He went on to explain,

> The days of leading companies via a one-way conversation are over. Power has shifted and our leadership must shift with it. The old system of "command and control" to exert power over people is fast being replaced by "connect and collaborate"—to generate power through people. Leaders and managers cannot just impose their will.[1]

As Seidman articulated, inspirational leaders don't just command or control those they lead. Nor do they merely coexist with the people in their organization. Instead, they collaborate, and most importantly, they *connect*. They invite people to join them on the journey. They build genuine connections with those whom they lead, and they also build connections between their organization's mission and each person's individual purpose within the organization. They do this by:

- Cultivating authentic relationships; recognizing a person's innate value, not just their usefulness.
- Asking questions and taking notice of personal details.
- Promoting a connected culture throughout the organization.

- Articulating a meaningful mission and each person's connection to it.

In this chapter I will share strategies, tactics, and lessons learned of inspirational leaders who realize the importance of building and establishing genuine connections with those they lead.

Cultivate Authentic Relationships

The most inspirational leaders excel in building connections. By "building connections" I don't mean merely corporate networking and exchanging business cards. "Building strong working connections is important. But I don't really like to network for networking's sake," says Curtis Rooney. "That gets pretty old, especially in Washington. I much rather work with someone and get to know them during the course of a common objective."[2] This approach to building connections that Curtis describes is much more authentic than simply going through the motions of corporate networking. While every leader typically engages in that kind of networking to some degree, inspirational leaders go beyond networking to build genuine relationships with those they lead and influence.

As already touched on in Chapter 5, authenticity is key to building trust and making genuine connections. Christine Márquez-Hudson put it this way: "When other people sense that you're being really down-to-earth and authentic, you break down a lot of barriers to connection."[3] While the depth of relationship will vary from individual to individual, inspirational leaders strive to make every connection authentic and purposeful. Whether colleagues, subordinates, board members, shareholders, clients, customers, janitors, coffee shop baristas, or food truck vendors, inspirational leaders recognize that every person and every relationship has value. But they don't value people merely for their "usefulness;" instead, they recognize the innate value of each person—apart from any perceived networking advantage or other self-interested benefit.

In a 2014 article titled "Leadership That Gets Results," author David

> Inspirational leaders strive to make every connection authentic and purposeful.

Bradford asserted that great leaders show true caring and concern for those they lead. He went on to note, "When people feel valued, a feeling of trust infuses itself throughout an organization. And when trust exists, business accelerates."[4] Joel Allison, CEO of Baylor Scott & White Health, is an example of just such a leader who shows true concern and fosters that kind of trust throughout his organization. Joel genuinely values other people and excels in developing authentic relationships. "It's important that you show that you care, that you value those you lead," Joel says. "You value their input and their opinions. You respect them, and you show respect to them. You also express appreciation, thanking them."[5] As *Inc.* magazine contributing editor Jeff Haden once wrote, "[employees] want to work with and for people they respect and admire—and with and for people who respect and admire them." Haden went on to explain,

> That's why a kind word, a quick discussion about family, an informal conversation to ask if an employee needs any help—those moments are much more important than group meetings or formal evaluations. A true sense of connection is personal. That's why exceptional bosses show they see and appreciate the person, not just the worker.[6]

Every colleague of Joel Allison's with whom I spoke attested to his talent for building authentic connections, unanimously describing him as a leader who truly cares about others. "Joel takes an interest in people's lives beyond the workplace," said Gary Brock; "he demonstrates a genuine interest in their success as individuals."[7] Steve Boyd said of Joel: "He has great people skills, treating everyone with dignity and respect."[8]

My friend and colleague Sheleza Mohamed, department manager at UT Southwestern Medical Center, told me about another inspirational leader for whom she worked who valued each of his employees and excelled at developing authentic relationships and building connections. She explained how she worked in an entry-level position at a local hospital very early in her career, registering patients for outpatient and inpatient services. Even though she was very "low on the totem pole," so to speak, she was impressed by the CEO's interactions with everyone—no matter their role: "The CEO's personality was charismatic and caring. He showed concern for all his employees. He knew their names and something about their personal lives. His uncanny ability to connect with people made every employee, regardless of title or position, feel connected and valued."[9] That is what building authentic connections is all about!

When speaking with me on this topic, Jack Lawless noted that an important aspect of building authentic relationships is a willingness to be vulnerable, sharing examples and even mistakes from your own life as a show of trust and empathy for others. He related the story of how he connected with a young direct report in his department who was struggling to succeed in a new leadership role. Jack sat down with him and shared about his own experience falling short as a young manager years before. Jack honestly and vulnerably shared about how he had failed and what it took to turn things around and for him to eventually succeed in that role. That conversation not only resulted in significant improvement in the young leader's performance, but also cemented an important and lasting relationship between the two men.[10]

As Jack told me that story I was reminded of my early days as a hospital CEO. One day I was down in the kitchen area, meeting with the food service employees and addressing some sort of issue—now long forgotten. Without planning it, I extemporaneously shared about my experience as a dishwasher working at a little airport restaurant while I was in high school. As I reminisced and we talked and laughed about washing dishes and wiping tables, an unexpected bond began to form. From that point forward, I had a special relationship with those employees—all because I chose to be authentic, connecting with them not just as their boss, but as a person with something in common. Had I gone down there planning to do that, hoping to gain their support and empathy by appealing to their emotions with a strategic personal story, I would have failed. Instead, I shared part of myself not because I hoped to "get them on my side," but because I was simply being authentic. Authenticity goes a long way toward building genuine connections.

Ask Questions and Take Notice

I am a naturally curious person. I tend to be a people watcher, observing individuals among the crowds, noticing unique details, and soaking in the sights and sounds around me. I also tend to follow the same pattern in conversation. My natural curiosity prompts me to listen carefully and notice details, seeking out more information by asking questions. I never thought about this much, but as I began to really study and research inspirational leadership, I discovered that asking questions and taking note of details is a valuable leadership skill.

Leaders who are really in tune to their organizations and the individuals whom they lead and serve tend to be people who ask questions and really listen to the answers. My colleague Richard Howe, CEO of HCG, agrees that a critical aspect of inspirational leadership and building connections is interacting with your team and asking sincere questions. "Every day, the leader should get up from his or her desk and greet and acknowledge each person on the team. In addition, I always try to ask a question about their personal life—just to make sure something did not happen that may have an impact on how that person feels today and if he or she may need some encouragement."[11]

> **Pay attention, ask questions, and take note of details to be remembered later.**

Inspirational leaders always want to know more. Whether people, situations, or processes, inspirational leaders want to better understand each. So they pay attention, they ask questions, and they take note of details to be remembered later. Harla Adams, CEO of NIHCL, explained how she tries to be very intentional when listening:

> During conversations I try to really listen. I pick up on little tidbits, and I often surprise people when I remember small details about their lives. It can make a big impact, and it just comes from listening and being more concerned about others than myself. I think that's how relationships are birthed. You have to be genuine, you have to be willing to listen, and you have to be willing to keep quiet and let others talk.[12]

Attorney Celina Caprio also discussed the importance of really listening and picking up on details during conversations, noting that she strives to always remember names and how she met someone. She also tries to ask meaningful questions: "I ask questions on what works for them, and I share my own insights. I find ways that our work, cause, or vision might relate to one another, and leave the door open for future potential collaborations."[13]

When I asked my friend and colleague Tim Orellano about the importance and impact of building connections, he related a story from early in his career about when he first joined a local association connected to his field (human resources). Upon joining, he received an unexpected phone call from the association's president, John Lee, who introduced himself, welcomed Tim as a new member, and sought to get to know him. Tim was floored that the president—a very experienced personnel manager—had reached out to make a personal connection with him. That early connection led to a lasting friendship, and also taught Tim a valuable lesson:

> Those individuals who put their hand out, make phone calls, introduce themselves, find out what you do, are interested in you, and are willing to help you—they make genuine, valuable connections.[14]

Hospital president Traci Bernard has been described over and over by her colleagues as a warm and personable leader who excels at building connections with individuals throughout her organization. One key way in which Traci does this is through paying attention to details and asking thoughtful questions during conversation. Her colleague Jessica Hill had this to say about Traci:

> I will never forget the way Traci made me feel when I was a charge nurse on the Inpatient Unit. She was always smiling and even remembered I had two dogs. She would ask about them and get personal with me. That is not something I ever would expect from a hospital president, and she inspired me to do the same. I remember how she made me feel when I was a frontline nurse, and those feelings have inspired me to be a relational leader. I learned from Traci that once people understand you care, they will follow your lead.[15]

As trite as the saying might be now, it is still true: "People don't care how much you know until they know how much you care!" Trust and respect are established when connections are made, and those connections are built by paying attention, noticing details, and asking questions.

Promote a Connected Culture

Due to demanding schedules, long commutes, and a variety of other factors, many people spend as much or even more of their waking hours with their coworkers than they do with their own families. While this trend brings up all kinds of questions and concerns about maintaining a healthy work-life balance, it also brings into focus the importance of a healthy workplace culture. Strong, authentic connections among coworkers are key.

So what does a healthy, connected culture look like? In a *Harvard Business Review* article titled "Proof That Positive Work Cultures Are More Productive," authors Emma Seppala and Kim Cameron listed six characteristics of a positive work culture:

1. "Caring for, being interested in, and maintaining responsibility for colleagues as friends.
2. Providing support for one another, including offering kindness and compassion when others are struggling.
3. Avoiding blame and forgive [*sic*] mistakes.
4. Inspiring one another at work.
5. Emphasizing the meaningfulness of the work.
6. Treating one another with respect, gratitude, trust, and integrity."[16]

Demonstrating and encouraging healthy and authentic relationship building is a critical responsibility of inspirational leaders. As with everything, a healthy, connected culture starts at the top—the leader sets the tone for the entire organization. According to Seppala and Cameron, leaders can foster a connected culture by promoting social connections, showing empathy, going out of their way to help, and encouraging people to talk to them about their problems.[17]

My friend and colleague Curtis Rooney is an excellent example of a leader who fosters a connected culture in his workplace. I had the privilege of gaining perspectives from many of his team members and colleagues, both past and present, and they all referred repeatedly to Curtis' knack for building and encouraging connections throughout his sphere of influence. Jennifer Bell noted, "Curtis genuinely cares about the people that he leads, and they all know that." She went on to talk about how Curtis has always been very welcoming to new team members, going out of his way to make sure they feel comfortable.

> We had a tradition (started by Curtis) that when a new team member joined they had to answer one random question (e.g. favorite ice cream flavor, a random hobby, etc.). We went around the table and everyone on the team had to answer. It was a fun ice breaker and it put everyone at ease.[18]

Another one of Curtis' colleagues, Michael Payne, explained how Curtis has consistently organized staff gatherings and fun outings to encourage connectivity beyond regularly scheduled meetings. "Unlike some of us who just do it around holiday time, Curtis thinks about it all year round,"[19] he said. Bob Van Heuvelen echoed those observations, noting that Curtis is always reliable in consistently connecting with those on his team, no matter how busy or relaxed the pace may be during a given workweek.[20]

Sandy Morford, CEO of Renovo Solutions, is another leader who takes connection seriously. He explained that he has always prided himself on staying in touch with all employees in his organization, communicating frequently via phone, email, and face-to-face whenever possible. However, Renovo has been rapidly growing over the last few years, and they now have over two hundred employees spread out all across the country—making staying connected more and more difficult. Even so, Sandy and his business partners all make a concerted effort to remain visible and connected to all their employees and clients, as well as to promote a connected culture throughout their organization. Sandy noted,

> We are constantly told by our clients that they see our senior management team more frequently than they've ever seen senior managers from other competitors with whom they've done business in the past… We make a habit of making sure that our senior leaders, the owners of our company, get out in the field and see our clients and our employees on a regular, consistent basis. I think that in itself has a huge impact on the individuals that work for us in this company, because they see the involvement of the senior management team, see us being involved at the very lowest levels in the organization, and I think it builds confidence in them that we are very involved in the success of this company and involved in what they each do.[21]

Like Sandy and his partners, inspirational leaders consciously try to foster connections throughout their organizations by modeling that behavior themselves, striving to personally be very connected and involved in the day-to-day activities and interactions. Here are a few other ways you can promote a connected culture:

- **Be proactive when hiring**. When interviewing potential new team members, make sure to focus on culture-fit as much as or even more than skill. Skill can be taught, so put more emphasis on finding people with the right character and values to connect with your team's culture.
- **Facilitate collaboration**. Design projects and plan assignments that allow for teamwork and collaboration. Be careful not to inadvertently isolate team members by giving them assignments that don't require connection and interaction with coworkers.
- **Celebrate successes**. Publicly recognize, affirm, and celebrate work well done, goals that have been achieved, and any other praise-worthy contributions and accomplishments. Emphasize group effort and celebrate as a team, as well as expressing appreciation for individual contributions.
- **Foster mutual respect**. In every meeting and team interaction, consistently model respect and support of others' input and ideas, and make it clear that you expect the same from everyone on the team.
- **Encourage camaraderie**. Plan get-togethers outside of work throughout the year, and inject fun into the workweek whenever possible—movie trivia to start off long meetings, silly socks day once a month, birthday shenanigans for every team member's special day, etc. Let loose, be creative, and encourage your team to do so too!

Articulate a Meaningful Mission

A connected culture isn't just about relationships, collaboration, and camaraderie. An organization's workforce must also be connected to the organization itself. Inspirational leaders understand that in order for their team members to truly be effective and engaged in their work, they must feel connected to the mission—namely, that their work is meaningful. Author Jim Collins put it very simply: "It is impossible to have a great life unless it is a meaningful life. And it is very difficult to have a meaningful life without meaningful work."[22]

Authors Teresa Amabile and Steve Kramer address this same concept in a *Harvard Business Review* article titled "To Give Your Employees Meaning, Start with Mission:"

> People's work lives are enriched greatly when they feel they are making progress on work that is meaningful—in other words, when they feel they are making a difference in the world... Why is meaning so important? Because when people find meaning in the work, they also feel a sense of ownership. The work means something to them personally... when people take ownership of the work, they are more committed to it, more intrinsically motivated, more engaged. And that makes for better performance on all dimensions.[23]

To truly engage those they lead, inspirational leaders must build a meaningful connection between the work being done and those doing it. Marc Reynolds, SVP of Payer Relations at Scripps Health, explained, "Inspirational leaders convey a greater purpose than just financial or organizational success, which, while important, do not necessarily inspire their followers." Marc went on to describe inspirational leaders as leaders who "can communicate and connect with people in a way around a mission or goals that creates the desire to become engaged and part of something... they show you that the mission is more important than any individual, but at the same time they make you feel that your individual contribution is essential."[24]

> To truly engage those they lead, inspirational leaders must build a meaningful connection between the work being done and those doing it.

Without a worthy mission and purpose, work is just something that has to be done to pay the bills, and deep engagement and fulfillment is virtually impossible. My good friend and colleague Ben McKibbens, a former health system CEO, put it this way:

> It's very important to realize that when you're in a position of leadership, what you do can have a very powerful impact on so many... So make sure the mission statement of the organization is worthy of everyone laboring under it. If we're going to put our lives and careers at stake with an institution, why don't we make sure that institution has a mission we can be proud of? And if we're going to sync our once-in-a-lifetime lives into it, it better be worthy. It better be in agreement with our personal values and with our perspectives.[25]

Ben is exactly right—those in positions of leadership have the opportunity and responsibility to impact the lives of those they lead in a powerful way. One such way is to ensure that those they lead find the work they do meaningful. Leaders can build that connection between people and their work in several ways, but an important starting point is to articulate the overall mission itself and how it touches people's lives. While official written mission statements aren't a mandatory element of every organization, group, or team, they can add clarity and convey purpose—when done well. Unfortunately, this is an area where many leaders and organizations unwittingly miss the mark. In a 2010 article for *Harvard Business Review*, author Eric Hellweg noted:

> Most companies, regardless of their sectors, have a mission statement. And most are awash in jargon and marble-mouthed pronouncements. Worse still, these gobbledy-gook statements are often forgotten by, misremembered, or flatly ignored by frontline employees.[26]

An effective mission statement should be specific and inspiring, giving those laboring under it a clear sense of how their work will positively impact customers, communities, and the world at large. In their *HBR* article, Amabile and Kramer offered this example of an actual mission statement that does little to inspire or communicate meaning about the work being done:

> The Company's primary objective is to maximize long-term stockholder value, while adhering to the laws of the jurisdictions

in which it operates and at all times observing the highest ethical standards.[27]

While maximizing stockholder value and adhering to laws and high ethical standards are certainly important goals for any organization, they're not particularly inspiring. Nor do these general objectives communicate anything about what kind of product or service the company provides! With a mission statement like this, the organization's leadership has little hope of really connecting and engaging their employees with the work being done. To contrast the above mission statement, the article's authors go on to share that of Starbucks:

> Our mission: to inspire and nurture the human spirit—one person, one cup and one neighborhood at a time.[28]

What a stark contrast! Starbucks could have chosen a mission statement that centers around the product for which they're famous, such as "to prepare and sell the best coffee in the world and create a warm and friendly environment for our customers." A statement like that is at least specific, and clearly conveys what it is that the company does. But instead they went one step further, addressing how their product *impacts* those who experience it. Theirs is a mission statement that is short, simple, and most importantly, can inspire those laboring under it.

> "If you're crafting a purpose statement, my advice is this: To inspire your staff to do good work for you, find a way to express the organization's impact on the lives of customers, clients, students, patients—whomever you're trying to serve. Make them feel it."[29]
>
> – *Graham Kenny*

If articulating the overall mission and how it touches people's lives is the first step toward building a meaningful connection between the work being done and those doing it, then the next step is to daily demonstrate that mission in action. While it should go without saying, it is critical that inspirational leaders lead by example, aligning their words, actions, daily tasks, and priorities with the mission that has been articulated. Only by living it out themselves will leaders be able to connect those they lead to the mission and purpose of the work being done. As the authors of the *HBR* article state,

> It's not enough to have good words down on paper (or on your website). Your organization's leaders need to live the values implied in your mission statement and expect others to as well. By making sure all people in power walk the talk, you can begin to give employees the meaning they crave.[30]

Another important way that leaders can help build that connection between the people they lead and the work they do is to make sure each person understands how his or her individual role makes a difference and supports the mission. As Warren Bennis once explained, "Good leaders make people feel that they're at the very heart of things, not at the periphery. Everyone feels that he or she makes a difference to the success of the organization. When that happens, people feel centered and that gives their work meaning."[31]

There are definitely jobs where feeling that connection between daily tasks and the overall mission is easier in certain roles than in other positions within the same organization. For example, most physicians or nurses can easily identify the very worthy mission they have of caring for the health and wellbeing of patients. But within a hospital or health system, there are typically hundreds of different non-medical staff positions, such as custodians, receptionists, and food service workers. For many of these employees, feeling that connection—that their work truly makes a difference in the lives of the patients—is a little harder. This is where an inspirational leader can have a powerful impact and help build that connection by communicating the significance of individual roles and how they contribute to the organization and support the overall mission.

> "Ninety percent of leadership is the ability to communicate something people want."
>
> – *Dianne Feinstein*

Another important step toward engaging people and really connecting them to the work they do is to encourage ownership and creativity within their individual roles. In a 2015 article for *Becker's Hospital Review*, Tamara Rosin referenced an example of a surprisingly satisfied worker in an unlikely role—that of hospital custodian:

> Luke, a pseudonym for a custodian in a major teaching hospital, has a long list of responsibilities in his job description, including "collect and dispose of soiled linen" and "stock restroom supplies." Not a single item on the list requires him to interact with another human being.
>
> However, after completing in-depth interviews with Luke and other hospital custodians, researcher Amy Wrzesniewski, PhD, discovered the custodians' "official" duties were only a small part of their jobs, and a large part was to make the patients and their families feel comfortable. The janitors told stories about times they cheered patients up when they were feeling sad, when they encouraged them or diverted their attention from their pain and fear and gave them a willing ear if they felt like talking.
>
> Luke and the other custodians wanted something more from their custodial work. What they sought was shaped by the goals of the organization: to promote health, cure illness and relieve suffering. These aims were embedded in their approach to their job.[32]

These custodians wanted something more from their work, and rather than simply accepting and conforming to their official—and rather mundane—job descriptions, they found ways to connect their work to a more meaningful mission. As a result, they had surprisingly high satisfaction levels with their job. Rosin noted,

> Satisfied workers are engaged in their work. They have autonomy and discretion, and they achieve a level of mastery or expertise. They learn things that help them develop as better workers and people. Most importantly, satisfied workers find the work they do meaningful—they believe they make a difference in the world and help touch other people's lives in positive ways.[33]

Inspirational leaders encourage initiative and autonomy, allowing those they lead, no matter their "official" titles or job descriptions, the discretion to craft their own roles in unique ways to further the mission and to really feel connected to the organization's overall purpose and vision.

KEY POINTS

To be a leader who builds connections:

- Cultivate authentic relationships, recognizing a person's innate value, not just their usefulness.
- Ask questions and take notice of personal details.
- Promote a connected culture throughout the organization.
- Articulate a meaningful mission and each person's connection to it.

11

MAKE INVESTMENTS

"The value of any organization resides in its people."[1] — *Deborah Maher*

Leadership coach Peter Baeklund once heard this exchange between an organization's CFO and CEO:

CFO: "What happens if we invest in developing our people and then they leave us?"
CEO: "What happens if we don't, and they stay?"

While the CFO was understandably concerned with the organization's expenditures and bottom line, the CEO wisely understood that investing in their people was something they couldn't afford not to do. As Steve Chase, cofounder and former CEO of AOL, once said, "Most businesses rise or fall not because of the product, but the people. At the end of the day, the team you build is the company you build."[2] Zig Ziglar summed it up even more succinctly: "You don't build a business, you build people, and then people build the business."

Sean Kelly is the founder of Awesome Office, an organization dedicated to maximizing employee engagement, productivity, and wellbeing. In a 2016 article titled "9 Simple Ways to Invest in Your Employees and Combat Turnover," Kelly wrote: "The fact is, if you're not investing in your people, you're not investing in the future of your business." Kelly went on to say, "…it's important to understand that an investment in your team can mean a lot of different things, ranging from personal development to financial incentives to activities that bring them happiness. The point is that you want to show genuine care for your employees, and in return, they will take care of your business."³

Inspirational leaders realize the importance of investing in those they lead, and are willing to invest time and resources in order to have great team members—and thus great teams and organizations. While monetary compensation and certain financial investments are a part of that, like Sean Kelly indicated, investing in those you lead—and the resulting ROI—goes far beyond money. Inspirational leaders make investments not only by providing competitive compensation and generous benefits (where applicable), but also by:

- Providing relevant training and education options,
- Creating opportunities for individual growth—personally and professionally,
- Nurturing a culture of leadership development, and
- Regularly showing appreciation and appropriate recognition.

In this chapter we will explore each of these ways in which inspirational leaders invest in those they lead, looking at real-life examples and examining specific strategies and tactics.

Provide Relevant Training and Education Options

Outside of generous compensation and benefits, probably the most obvious way in which leaders can invest in those they lead is by providing relevant training and education options. Exactly what kind of opportunities you offer will of course depend on what will be of greatest value to those whom you lead. This might include job-specific training courses, leadership conferences, educational seminars, team-building events, scholarships for continued education, or maybe a special stipend for outside courses and events of choice.

In an interview for this book, my friend and colleague Dan Neufelder talked about the rewards of being able to assist those he leads with educational programs: "Sometimes it may be a masters program. Many other times it's some type of development program within our own company or something they can get elsewhere. That, I think, is really positive." He added, "We also get to encourage people that it's not just about your job. It's about the person that you are. Really thinking about mind, body, and spirit, so that these conversations aren't just about how to be a better healthcare executive, but how we can help the whole person develop." Dan went on to acknowledge that the financial investment can sometimes be hard, but it's worth it. "You always have to pay the bills... but people are worth far more than this month's income statement... people are a value just in and of themselves. They're not valuable because of the role they play, they're valuable because they're human beings."[4]

Traci Bernard is another leader who truly grasps the individual value of every person, and it shows in her leadership and the way in which she invests in her people. When talking about investing in the growth of those she leads, Traci explained that every year she sits down with members of her team not only to talk about organizational goals, but also to discuss personal and professional goals and how she can help them accomplish those goals as well. Traci's colleague and direct report Laura Redman noted that Traci encourages her team to read leadership books

> "You have to be intentional in developing your people."
> – Traci Bernard

and to enroll in classes in their area to continue learning and growing. "She's a huge proponent of education and to never stop learning."[5] Traci herself noted, "We have leadership development institutes that all of our leadership team goes to, from front line on up. We have all kinds of training opportunities. We do bag lunches. We promote certifications. We send people to training. We have tuition reimbursement... you have to be intentional in developing your people."[6]

Inspirational leaders don't merely rely on previously established programs and customs, they thoughtfully consider the needs of their team and seek out the best options and resources to add value to those they lead; and when necessary, they create those opportunities and programs themselves. Jim Wetrich's creation of the Women at Mölnlycke event (described in Chapter 8) is one such example. Recognizing a need, Jim created a program specifically geared and tailored to the needs of the women in his organization—with tremendous results. His colleague Sanchia Patrick Rasul said of Jim, "his commitment to growth in business, in others, and in himself is evident, contagious, and rare."[7]

Another example of a leader who spearheaded an innovative and valuable opportunity for his team is Mark Dixon. While serving in a senior leadership position in one organization, Mark established the practice and expectation that each of his direct reports had to visit an external organization for one day once a year in order to seek out best practices and learn from others in the industry. Mark noted that initially they were a little skeptical about the assignment, but after doing it, were grateful for the opportunity. "The feedback I got after doing that for some period of time is they just thoroughly enjoyed it. They learned. They wished they had been doing that for a long time before."[8]

One more example of a leader who invests in those he leads by providing training and education opportunities is my good friend and respected colleague Jack Lawless. His former direct report Arthur Sparks described Jack as a leader who "championed numerous training opportunities."[9] Another colleague, Jay Niner, wrote, "Jack invested in the careers and lives of the people in the organization. He believed in investing in people through internal and external training programs, which I believe was one of the most important commitments he could make as a leader of our organization. This is one reason why year after year we were voted one of the top 100 training companies in America."[10]

> A sincere and generous investment in people lies at the core of true inspirational leadership.

As exemplified by each of these leaders, a sincere and generous investment in people lies at the core of true inspirational leadership. No matter what specific resources and opportunities they offer, inspirational leaders know those they lead are worth the investment. They understand, as Robert Half once said, "Giving people a little more than they expect is a good way to get back a lot more than you'd expect."

CREATE OPPORTUNITIES FOR INDIVIDUAL GROWTH

In investing in those they lead, inspirational leaders don't just offer general job training and educational programs to their people as a whole; they go beyond group solutions to really focus on specific needs, customizing growth opportunities according to individual roles, interests, and strengths. Inspirational leaders recognize potential in those they lead and push them to achieve it by providing opportunities to grow and stretch the boundaries of their comfort zones. Most importantly, inspirational leaders offer plenty of support and encouragement to help their people meet those challenges and achieve success.

Dr. Robert Pryor, former chief medical officer at Baylor Scott & White Health, described his colleague Joel Allison as one such leader: "I see Joel as a coach who watches people, understands their abilities, and makes everyone with whom he comes in contact a much better leader and operator. He goes out of his way to find out how people think, work, and produce results, and he is always around to help them through difficult times."[11] Baylor EVP Gary Brock echoed that description of Joel, noting that he regularly discusses career paths and aspirations with each of his direct reports. "He demonstrates a genuine interest in people's success as individuals,"[12] Gary explained. Through his regular investment in the growth of those he leads, Joel lives out true inspirational leadership. As Jack Welch once said, "Leadership is helping other people grow and succeed. To repeat myself, leadership is not just about you. It's about them."

My friend and colleague Sheleza Mohamed shared an excellent example of another inspirational leader—one who recognized her potential, gave her a chance, and challenged her, supported her, and provided her with opportunities for growth. Sheleza explained how several years ago she interviewed for a position at a prestigious medical university. By many standards she was extremely qualified—having two relevant graduate degrees—but she lacked applicable work experience, and was nervous about the interview. Despite her lack of confidence, the interviewer saw Sheleza's potential and hired her for the position. "I had no idea how that interview and interviewer would forever change me as an individual and shape the leader I've become," Sheleza said. The leader who interviewed and hired her was an assistant vice president at the organization, and Sheleza described him as an intense figure who was very busy and often seemed difficult to please—yet was an incredible leader. "I struggled initially in that position," Sheleza noted, "but his trust and confidence in my abilities were enormous." She went on to explain how this inspirational leader took the time to invest in her:

> He took time in his schedule to train, problem solve, and mentor. I attended several organizational development and training classes with his support. By his appointment, I led several system implementations and upgrades that impacted over 10,000 employees. My self-esteem grew and I truly learned to "lean in." With his continued mentorship, I received five promotions, doubled my salary, and completed a leadership program in six years.

What an excellent example of how an inspirational leader's commitment to create opportunities for growth for one individual not only greatly impacted that individual's life and career, but because of the resulting growth had an impact on thousands of others! And that investment continues to resonate and grow: "I continually strive to be better," Sheleza explained, "because a great leader once invested in me."[13]

Mark Dixon is another inspirational leader who practices the critical habit of creating growth opportunities for the individuals he leads. He takes a genuine interest in their success, and offers personalized encouragement, support, and mentoring. His colleague Jeff Kirkham noted, "Mark has an exceptional ability to evaluate talent and identify areas of opportunity. He is perpetually coaching, and provides the time and resources needed to support his team."[14] Brad Beard said of Mark: "he is a tremendous leader, and he loves to teach those around him to become better leaders." Brad went on to say, "Mark is an inspirational leader who encourages his direct reports to achieve more than they thought possible, and my experience is that he had more confidence in me than I had in myself. He sets high goals and provides wonderful support for leaders to achieve those goals."[15]

> **Inspirational leaders encourage others to achieve more than they thought possible.**

The way in which inspirational leaders invest in individuals' growth is as varied as the leaders and individuals themselves. Celina Caprio, an attorney who volunteers as a mentor for young women and serves as a board member for MANA, A National Latina Organization®, explained that she helps those she leads learn and grow by delegating tasks to them that she knows will stretch their comfort zones—challenging them to do things they haven't done before. She gave the example of an occasion when she was scheduled to lead a seminar for Hermanitas—the MANA mentoring program she was directing at the time, and for which she still volunteers. Due to a change in her work schedule, Celina realized she was not going to be able to attend and lead the seminar as planned, so she delegated the task to the program's assistant director. "She did not like to speak in public, and was nervous that things would not go well," Celina explained. "But I knew she could do it. So I worked with her on what to say, helped her write her message, and reassured her of her skills. I also reminded her that she knew a lot of the people that were going to attend, so to view the event as being in the company of friends. She did just fine, it went well, and I got a big 'thank you' for believing in her."[16]

An important aspect of the example above is that Celina knew her assistant director could handle the challenge, but she didn't simply delegate the task and leave her to figure it out on her own. She offered assistance and encouragement, making sure to prepare her appropriately so she was equipped and empowered to succeed. Likewise, inspirational leaders always provide support and reassurance while they challenge and push people to greater heights.

Another example comes from the leadership of Jack Lawless, who has greatly impacted the lives and careers of countless colleagues over the years. During the interview Jack so graciously agreed to do for this book, he recounted a situation where a promising young leader in his organization was rather suddenly given the opportunity to stretch and grow when he was thrust into a more senior leadership role. Though he did well at first, the new leader soon began to struggle. Jack explained,

> This was a young man who had been a clinical director of nutrition, working for us in a facility that was going through some struggles and where we needed to make a leadership change. We needed to pull the food service director quickly and we asked this young clinical director to step in as interim. He was extremely anxious

> about it. He had gone to school for it, but he had not really worked in the operational position. But he had a lot of common sense. We were asking him to hold down the fort, so to speak, while things were rocky and until we could get great leadership in place. Well, over the course of a couple of months, the client came to really like and respect him. We liked him as well, and we said, "Hey look, we'd really like you to step into this position permanently," and he finally agreed to do that. Then a short time later the department started having some struggles again.[17]

Jack went on to describe how the new leader was losing confidence, and the more he struggled, the more fear he had about taking action. The young director, Arthur Sparks, continues the story:

> I was probably in over my head, and I was struggling immensely. The hospital had a new CEO that was stepping up every level of service the hospital provided… our department had made strides in the right direction over the time I had been director, but we were far from what anyone would consider a high-performing part of the hospital. While I was focused on the changes we had made, Jack and the new CEO clearly saw the changes that still needed to be made. Unfortunately, as the pressure increased on our department to step up our game, I became less and less confident to make the changes that needed to happen. I believed that every decision was going to be the decision that got me fired. I did not see that the failure to make a decision was worse than making the wrong choice.

Arthur went on to explain that Jack could see he had lost all confidence and was operating out of fear. Instead of reprimanding him or pulling him from the position altogether, Jack sat down with Arthur for an honest conversation, first encouraging him by sharing some of his own experiences, challenges, and failures, and then plainly laying out what needed to happen for Arthur to turn things around.

> Keep in mind, I was a lowly food service director and Jack was the president of the entire division. However, within minutes Jack had established a comfort level that let me know this was not going to be a regular "here are the things I saw on this visit" discussion. Jack and I talked about everything from his family growing up, to

> his career, to what was going on in my head. As the conversation progressed, we started to discuss what was going on at our hospital and with me personally. Jack was extremely honest and let me know that my inability to make the decisions that needed to be made had certainly made the CEO question if I was the person to lead this department. He was looking for "A" players, and I simply was not performing anywhere close to that level. Jack also asked the question, "If you were removed from your position today, how many times would you say to yourself, 'I just wish I had done this or done that?'" Jack had the confidence that I knew what needed to happen, I just was not making it happen… I was definitely headed for a crash if I did nothing. He made me realize if I started taking action and still got removed, at least I would be able to know that I gave everything I had.

As their conversation drew to an end, the two men looked at the clock and saw it was 1:21 in the afternoon. They decided that this would be their "1:21 conversation," agreeing that from that minute on, Arthur would run the department the way he knew it ought to be run, making the decisions that had to be made, and that Jack would support him in that effort in whatever way was necessary. There were many more tough days after that conversation; tough decisions were made, and changes were implemented. But that conversation and Jack's support made all the difference.

> Jack and I would reference our 1:21 conversation many times over the next few years. Jack helped me understand a lot of things that day. Trust yourself. Be honest with yourself. Be honest with your team. Use your resources. Do not be afraid to act. Jack knew he would impact me that day. What I'm not sure that Jack knew is how many more people he would impact as a result of that day. As my career has progressed, I have had the opportunity to have conversations very similar to our 1:21 conversation with mangers I support. I have gone back to that afternoon in my office more times than I can remember. Sometimes because I am struggling, sometimes because I think someone might benefit from hearing about that day.[18]

Obviously, the investment Jack made in his direct report had a huge ROI—not just for that one young man and the department he led, but for countless others down the line. Every one of Jack's colleagues whom I interviewed echoed the same thing—Jack truly invests in those he leads. Here are just a few of the comments regarding Jack's habit of making investments:

- "Jack invested in others by finding time to have personal conversations, by making personal connections, and by growing relationships."[19] – *Kathy Dagg*
- "Many people, including myself, owe part of their success to Jack's vested interest in their success. He was always encouraging others to grow… to go for promotions and other opportunities."[20] – *Ed Clark*
- "Jack had a natural talent for understanding when he needed to lift people up by recognizing their efforts, holding them accountable when execution lacked effort, and when to push for further thought when alternatives were available but not presented. To me this was inspirational leadership because it made us better leaders."[21] – *Scott Lewis*
- "He is a very caring man who puts people first but at the same time holds people accountable for their actions in a very fair way. He does a good job providing constructive criticism and insight… it is an honor to consider him a friend."[22] – *Michael Svagdis*
- "I am not sure Jack facilitates growth as much as he requires it. This does not necessarily mean that one is either moving up the corporate ladder or he is moving them out. However it does mean that he requires his team to consistently push what they are doing, what they know, and how they operate."[23] – *Arthur Sparks*

Jack's investment in Arthur Sparks and so many others is an excellent example of an inspirational leader investing in people by creating opportunities for individual growth, then supporting and encouraging throughout the ups and downs. And thankfully, the story of Jack and Arthur had a happy ending. But what happens when a leader gives someone an opportunity to grow and stretch, and it proves too much for them? My colleague Bruce Lawrence addressed this, stating, "I think as leaders, we always have to look for those growth opportunities… where can we find opportunities to stretch someone? But when we ask someone to stretch, we should also let them know that they've got a safety net to fall back on if that doesn't work for them or for us." Bruce went on to share an example from his own organization about a leader whom he encouraged to move into a new role that he knew would be challenging, but also knew would be a great stretching and learning experience:

> We sat down with him and asked him if he had an interest in exploring that, but the first thing we said to him was, "Hey, look, if this doesn't work for you or it's not working for us, you can move back into your other role. There's not going to be any negative attached to that. We're not going to think less of you, because we're asking you to really step out there on the edge, and it's an experiment. It may or may not work." He agreed to take the challenge. He did a very good job for probably close to a year, and then he came to us and said, "I've taken this as far as I can, and I can see it's going to take somebody with another level of expertise to get it to where it needs to be in totality, and I would like to go back to my old job now." So without any hesitation, we said, "You got it, that was our deal." Guess what? He goes back into his old job. He's even better there today than he was before because of what he learned through that stretching capability, and we didn't run the risk of losing him from the organization. It really worked out well for him, and it worked out well for the organization. His current areas of responsibility are more effective and efficient now from the things he learned, and so I think it was a win-win-win all the way around.[24]

Inspirational leaders like Bruce Lawrence understand the critical importance of balancing a challenging stretch opportunity with adequate support and a fallback plan—a "safety net," as Bruce calls it. Had Bruce never pushed that leader to try, he would have missed a great opportunity to leverage and improve his strengths. But if Bruce had not also provided the reassurance of a safety net, that leader may have felt no other option than to quit the organization feeling like he failed, rather than recognizing the experience as the positive stretching opportunity that it was. When designed and implemented well, a safety net serves not as a crutch or excuse to back out, but as additional encouragement to "go for it," reassuring those you lead that you'll be there to catch them if they fall.

In describing her colleague Tim Orellano, Breda Turner succinctly sums up how inspirational leaders focus on individual growth: "Tim is really great at spotting a special talent in a person, and he guides and cajoles them to expand their abilities. (We give him a hard time about that!)… He manages to spot a talent and give that person an opportunity to do more, to give more, and to learn more about who they are."²⁵ How about you? Do you spot talent and give those you lead the opportunity to do more, give more, and learn more about who they are? That's what making investments is all about!

NURTURE A CULTURE OF LEADERSHIP

Inspirational leaders believe in raising up other leaders. As Bill Murphy, Jr. wrote for an online *Inc.* magazine article, "The mark of a great leader isn't creating followers—but instead developing other leaders."²⁶ Inspirational leaders do just that—they are intentional and strategic in terms of developing and building up more inspirational leaders. Whether it's called "leader development," "talent management," or "internal succession planning," a commitment to raising up new leaders is a mark of inspirational leadership and a critical aspect of healthy and growing organizations.

Dan Neufelder, founder and CEO of The Neufelder Consulting Group and former president and CEO of Ministry Health Care, takes leader development very seriously. While at Ministry Health Care, he had a simple yet effective talent review process in place for evaluating people on their performance in their current role and on their potential for promotion. Dan explained that part of the review process was to speak with each individual about where they're at in their career and where they want to go. "What support, education, or experiences do they need? We have a conversation about what they feel like they need and what we feel like they need to kind of take the next step in the direction for their career."²⁷

Peter Fine, president and CEO of Banner Health, is another leader who believes strongly in the importance of building up new leaders within his organization. Banner Health has what Peter calls a very sophisticated talent management program. "We take talent management seriously. Virtually all of our top people in the organization—several hundred—have development plans in which we have identified what they need to do and what skills they need to gain to migrate further up into the company." Peter went on to explain:

People *thrive* —*and so does their work*— when they are **VALUED, RECOGNIZED,** and **CELEBRATED**

> We look at their relationship within Banner as a journey of a lifetime So if it's a journey of a lifetime, we have a certain responsibility to enhance their skill levels and provide opportunities for them to develop and grow. So the development plan has become important for us because it guides us as to what responsibilities they need to gain, with input, to advance.[28]

Just as Peter Fine and the senior leadership of Banner Health consider the investment in leader development to be part of equipping people for a "journey of a lifetime," inspirational leaders recognize that the investment they make in building up new leaders will have a lifelong impact.

Traci Bernard, president of Texas Health Harris Methodist Hospital in Southlake, Texas, is another example of an inspirational leader who invests in the lives of those she leads by building them up to become better leaders. Traci explains that in her organization they identify people who aspire to lead and are already inspirational leaders in their current role, then develop them for the next level by providing the education, training, and mentoring they need. "We have a phenomenal succession plan here. We always try to promote internally. The majority of my leadership team were staff-level people when they originally started at the organization, and have moved up through the ranks."[29] Traci gave the example of one staff member who started as a floor nurse, then became a charge nurse, then the quality director, and eventually the chief nursing officer.

That's just one of countless success stories made possible by the emphasis Traci and her leadership team place on leader development. The leadership culture that Traci has nurtured within her organization impacts each and every person who works there. One of her direct reports, Karen Adams, had this to say about Traci:

> With her encouraging and supportive leadership, she inspires me to be the best I can be. She invests in my growth as a leader and mentors me, always having an open door. Traci has great solutions when I need help with a situation. She believes in me and will always build me up—not tear me down—when the chance comes. This allows me to have the confidence to do great things, to make this hospital great, to make her look great, and for her to be proud of me. She has created the most positive culture of any hospital I have ever worked for in the thirty years that I have been in healthcare.[30]

Another colleague of Traci's, Anthony Romero, credited Traci for her guidance and encouragement that led him up the ranks to ultimately achieve his current position in management. He also echoed Karen's comments about the positive work culture Traci has nurtured, noting, "The culture she has created here is like none I have ever worked in. It's a culture of teamwork, development for all levels, and caring for each other, our families, and the community we serve."[31]

One significant aspect of a positive, leader-developing culture like that which Traci Bernard has helped create and nurture, is the presence of mentoring. Joel Allison made the point that as leaders, we have all benefited from having mentors, whether we have formally recognized them as such or not. "So I think it's our responsibility to give back and to mentor other young, aspiring leaders," Joel said. "You do that by spending time with your people; you spend time with your team, you get to know about them personally. And you don't just know them in a workplace setting, you really invest time in them by knowing their families and showing that you care and have a genuine interest in them."[32]

Like Joel Allison, Jack Lawless also believes mentoring is a critically important aspect of developing leaders. Jack explained that when he worked at Morrison, they really focused on mentoring. "We didn't have a mentoring program per se, but rather tried to create a mentoring *culture*. It wasn't a promise of anything. It was basically trying to establish a culture where everyone had a mentor and was a mentor."[33] Jack's colleagues Michael Svagdis and Arthur Sparks both mentioned how Jack himself served as a mentor for many of the young leaders under him. Arthur described Jack's commitment to mentoring as one of the most important and significant aspects of his leadership, explaining:

> Jack always takes the time to mentor those he leads, either formally or informally. Jack has mentored me since I first started working closely with him. This has included professional and personal mentoring. As I started in my current role, which requires significant travel, Jack has taken the time to discuss techniques that he or others have used to attempt to find some balance between the work and family life. Not only does Jack provide mentoring on situations you are currently dealing with, he provides insight into upcoming opportunities, pitfalls, etc. Jack and I have discussed dealing with clients that may seem unreasonable, and how to get in front of

those situations. We have discussed ways to keep my wife and kids involved in my life when it seems that work is taking over. Basically, Jack not only seizes any opportunity to provide mentoring, he creates those opportunities.[34]

Another excellent example of an inspirational leader committed to building up young leaders through mentoring is Celina Caprio, who has volunteered as a mentor for young women for more than a decade. In 2013 Celina was recognized as the Inspirational Leader of the Year by *San Diego Magazine* as part of the Latino Impact Awards. Reflecting on that experience, Celina humbly explained, "I was up against both men and women who are very highly regarded in our community, and to my surprise I was the one who won… and speaking to those who gave me the award, I asked, 'Of all of these people, why me? What did I do differently than all of them?'" Those bestowing the award pointed out that the mentoring Celina does is all volunteer work—she doesn't get paid for the countless hours she invests volunteering in addition to her full-time job as an attorney.[35] It was apparent when speaking with her that Celina invests in these young women—encouraging and empowering them in practical ways to pursue their goals and dreams—not for any sort of compensation or recognition, but because she sees their potential and deeply cares about them and their futures. Harvey S. Firestone once said, "The growth and development of people is the highest calling of leadership." without a doubt, Celina is fulfilling that calling, and nurturing a culture of leadership that will dramatically and positively impact the lives of the young women whom she leads and mentors.

> "The growth and development of people is the highest calling of leadership."
> – *Harvey S. Firestone*

When I first started writing this chapter, I tentatively titled this section "Implement a Leader-Development Strategy." But upon further thought and research, I realized that implementing a specific strategy to develop leaders is far less effective than nurturing a *culture* of leader development. While there's nothing wrong with having a strategy—and I've shared several examples here—strategies and processes are inherently limited, whereas a thriving culture where leader development is the norm has a greater and more widespread impact. As Tim Stevens put it in an article for *Entrepreneur*, "It's just better when leadership development is in the air you live and breathe rather than a process to follow." Stevens went on to explain, "A successful leadership culture can't be seen, touched, or picked up, but it permeates a business at every level… it is more of a philosophy, a way that you think about the people on your team and in your organization."[36] I think this philosophy accurately reflects the attitude and actions of inspirational leaders; they think of everyone on their team as leaders in the process of being further developed.

SHOW APPRECIATION AND RECOGNITION

Showing sincere appreciation and recognition for work well done is one of the simplest but most significant ways in which inspirational leaders engage those they lead. It's a basic truth of life that people want to be recognized and appreciated for what they do—especially when they achieve particularly challenging goals, go above and beyond their areas of responsibility, or exceed expectations with their assigned tasks. Sadly, this very basic tenet of employee engagement is often overlooked in the workplace. Whether some leaders don't believe their direct reports have earned their praise, or they simply don't think about it, far too many leaders fail to express appreciation, and as a result, those they lead feel their work goes unrecognized and efforts unappreciated. In an article for HR.com, Sasha Bricel noted the negative ramifications of neglecting employee recognition:

> When hard work goes invalidated, why would anyone feel inclined to repeat the positive behaviors they exemplified to deliver those results again? For the workforce, experiences like these are extremely detrimental when it comes to employee engagement. But the repercussions are equally damaging for leadership. When management fails to recognize other's accomplishments, they decrease their reputability—meaning they are not seen as a team player, which affects their ability to retain top performers and to recruit great talent in the future. Not to mention future results remain unsecured due to de-motivated teams.[37]

On the other hand, the positive effects of frequent and appropriate praise and recognition are just as significant. When people are recognized for their efforts and made to feel a sense of pride in their accomplishments, they are dramatically more engaged in their work and will be motivated and driven to continue producing outstanding results. As Sam Walton once explained, "Outstanding leaders go out of their way to boost the self-esteem of their personnel. If people believe in themselves, it's amazing what they can accomplish." Nothing boosts self-esteem and encourages engagement like praise for work well done. Author and speaker Michael Hyatt echoed Walton's statement, writing, "Inspirational leaders help people believe in themselves." He went on to explain,

> We all get bumped and bruised as we go through life. Circumstances constantly conspire to undermine our esteem. It's easy to lose heart—to begin doubting our ability to handle the challenges we face. That's why it is so refreshing to meet someone who believes in us and is willing to verbalize it. It gives us confidence that maybe we do have what it takes. Great leaders—like great parents—help people believe in themselves. They look for opportunities to catch people doing something right. They focus on their people's strengths, not their weaknesses. And, they have a knack for offering encouragement at strategic moments—when the team needs it.[38]

In an article published on LinkedIn, author Jeff Haden reminds us that everyone does *something* well, and every employee deserves praise and appreciation. He writes,

> It's easy to recognize some of your best employees because they're consistently doing awesome things... You might have to work hard to find reasons to recognize an employee who simply meets standards, but that's okay: A few words of recognition—especially public recognition—may be the nudge an average performer needs to start becoming a great performer.[39]

Haden's mention of public recognition is an important point; while not all people enjoy the spotlight, most people do crave some measure of public praise. For many people, having their efforts and accomplishments acknowledged in front of their peers means a lot—boosting their confidence and inspiring them to achieve even more. And they're not the only ones who benefit from being publicly recognized for their work—seeing hard work praised and appreciated is encouraging and motivating for their coworkers as well.

One organization that has really leveraged the power of public recognition to encourage and engage its workforce is Morrison Management Specialists. Jack Lawless worked for Morrison's Healthcare Food Services for more than three decades, and served as division president for 12 years. During that time, he and his colleague Michael Svagdis were instrumental in developing a culture of service throughout the organization. Part of that culture is a program called "People First," where stories are shared and employees publically recognized for the remarkable ways in which they have served others. Jack explained that sharing those stories throughout the organization not only affirms the excellent work being done, but helps to further engage and inspire everyone who hears them. Jack went on to share a specific story about one of their catering associates who impacted a patient's life with a simple but significant gesture of kindness: In the course of her job, as she finished delivering a food tray to a patient, the catering associate asked, "Is there anything else I can do for you?" The woman responded, "I would love a brush and a mirror so I can do my hair." Upon further inquiry, she learned that the patient didn't have those basic items, and had no family to bring them to her. "So the catering associate went downstairs to the gift shop," Jack explained, "and with her own money, came back up and gave that woman a brush and a makeup kit, then helped her to do her hair. She found out that the woman was actually leaving the hospital and going to hospice. She didn't have anybody left in her family, so the catering associate and her family ended up 'adopting' that patient, so to speak, staying in touch with her through the rest of her life."

Stories like that are published and shared throughout the organization. So the catering associate's actions not only impacted that one patient, but have since impacted and influenced the work of hundreds of Morrison employees who have come to be familiar with that story, and through them, have impacted thousands of patients. Every year thousands of stories of outstanding service are submitted as part of the People First program, and every individual whose story is submitted receives a letter from the CEO and a small token of appreciation. Then a dozen or so individuals with the most inspiring stories are selected for special recognition and celebration, and are given a customized reward to thank them for going above and beyond. Jack explained,

> For one individual, they had always wanted to attend culinary school, so we sent them to the culinary institute of America for three weeks. For another one, they had never been able to afford wedding rings. So we bought them wedding rings, put together a little ceremony to celebrate it, and sent them on a little honeymoon. For another one, this individual had come to work during a hurricane; his car had been flooded, so he had to walk to work. We ended up buying him a car... so we celebrate service to others, whether it's to another associate, the community, or to the patient. That's what we celebrate, and it's great.[40]

Without a doubt, Jack and his fellow leaders' commitment to show genuine appreciation and to recognize and celebrate the service and success of those they lead makes an enormous difference in the organization. As Colleen Barrett and Ken Blanchard discuss in their book, *Lead With LUV*, celebrating successes is an important part of a healthy company culture.

> To sustain our Company Culture, we cheer People on all the time. We celebrate little things, big things—we celebrate everything! Although we do have some formal celebrations, a lot of them are informal, spontaneous celebrations that cost little or no money... What's important is the fact that you're honoring them and acknowledging that what they do makes a positive difference.[41]

Like Colleen Barrett, inspirational leaders understand that people thrive—and so does their work—when they are valued, recognized, and celebrated. Making an investment as simple as a sincere "Thank you" and a box of chocolates can go a long way. Whether it's a small investment like a moment of recognition for a job well done, or a large investment like covering the cost of further education, inspirational leaders make intentional, personal, continuous investments in each individual whom they lead. As author Sheri L. Dew once wrote, "True leaders understand that leadership is not about them but about those they serve. It is not about exalting themselves but about lifting others up."[42]

KEY POINTS

To be a leader who makes investments:

- Provide relevant training and education options.
- Create opportunities for individual growth.
- Nurture a culture of leadership development.
- Regularly show appreciation and appropriate recognition.

INSPIRE

"You get the best efforts from others not by lighting a fire beneath them, but by building a fire within." – Bob Nelson

12

CREATE VISION

"Good business leaders create a vision, articulate the vision, passionately own the vision, and relentlessly drive it to completion." – Jack Welch

Great success almost always starts with great vision. As Peter Drucker once said, "Leadership is lifting a person's vision to higher sights, the raising of a person's performance to a higher standard, the building of a personality beyond its normal limitations." Inspirational leaders do just that—lift the vision of their team or organization to higher sights, then engage, inspire, and empower them to achieve that vision by performing to a higher standard and beyond their normal limitations. When asked what comes to mind when he thinks of inspirational leadership, my colleague Dan Teeters immediately responded, "Capturing and effectively communicating a vision."[1] By creating and communicating a compelling vision, inspirational leaders stir up passion and enthusiasm in those they lead and help overcome apathy and disengagement.

Clearly, vision is important. It's one of those words you hear all the time in connection to leadership, and it goes without saying that leaders should have vision. But what does it really mean to lead with vision? How does vision differ from mission and strategy? How does a leader create vision and inspire people to work toward that vision? Can any leader be "visionary," or is that a label reserved for special leadership virtuosos? In this chapter we will address those questions and take a look at practical ways inspirational leaders create vision and communicate it to those they lead.

Answer the "What" and the "Why"

As former University of Notre Dame president Theodore Hesburgh once said, "The very essence of leadership is that you have to have vision. You can't blow an uncertain trumpet." Simply put, leaders must have an idea of what future they are leading toward if they are to have any hope of getting anyone to follow! Having vision is having a picture of future possibilities. Without a picture of where you are going—without a hopeful vision of what *could* be—it is virtually impossible to inspire people to go there with you.

A hopeful vision of the future provides the framework for a meaningful mission, which in turn gives significance and purpose to daily tasks. Michael Hyatt refers to this as the "why" behind the "what." Both are essential, but vision (why you're doing what you're doing) must come first. Hyatt explains, "Vision and strategy are both important. But there is a priority to them. Vision always comes first. Always. If you have a clear vision, you will eventually attract the right strategy. If you don't have a clear vision, no strategy will save you."[2]

Different people and organizations define and differentiate between terms like *vision*, *mission*, *strategies*, and *tactics* in many different ways. I like the way Saul Kaplan puts it: "Vision is a clearly stated picture of the future state you are trying to achieve. Strategies are what you are going to do to achieve the vision. Tactics are the specific actions necessary to carry out each strategy."[3] And what about mission? We discussed mission a little bit in Chapter 10. Essentially, I believe mission is the bridge between vision and strategy; it puts the overall vision into practical terms with achievable objectives for which strategies can be developed. Another way to think of it: *tactics* are the very specific actions that are carried out as part of the *strategies* intended to achieve the *mission*, which aims to make the *vision* a reality.

So if mission and strategies are the "what" and the "how," then vision is the "why." It is critical that inspirational leaders have a clearly defined "why"—a clear picture of the future toward which they are striving and leading others. Without a compelling "why" behind what you're doing, true and lasting inspiration is virtually impossible, and very few will want to follow you.

So in practical terms, what does it mean for a leader to have and create vision? Jack Welch puts it plainly: "A leader's job is to look into the future and see the organization not as it is, but as it should be." My friend and colleague Bill Brown shared a story with me about a leader who did exactly that. Here's his story:

> It was my privilege in the late 1970s to work for a man who embodied the characteristics of a truly inspirational leader. I was in Abilene at the time, a west Texas city with a population of about 75,000 and with a pronounced dearth of mental health services—especially for children and youth. Everett E. Woods had a vision of a place to meet those needs and needed management assistance to implement his vision, so I joined his firm. Woods was a clinical social worker by profession who had a failing residential treatment center thrust into his lap by other investors who literally walked away from the enterprise. But instead of worrying about his troubles—and there were many—he cast a vision of a comprehensive treatment facility for children and youth and set about to make it happen. Without him even knowing who Peter Drucker was, Woods exemplified Drucker's definition: 'Leadership is lifting a person's vision to higher sights, the raising of a person's performance to a higher standard, the building of a personality beyond its normal limitations.' Throughout the brief time I was part of his organization, I was constantly amazed at Woods' ability to bring divergent—and sometimes hostile—interests on board to accomplish his vision.
>
> Our paths diverged in 1980 and I did not hear much from Woods until I had relocated my consulting practice back to Texas in the mid-1990s. He called and invited me to Abilene to assist with some issues he was facing at that time. Upon arriving, I was amazed to see what he had accomplished. Embodied in impressive, modern buildings staffed by a host of competent professionals, his dream had come to life, all because he was determined to have it and gain the support of others necessary to achieve it. Lifting a person's vision to higher sights? Absolutely. The creation of the Woods Psychiatric Institute was a classic case of accomplishing what others said could not be done. Building connections? Again, right on target. Abilene was not particularly interested in, nor sympathetic to troubled children and youth. But Woods not only persevered, he demonstrated the value of a comprehensive mental health service to the well-being of the community at large. In sum, Everett E.

Woods meets my definition of a very inspirational leader.[5]

Bill's story about the vision and determination of Everett E. Woods reminds me very much of my own story, starting a hospital from scratch back in the early 1970s. I was thirty-years-old, just a couple years out of graduate school and into my career, and I was hired to be the CEO of a medical center that was only a hope and a dream at the time. In the beginning, the organization was without funding, property, buildings, employees, medical staff, or patients. I was the very first employee, hired to turn a dream and vision into reality. Thanks largely to the significant impact and positive foundation provided during the first two years of my career by one very inspirational leader—Max Coppom—I was able to develop a plan, answer the "what" and the "why," and build and lead the organization from the ground up. Thanks to great vision and determination, the Dallas-Fort Worth Medical Center was the fastest growing hospital in the state of Texas at that time, and I enjoyed fifteen incredible years at its helm.

Whether you're a leader in a large corporation, a coach of a sports team, or a teacher in an elementary school, you are leading people somewhere, and you must have a vision of the future you'd like them to reach. Inspirational leaders must be farsighted, not only concerned with the daily life of their teams or organizations, but continuously keeping the end in mind as well. As Warren Bennis once said, "Leaders keep their eyes on the horizon, not just on the bottom line."

But as a leader, it is not solely up to you to envision the ideal future. On the contrary, it's important that those you lead be a part of the process. The people you lead need to own the vision as well. They need to be bought in—they need to feel like the future you're trying to lead them toward really is *their* future, and not just what *you* want. As Michael Hyatt has noted, "Some leaders just expect people will follow them just because of their position. Wrong. If a leader can't enroll others, failure looms."[6]

> **Vision must be developed, not dictated.**

Creating vision should be a somewhat inclusive, collaborative process, directed and finalized by the leader. Obviously this should be done carefully so as not to get bogged down in the process of trying to reach a consensus, but the bottom line is that a leader cannot be a lone wolf when it comes to creating vision for a team or organization. Vision must be developed, not dictated. Jack Lawless emphasized the importance of this; you should collaborate with your leadership team and get buy-in for your vision before announcing it and expecting everyone in the organization to just jump on board.

> Be passionate about and committed to your vision, and make sure that you get buy-in from all of your senior leaders before announcing it. So many times somebody comes up with an idea, then they run out and say "this is where we're going to go," and the organization hasn't had a chance to actually get on board with it. By bringing the idea out and allowing others to shape it a little bit first, to touch it and create their own ownership of it, when you deliver that inspirational message, you have an organization that's already anxious and wanting to get on board with it. If you have to own that idea by yourself, then it's going to be hard for you to inspire others; but if you let others own that and feel like they created it, that it's their vision and culture, then you're going to be able to move miles further than you could otherwise.[7]

Christine Márquez-Hudson, who spent over seven years as executive director of Mi Casa Resource Center before taking on her current role as president & CEO of The Denver Foundation, shared about her experience with creating vision while at Mi Casa. She explained how when she first came on board as executive director the organization was going through a very difficult period; programs were being cut, success was waning, and morale was very low. So Christine began by leading the organization through the process of creating vision and aligning their mission and strategic plan with that vision.

> We went through a strategic planning process that exercised the idea of getting a lot of input from a lot of angles. We had that data from people. We also had the data from the economic growth of the city. As a result, we changed our name to Mi Casa Resource Center. We used to be Mi Casa Resource Center for Women. We changed our mission to advance the economic success of Latino families, whereas before we had been about women and youth. We also overhauled our career programming, our business programming, and our youth programming to really align around this idea of economic success. That really helped crystalize our identity,

who we wanted to be, and how we were going to be that.

Christine went on to explain that the strategic plan they developed as a result of that process was really a manifestation of that identity. "I think that was really key, because as we went out to 'shop around' the strategic plan, we had data to substantiate why we were moving in this direction, what the need was, where we had gotten the input, etc. It wasn't just me saying, 'I think this is where we should go,' off the top of my head. It was substantiated." Later during her time at Mi Casa, the organization went through another phase of growth and change. However, this time Christine didn't begin with the same careful process of gathering data and input to create the vision before trying to move forward. As a result, she experienced a surprising amount of pushback. "I got ahead of everybody else, and ended up having to pull back and gather everyone around that idea again," she explained. "It's a lesson learned."[8]

As Jack Lawless and Christine Márquez-Hudson's real-life experiences demonstrate, involving your team in the process of creating vision is an important step leaders shouldn't skip. Those you lead need to feel connected to the mission (the "what") and bought in to the vision (the "why")—and the best way to achieve that is to include them in the process of creating it. Or as Charles Lauer once said, "Leaders don't force people to follow; they invite them on a journey."

Paint a Vivid Picture

My wife is an extremely gifted interior designer, and she loves what she does. She regularly envisions gorgeous kitchen renovations, stunning bathroom makeovers, and incredible contemporary updates for homes and businesses. But in order to bring those visions to reality, she must first get her clients to see what she sees. Without first painting a vivid picture of what could be (aligning that vision with her client's needs and desires) her client might get lost and overwhelmed by all the details—the time, money, and effort required to bring the vision to fruition. She has to get that buy-in before she can get started, and to get the buy-in, she has to help her clients visualize what it is she is envisioning.

In the same way, inspirational leaders must paint a vivid picture of the future in order to inspire those they lead to follow them toward that vision.

One of the most important parts of creating vision is painting that picture—or articulating it—for those you lead. Once you have the vision in mind and have sought input and agreement from key members of your team or organization, it is time to communicate it to everyone you lead. Michael Hyatt explains, "Inspirational leaders believe in the future. They are able to paint a vivid picture of a different and better reality. They make it concrete, so people can see it, touch it, smell it, and taste it. They give people hope that things can be better, and they have a plan for making it so."[9]

Peter Fine, president & CEO of Banner Health, offered some great insights about creating vision: "You have to give people a sense of direction," he noted, "and creating vision—or in my mind, creating a picture—is necessary for people to rally around not only the certain tactics that you want to use or to accomplish a desired end, but to work through the very hard process to achieve those desired ends. Without giving people a picture of reality, they get lost in it."[10]

> "Without giving people a picture of reality, they get lost in it."
> – Peter Fine

In an excellent episode of the *EntreLeadership* podcast, featured guest and best-selling author Marcus Buckingham talks about the critical importance of painting a vivid, detailed picture of the future. "Whether it's the values on the walls or whether it's the anecdotes you tell about customers, if you're going to drag me into the future, if you're going to say this is the land of milk and honey, then like Moses you've got to say, 'This is what the milk will taste like, this is what the honey will taste like.'" You've got to help those you lead see the future as vividly as you can see it. Do that, Buckingham says, and people will follow you into that future with confidence.[11]

My colleague Mark Dixon, president of The Mark Dixon Group, LLC, echoes that insight:

> I love the word vision. It's used kind of as a boilerplate by so many different people… vision, values, mission, etc. But vision is so important. To me it's creating that vivid picture of what a successful future will look like, and doing it in such a way that everybody in the organization wants to be part of that. Doesn't have to be part of it, but wants to be part of it.[12]

Mark went on to note that creating vision requires engaging people across the organization to get involved in thinking through and developing that vision, and that it's important to let the creative people on your team help make it come to life. "I use the word vivid—paint a vivid picture of what you want to be." He offered an example from his own experience, while serving as a hospital CEO, of a vision-creation process that eventually resulted in a very simple but compelling vision and mission statement:

> We worked so long on creating and articulating the vision for our rehabilitation unit. We had tried "smile for rehabilitation," and other post-orthopedic sorts of things. But when we broke it all down, we realized our vision was really "to make lives work," to help patients and their families get back to work, get back to functioning and working at home again. And that was really compelling. That's what we were all about; we were making lives work. That kind of compelling vision gets people engaged in the organization, makes them say, "I want to be part of that. I want to be part of where we're going as an organization."[13]

In a sense, visionary leaders are artists, skilled at painting a vivid picture of the future they strive to reach. But as any good artist does, they know and utilize their tools well; so even if you as a leader are not personally strong in the area of creatively articulating vision, you likely have people on your team who are. Use them. Leverage your resources, involve your team, think outside the box, and paint that picture. Because to truly be strong, effective, and inspiring, your vision must be communicated well.

Share Passion, Build Excitement, and Maintain Enthusiasm

Congruent with the articulation of your vision should be your own excitement and passion for that vision. It should go without saying that in order for leaders to inspire others with their vision for the future, they themselves must be inspired and passionate about it. Or, as my friend Tom Furman, a veterinarian from my hometown of Alliance, Nebraska, put it, "If a leader cannot be honestly excited about his or her organization's mission and vision, then he or she will never be effective at inspiring and coordinating other people to follow in pursuit of it."[14] Another one of my colleagues, Richard Howe, expanded on that concept, explaining:

> Leaders must lead by example. They must be excited about what they are doing; must express enthusiasm and encouragement toward achieving goals, and must celebrate successes all the time—both the little ones and the big ones. Excitement and celebrating successes creates inspiration!

Richard went on to describe inspirational leadership as the "fuel" that pushes individuals to achieve more and drives teams to function at their very best. "Team members will go out of their way for a passionate, visionary leader. The atmosphere turns from just pure work to something that all team members aspire to be a part of."[15] That inspiration starts at the top, with a passionate, excited, enthusiastic leader! As Ralph Nader once said, "A leader has the vision and conviction that a dream can be achieved. He inspires the power and energy to get it done." Jack Welch has also commented on the importance of passion and energy, noting that the future "will not belong to 'managers' or those who can make the numbers dance. The world will belong to passionate, driven leaders—people who not only have enormous amounts of energy but who can energize those whom they lead."

Lisa Hill received Denver's 9News Leader of the Year Award in 2014. Lisa has worked at Invest in Kids, which is a non-profit dedicated to improving the wellbeing of young children in Colorado, since 2000, and has been the executive director since 2009. Asked about what it means to be considered an inspirational leader, Lisa responded, "When I hear people give me feedback and say, 'Oh, you're so inspiring,' what I hear them saying is that I have a commitment to a mission. I have a vision for the organization's impact. I have a tremendous amount of passion and optimism and commitment to those things. I'm able to articulate a bright future, and able to articulate a path from here to there. I'm able to see that bigger picture, but not lose sight of the details." She concluded, "When I think of inspirational in particular, I think of the energetic, passionate, committed. I think it's my energy that inspires people."[16]

Mark Dixon is another leader who demonstrates great energy and passion for reaching the vision. His colleague Bob Solheim said of Mark, "Alongside of character, perhaps Mark's greatest strength is his ability to not only be a visionary leader but to be able to share this vision and inspire others with it." Bob went on to say,

> I give Mark the highest possible ratings for his ability to build excitement and passion within those he leads. I know that, because I am someone who is not easily impressed by some of the topics Mark has needed to speak about in the hospital system he enjoyed a leadership role in—i.e. operating margins, revenue cycle tactics, labor issues, just to name a very few—yet I was always moved by what he said and felt empowered by his words to be a part of the solution to the issues he would raise as challenges for us. The passion and excitement begins within Mark and he is able to communicate this passion so effectively as to infect others by it.[17]

Bob's description of Mark's infectious passion fits well with something Ted Turner once said: "A leader is someone who creates infectious enthusiasm." It's that infectious enthusiasm, that sincere passion for and belief in the vision, that will inspire people to follow you into the future—not just at first, but day after day. Because building excitement and passion for the vision is only the first step. You then have to keep that enthusiasm alive. As Andy Stanley puts it, "Vision leaks." You've got to keep pouring vision into your organization, day in and day out, or it will slowly leak out and dry up.

> "Vision leaks." You've got to keep pouring vision into your organization, day in and day out, or it will slowly leak out and dry up.

Beyond consistently sharing their own passion for the vision, inspirational leaders also work to build and maintain excitement by connecting the vision to daily tasks. As John Maxwell points out, "Vision comes alive when everyone sees where his or her contribution makes a difference." Mark Dixon explained that connecting the day-to-day activities within an organization to its overall mission and vision helps build excitement and passion for the vision by making it less abstract; "so people can see where they fit and know that they're building towards that vision." Mark went on to note that inspirational leaders make those connections—reminding their people of why they're doing what they're doing—by being present and engaged in the little things.

> There's many different ways you can do that, whether it's town hall meetings, or management by walking around, being available for conversations, attending little staff meetings, etc. Just being in front of your people on a very regular basis—to me that's what I found is the most successful way to build excitement and passion for where you're trying to take your company.[18]

Bob Furman, former executive director of YMCA Camp Kitaki, offers additional insights about maintaining that enthusiasm and commitment: "Excitement and passion come from thoroughly engaging the mission. Constant reminders, stories, and reports of accomplishment shared with your staff keeps them enthused about what they do."[19] Bob's comment about using stories to sustain enthusiasm for the mission and vision is echoed by Lisa Claes in an article titled "Inspirational Leadership: Engaging Staff in Times of Change." Claes notes that people relate to stories, and that storytelling "builds authenticity and makes the business of leadership real."[20]

So what does storytelling look like? For some organizations, like the example of Morrison Management Specialists in the previous chapter, storytelling may take on a life of its own, becoming an official company program and publication intended to showcase the most inspiring stories throughout the organization. For other organizations and leaders, storytelling is a more natural process, effortlessly incorporated into their teams' daily interactions. In the interview he did for this book, Dan Neufelder, founder and CEO of The Neufelder Consulting Group, spoke about storytelling and celebrating successes as one of the most important strategies for inspiring those he leads. "I like to lead with celebration and appreciation," he said. He explained how years ago he read about the power of positive affirmation in the workplace, and so began incorporating it into some of the most common and mundane aspects of the job: meetings.

> So at the beginning of our meetings with our whole leadership team, at the very beginning, we'd start with celebration and appreciation. Sometimes there would be fifteen or twenty minutes where people were just talking about "we got this recognition," or "we accomplished this," or "we finished that project." It was great. I think it created a real pride in the organization and a sense of togetherness.

Dan went on to talk about the impact that sharing success stories had on the individuals in those meetings:

> It really made a difference. I once had an HR leader who joined us, and after one of our first meetings like that, he told me, "I feel like I've just joined the New York Yankees." I asked, "What do you mean?" He said, "All the other organizations I've ever been a part of, people dread meetings like that because generally the focus is what's not working right, or what's wrong with this area or that area. But here, it's like a pep rally."[21]

As Dan has noted, recognizing and celebrating small successes is an extremely important part of inspirational leadership. By noticing and corporately celebrating those small steps toward the greater vision, you help maintain your team's enthusiasm and keep their focus on the big picture. Celebration of small successes becomes particularly important when your team or organization is facing difficulty. It's a fact of life that things don't always go smoothly or according to plan, and at times forward progress sometimes halts or even reverses. At times like that, it is critical that inspirational leaders help their people maintain hope; one way they do that is by celebrating the things that *are* going well. Hope might not be a term you hear a lot in most organizations, but it's an essential element of inspirational leadership. Hope is powerful and productive—and conversely, lack of hope is draining and destructive—personally, professionally, and organizationally. In his book *Sometimes You Win – Sometimes You Learn*, author John Maxwell devotes an entire chapter to hope. He writes, "Hope-filled people are energetic. They welcome life and all that it brings—even its challenges." Maxwell also includes a quote from Napoleon that I think is spot on: "Leaders are dealers in hope."[22]

When it comes to creating vision, inspirational leaders understand they must first answer the "what" and the "why," and engage those they lead in forming the vision and painting a vivid picture. They also understand that creating vision isn't something you do just once; vision creation is an ongoing, continuous process, embedded in daily assignments and found in everyday, ordinary work. I think Erika Anderson summed it up pretty well in her article for *Fast Company* titled "What Leading With Vision Really Means:"

> We are drawn to leaders who articulate a possible future in a way

that speaks to us and includes us. Farsighted leaders use their clarity of vision and their articulation of a successful future to pull people out of fear or shortsightedness and into hopefulness and a sense of purpose.[23]

Are you creating and leading with vision? Be an inspirational leader, and create vision and inspire hope for those you lead!

KEY POINTS

To be a leader who creates vision:

- Answer the "what" and the "why" for your organization
- Paint a vivid picture of the future you're striving toward.
- Share passion, build excitement, & maintain enthusiasm.

13

DEMONSTRATE VALUES

"A leader leads by example, whether he intends to or not." – Author Unknown

In the previous chapter we looked at the critical role vision plays in inspiring those you lead. Your organization's vision should be a vivid picture of the future you strive to make a reality. A compelling vision not only gives those striving toward it a sense of purpose and mission, but it also innately communicates some of the organization's core values. For example, the vision of IKEA (the international home furnishings retailer) is "To create a better everyday life for the many people." They explain that their business idea is "to offer a wide range of well designed, functional home furnishing products at prices so low that as many people as possible will be able to afford them."[1] Innate in that vision are values like working with excellence and caring about the consumer. Their vision is based on their values—which is essential for a vision to be truly compelling and worthy of laboring toward.

While it is important that an organization's vision be based on values, even more critical is that the leaders demonstrate those values. Too often a devastating disconnect between task and mission occurs because an organization's leadership does not demonstrate those core values. As Susan M. Heathfield writes, "If the organization's leadership has a code of conduct and ethical expectations, they become an organization joke if the leaders fail to live up to their published code." She goes on to say, "Leaders that exhibit ethical behavior powerfully influence the actions of others."[2] Leading by example may seem like a clichéd and worn out idea, but it is still an extremely important principle of inspirational leadership.

So what does it mean for leaders to demonstrate values? In this chapter we will explore how inspirational leaders and their organizations establish core values, hold integrity in high esteem, and—above all—lead by example. While these topics might seem obvious or even rather trite, they are critically important—enough so to warrant a closer look.

Establish Core Values

You probably don't have your personal values written out and posted on the wall somewhere. You likely haven't even thought through and named each of the values you strive to embody. But whether articulated or not, everyone lives by a set of values, and organizations should too. Some may argue that "corporate values" just end up as a meaningless poster on the wall or paragraph in the employee handbook and don't really make a difference. That may be the case for some organizations, but it definitely shouldn't be the norm.

In an online article for *Forbes* magazine, contributor Gary Peterson makes an argument for why corporate values matter. He offers three reasons why they are important to the long-term growth and value of an organization:

- Values are how you hire.
- Values are how you change your behavior.
- Values are the heart of your culture.

Peterson writes, "By hiring based on values and holding each other accountable to the company's standards, the values become the fabric of the organization's culture—regardless of who is in charge."[3] This is absolutely true; an organization is made up of people, and the values of those people are woven together into the "fabric of the organization's culture." So it's important that you have corporate values in place in order to align your hiring process with your desired culture; if the values of the people you hire don't align with your corporate values, you're definitely not setting them—or your organization—up for success.

Mike Williams, president & CEO of Community Hospital Corporation,

Your **VALUES** become the **FABRIC** *of your* organizational **CULTURE** puts such an emphasis on his organization's culture and values that he takes the time to personally interview potential employees before they are offered a job—at any level. Although a healthy and growing organization, the number of employees at the CHC corporate office is still small enough that Williams can do this. Even so, it is still a significant investment of his time and energy—but it is worth it. By having a personal conversation with every potential employee, Williams is able to impress upon them the values he wants represented in the culture of CHC, and is also able to "weed out" job candidates who appear unable to meet that standard. "There are many qualified and competent folks out there. There are fewer who understand and meet our cultural expectations,"[4] Williams explains. Without a doubt, the positive, long-term results of that values-based hiring process are absolutely worth the investment of the CEO's time!

My colleague Bruce Lawrence, president and CEO of INTEGRIS Health, spoke to me about this topic as well. He explained that during new employee orientation he shares about the organization's mission, vision, and values, saying:

> Here's our mission, here's our vision, and here are our values. In your life, you have a mission statement, you have a vision for your life, professionally and personally, and you have a set of core values. You may not have written them down yet, but they're there, that's how you live your life. I just ask you to put your life values up against our organizational values, and if there's a strong correlation, I think you can be very happy working here. If there's not a strong correlation, then I would suggest you go ahead and go find someplace else to work, because you're not going to be very happy here. Because this is how we do business, this is how we expect everyone to act, and we're going to hold everybody accountable to this. I'm just giving you a free bit of advice on the front end; so if your values don't correlate, save yourself a lot of time and pain and discomfort, and go ahead and work for somebody else.[4]

The values upon which INTEGRIS Health is built are summed up in three words: Love, Learn, and Lead. These individual values are further defined by specific value statements, including "Treat self and others with kindness, dignity and respect," "Improve every day," and, "Expect and acknowledge excellence."[5] These are just a few examples of the kinds of core values organizations name as the bedrock of their corporate culture; others might include principles like honesty, authenticity, professionalism, transparency, passion, teamwork, innovation, caring, commitment, etc. There is an endless list of core values and guiding principles you could choose; what matters is that those values don't just sound good, but actually reflect the culture and vision you are creating for your organization.

Like INTEGRIS Health, another example of an organization that puts great emphasis on its values is Zappos. In an online article for *Fortune* magazine, Holly Lebowitz Rossi wrote, "Employees at the online retailer Zappos.com aren't expected to memorize the company's 10 core values... But they are expected to embody those values in their personalities—and not just at work." Zappos chief of staff, Jamie Naughton, explains, "The best employee is the person who can be the same person at home that they are at work." The article continues, "When they are hired, employees sign contracts saying they understand the values, agree to be reviewed based on them, and understand that they can be fired if they fail to live up to them. This commitment makes the values 'a living breathing thing, more than just a plaque on our lobby wall,' says Naughton, and it fuels the company's reputation as a place where employees are happy and motivated."[6]

No matter what your company values are, it's important that they are firmly established, clearly articulated, and that your leadership team and everyone in your organization is familiar with and committed to those values. It is especially important that you as a leader stick to those values—no matter what. Author Ken Blanchard relates a story about one leader standing by his company's values even at the cost of a customer:

> Southwest founder Herb Kelleher once got a letter from a grumpy customer complaining about how much it bothered him that the flight attendants goofed off during the safety announcement. Because a Fun-LUVing Attitude is a Southwest value and this was a customer who tended to complain a lot, Herb didn't apologize or offer him a coupon. Instead he wrote back, "We'll miss you." He stood by the values and the people of Southwest.[7]

Now that is a great example of a leader—and an organization—demonstrating values and depending on that foundation when faced with a difficult situation. Kelleher didn't default to "the customer is always right;" instead, he reflected on his company's core values and made the decision most in line with those values. My friend Bill Keogh related a similar anecdote from his time working for Hertz car rental about a leader who stood behind his people and his organizational values. "The chairman at the time, Mr. Frank Olson, made a wonderful impression on me with how he handled a complaining customer," Bill said. He went on to explain,

> Mr. Olson looked into the situation and determined that the customer, president of one of Hertz's large customers, had read the riot act to one of our young managers—cursing, and perhaps a little inebriated. The young manager, an acquaintance of mine, was a very good employee who tried to please the customer who went into a tirade. Mr. Olson, after investigating, supported the Hertz employee and told the customer that if he didn't apologize to our employee he'd pull their company's contract. Mr. Olson was a very strong chairman who showed that these things have two sides and inspired all of us.[8]

Certainly another great example of an inspirational leader whose established values dictated his actions in a sticky situation. As Robert Townsend once put it, "Values are critical guides for making decisions. When in doubt, they cut through the fog like a beacon in the night."

> "Values are critical guides for making decisions. When in doubt, they cut through the fog like a beacon in the night."
>
> – *Robert Townsend*

In an article for CNN, author Dov Seidman wrote that leaders and organizations who "inspire their people through values significantly outperform those who don't. These companies experience higher levels of innovation, employee loyalty, and customer satisfaction, and lower levels of misconduct, employee fear of speaking up, and retaliation."[9] Bottom line: organizations thrive when their people are inspired, and people are inspired when their organizations establish well-chosen corporate values that authentically reflect the organizational vision and culture.

Avidly Promote Integrity at All Levels

We've already touched on the critical importance of leading with integrity back in Chapter 4. As Michael Josephson explains, "Great leaders are principled; they are not merely effective, they are ethical. They adhere to moral principles in forming their objectives and using the methods of influence. They engender trust and credibility because of their integrity and loyalty and because they care about their followers and treat them with respect."[10]

But integrity is not just a personal virtue that leaders should exemplify—they must also hold those they lead, and their entire organization, to a standard of high integrity. In their book *Leading to Ethics*, authors Eric Harvey, Andy Smith, and Paul Sims write, "High-integrity workplaces don't get that way by accident, coincidence, or luck. They're molded, shaped, and built by leaders at all levels."[11]

So how do inspirational leaders mold, shape, and build a high-integrity workforce? It starts with holding integrity in high esteem. By this I mean that leaders should continually emphasize and reinforce the importance of integrity through small gestures and everyday reminders, such as:

- Being transparent and honest, even about bad news.
- Commending a direct report for admitting his mistake and owning a problem instead of making excuses.
- Consistently following through on commitments—no matter how small—and thanking others for doing the same.
- Not letting too many small infractions slide, kindly but firmly reminding workers to be on time and focus on work while at work.
- Insisting on honesty and fairness in all dealings—with colleagues and customers alike.
- Frequently reviewing company policies to ensure daily activities and actions are in alignment with those policy statements.

Mark Dixon is a leader who consistently demonstrates and promotes integrity, holding those he leads accountable to maintaining integrity in all they do. His colleague Jeff Kirkham said that Mark's most distinct leadership strength is "his ability to hold people accountable and maintain positive personal relationships with them."[12] Bob Solheim noted that Mark embodies integrity both personally and professionally, stating,

> Mark continuously exhibits qualities of character so important to a leader—qualities like integrity, ethical behavior, and genuineness in his business and personal dealings with others. Mark is recognized in the community as a man of unusual character, embodying these values in his daily walk. His trustworthiness is absolute—that is authenticity at its best.[13]

Holding those you lead accountable to living and working with integrity is not easy, but it is an absolutely essential part of inspirational leadership. The impact of a leader who does not hold integrity in high esteem is highly toxic. When leaders don't demand integrity from those they lead, when they turn a blind eye to dishonesty and irresponsibility, what might start as small offenses slowly escalate until the organization's culture becomes dotted with deceit, manipulation, selfishness, entitlement, discrimination, and laziness. On the other hand, when leaders demonstrate and promote integrity at all levels within the organization—in small matters as well as large ones—the company culture soon becomes marked by traits such as honesty, fairness, selflessness, hard work, trustworthiness, respect, and outstanding service. That is inspirational leadership!

Lead by Example

Leading by example may seem like an overly simple (and endlessly repeated) concept—so much so that you might be tempted to skip over this section because you already *know* that leading by example is important. But I hope you don't skip over this section or dismiss this age-old principle as too obvious to even warrant reflection. Because the concept of leading by example is so critically important to inspirational leadership, I firmly believe it is always worth revisiting. As Albert Schweitzer once said, "Example is not the main thing in influencing others; it is the only thing."

When leaders don't lead by example, when they don't demonstrate the values touted within their organization, the consequences are highly destructive to the health and growth of the organization. This really comes back to vision; a strong and compelling vision is built upon core values, and that vision can only be realized if those working toward it practice those same values. To achieve this, the corporate culture must revolve around those core values, and that is only possible if the organization's leadership nurtures such a culture by leading by example.

Inspirational leaders know that whether they intend to or not, they are *always* leading by example; therefore they are very intentional about setting the right one. As Michael Hyatt puts it, inspirational leaders "model the behavior they want others to manifest."[14] Day in and day out, they demonstrate core values through their words, actions, and attitudes—sometimes in big ways, but most often in little, everyday ways. In an interview for Lifehack.org, author Scott Berkun reminds us that a critical element of leadership is doing whatever you ask others to do. "I think there are non-obvious ways to lead. Just by providing a good example as a parent, a friend, a neighbor makes it possible for other people to see better ways to do things. Leadership does not need to be a dramatic, fist in the air and trumpets blaring activity."[15] My good friend and colleague Harla Adams, CEO of NIHCL, gave some examples of ways in which inspirational leaders can demonstrate values on a daily basis:

> Inspirational leaders know that whether they intend to or not, they are *always* leading by example.

> Show up on time for meetings, follow through on commitments, over deliver, be genuine, work on building strong relationships, extend grace, don't put down others' ideas or thoughts, always be willing to help others… When you lead by example people have a desire to return the same, to live up to the things that are important to you the leader, and hopefully to them as an individual. People are going to follow someone. Make them desire to follow you as an inspiring, caring, well-intentioned leader.[16]

When thinking about inspirational leaders who have consistently demonstrated core values through little, everyday ways, I cannot help but think of the late Marlowe Senske. Marlowe was a dear friend and colleague of mine who lost a hard-fought battle with cancer on Father's Day, June 21, 2009. I was incredibly privileged to have had one last, wonderful conversation with Marlowe and two of our mutual friends and colleagues just two days before he passed away. Before I left his room, I handed Marlowe a copy of an article I had written entitled "Be an Inspirational Leader." I attached a personal note that read in part:

> Marlowe. This article describes you. You are an excellent role model. You are, without question, a world class Inspirational Leader! All who know you would and do agree... Your positive impact on your family, friends, colleagues, and on many people you will never meet will continue for decades to come. Thank you for who you are and for all you have done for so many.

I had no idea that would be the last time I saw or spoke to Marlowe. I am eternally grateful that I had that opportunity to tell him how much he meant to me and so many others. A few days after Marlowe's funeral, I wrote and published a tribute titled "A Blueprint for Success: The Life, Leadership and Legacy of Marlowe Senske." In that tribute I described the example and impact of this incredibly inspirational leader:

> Marlowe was passionate about every aspect of life. He loved living... and he lived and served so very well. Marlowe was all about strong, effective and long-lasting relationships. He was a world-class role model in creating, nurturing and appropriately leveraging excellent relationships for the benefit of all. He led by example.[18]

Without a doubt, leading by example is the most important and effective way to establish and communicate core values. And like Marlow Senske, inspirational leaders who lead by example almost always have a wider and greater impact on people than they ever know.

In talking about INTEGRIS Health's corporate values, Bruce Lawrence agreed that leading by example is one of the most important habits of an inspirational leader. He explained, "If I'm not out there being consistent with how I live out our values day to day, others will see that immediately, and then think, 'Well, those don't really apply to everyone.'" Bruce went on to say, "I think our organization has benefited greatly from many years of consistent leadership in this area, and it has to continue."[17]

Consistently leading by example is a habit at which inspirational leader Traci Bernard excels. Her colleagues and direct reports have nothing but high praise for Traci in this area—a testament to the significant impact of leading by example. Asked what words first come to mind when describing

Traci, Anthony Romero immediately responded, "Role model." He went on to explain that Traci "conducts herself in an ethical way and models the traits she wants to see in others. In doing so she has earned the respect of those around her."[18] Laura Wahl commented, "Traci Bernard leads by example, always. There is never a moment that she does not ask of you something that she would not do herself."[19] Another colleague, Jessica Hill, noted that Traci is consistent in how she demonstrates values on a daily basis,[20] and Karen Adams stated, "Traci inspires me by the way she leads by example. She is positive, caring, and genuine." Karen went on to say, "Traci is very transparent and honest. She leads us to always do the right thing even when no one will know. She lives this example for all of us every day."[21]

Without a doubt, demonstrating values is a key ingredient of inspirational leadership—and it is powerfully effective. Not only should leaders personally embody core values and ethical behavior, they should establish those same values within their teams and organizations, maintaining the expectation that everyone within the organization adhere to those values and demonstrate high integrity. It all starts at the top; inspirational leaders are devoted to a set of core values, and expect those they lead to do the same. As Susan M. Heathfield writes, "Living your values is one of the most powerful tools available to you to help you lead and influence others. Don't waste your best opportunity."[22]

KEY POINTS

To be a leader who demonstrates values:

- Establish core values within your organization.
- Avidly promote integrity at all levels.
- Most importantly: lead by example.

EMPOWER

*"Leaders become great, not because of their power,
but because of their ability to empower others."*
— John C. Maxwell

14

FACILITATE GROWTH

"Before you are a leader, success is all about growing yourself. When you become a leader, success is all about growing others." – Jack Welch

In this day and age, I think very few leaders want their employees to perform their duties like mindless drones as opposed to the thoughtful, innovative people that they are. Scores of leadership articles and books tout the strategies of team collaboration and employee empowerment, declaring the age of "command and control" to be over. But even so, many leaders continue to micromanage, and fail to really empower people to think innovatively, try new things, and do their jobs with excellence. As Bob MacDonald puts it, "Rare is the business executive who does not avow devotion to empowering employees and the benefits derived from employing it. And yet, for something so universally touted as an invaluable management tool, it's amazing how rarely it is taken out of the toolbox."[1] This disconnect between what is preached and what is practiced may not be intentional, but it is real.

So why do so many leaders fail to empower those they lead? I believe many leaders do not fully understand what it means to empower people, and unfortunately, they may also fear "giving away" some of their power to others. But that's not really what empowerment is about. MacDonald explains: "The empowering of employees does not mean giving your power away; it means retaining your power, but sharing it." He goes on to note,

> Most employees really don't want the risk and responsibility that comes with actual power, but they do want the feeling that they

can make a difference in the organization and that their talents and experience are valued in a way that can influence decisions that are made by those in power.[2]

Empowering others isn't about abdicating any of your own power or responsibility as a leader, but rather it's about giving those you lead the opportunity to leverage their talents and use their own skills and common sense to influence decisions, add value, and make a difference. In an article for Forbes.com, contributor Lisa Quast writes that empowering your employees is about giving them the permission to "use their creative talents to find solutions when issues arise, without having to run to management and ask for permission to do something." However, Quast goes on to point out that empowering employees isn't easy, "because it requires that a company and their management be committed to continuous employee development. It means fostering an environment of trust and helping employees learn from successes and analyze failures."[3] In this chapter we will look at that critical element of empowering those you lead: facilitating their growth.

Inspirational leaders understand that in order to truly empower others, they must first help them grow. Facilitating the growth of those you lead includes things like equipping them beyond the essentials required to do their job, giving frequent, consistent, and honest feedback, building and valuing their confidence as much as their competence, and preparing them for future opportunities.

Equip Beyond the Essentials

We've already discussed the critical importance of investing in those you lead, back in Chapter 11, including providing relevant training and education options and creating opportunities for individual growth. Another way in which inspirational leaders invest in and empower those they lead is by equipping them beyond the essentials required to fulfill their job description. If you want to empower your people, you must equip them. Instead of just providing the bare minimum of job training for necessary hard skills, leaders should offer additional development opportunities for those hard skills, as well as plenty of training and coaching for important soft skills. By facilitating employees' growth in their area of focus and expertise as well as complimentary areas, inspirational leaders empower them to

If you want to
EMPOWER
your people,
you must
EQUIP
them.

achieve greater success—personally, professionally, and organizationally.

Obviously every organization and employer wants their people to be proficient in the necessary "hard skills" (e.g. typing speed, mathematic ability, financial acumen, programming knowledge, etc.), and leaders should find or create opportunities for their people to further develop those skills. But even more important are the "soft skills" (e.g. working in a team, decision making, problem solving, verbal communication, organizing and prioritizing tasks, etc.). When they grow in those areas and become equipped with valuable soft skills, those you lead will be more empowered to leverage their strengths, weigh-in on big decisions, and add greater value to their role and the overall mission. As John Maxwell says, "As a leader, it's your duty to enrich and empower your people by fully equipping them to excel on the job."[4]

Another way in which inspirational leaders equip their people and facilitate their growth is by providing knowledge and information. Clancy Hayes explains, "They need information about organizational goals, plans, and changes. Workers are motivated when they know what is happening in the organization. It makes them feel important and valuable, helps them desire to do a better job, and enables them to do a better job. Without information, people cannot take responsibility, will not be as creative, and will not be as productive."[5] Resist the temptation to only tell employees what they "need to know;" choose to be transparent and generous with information and you will not only further equip those you lead, but also gain more of their trust and respect. Chris Van Gorder, president and CEO of Scripps Health, told me in an interview, "There are many managers and leaders who think that being 'in the know' makes them somehow more powerful than everybody else." Chris explained that yes, "information is power, but it's only powerful if it's shared." He went on to illustrate this point with a story from his own experience as a leader:

> I learned something when I was a director of security years ago. Security officers usually didn't make a big salary or anything like that, especially back then. A lot of them were ex-military, and there was a lot of turnover. After running the department for a year or so, I looked at my statistics, and nobody had left the organization. I had two retired army sergeants working for me, and I asked them, "Why is nobody leaving? It's really kind of strange." They said, "Don't you get it, Chris?" I said, "Probably not, or I wouldn't be

asking the question!" They said, "You respect them so much." And they explained, "If you go to a department-head meeting or something like that, you immediately come back and you gather all the employees together and say, 'Look, let me tell you what's going on here.' You respect them and share that information with them." It turns out most other managers weren't doing that, so the source of information in that hospital was the security officers. They literally had doctors going to them asking, "Have you heard about this?" And that security officer could say, "Well, doctor, as a matter of fact, I have. Let me tell you what's going on." So those sergeants explained, "They feel so respected; why would they want to go anywhere else?" I went, "Wow." That was an eye opener for me.[6]

Chris noted that through that experience he learned people really want to be informed and to understand what is happening and why. "So leaders have to create opportunities for people to get that information—in all sorts of different ways, because people learn things in different ways." He said. "I think sometimes leaders get so busy doing their job that they forget that one of the biggest things that they have to do is communicate and teach. You've got to make time for that."[7] Chris is absolutely right—inspirational leaders must be intentional and make time to communicate and share information with those they lead, further equipping and empowering them for success. As Jody Livingston put it, "Training and equipping your team does not happen automatically, it requires being intentional."[8]

GIVE FREQUENT FEEDBACK

Motivational speaker and personal development guru Jim Rohn once said, "A good objective of leadership is to help those who are doing poorly to do well and to help those who are doing well to do even better." The key to achieving that objective is to offer consistent and constructive feedback. Giving and receiving feedback is one of those things that we all know is important, but in practice, can be daunting and uncomfortable—for both the giver and receiver. However, inspirational leaders recognize the critical value of frequent, honest feedback, and approach it in a positive way.

The editorial team for mindtools.com put together a great article about giving feedback in which they write: "When you make a conscious choice to give and receive feedback on a regular basis you demonstrate that feedback is a powerful means of personal development." They go on to say, "Done properly, feedback need not be agonizing, demoralizing, or daunting and the more practice you get the better you will become at it. It may never be your favorite means of communicating with employees, co-workers, or bosses but it does have the potential to make your workplace a much more productive and harmonious place to be."[9]

One key element of successful feedback is its frequency. While most leaders and organizations have processes in place for conducting annual or sometimes quarterly performance reviews, if that's the only time those you lead receive honest feedback, its not going to be all that effective. The team at mindtools.com addresses this as well:

> Feedback is a process that requires constant attention. When something needs to be said, say it. People then know where they stand all the time and there are few surprises. Also, problems don't get out of hand. This is not a once-a-year or a once-every-three-month event. While this may be the timing of formal feedback, informal, simple feedback should be given much more often than this—perhaps every week or even every day, depending on the situation. With frequent informal feedback like this, nothing said during formal feedback sessions should be unexpected, surprising or particularly difficult.[10]

In the interview he did for this book, Bruce Lawrence said, "I think we've got to use every opportunity as a teacher or coach moment… I believe there's a coaching moment at every opportunity, and so we just have to be open to that." Bruce went on to say, "A good teacher coach has to have not only the ability, but also the courage to use every situation as a learning opportunity." He explained that he has often seen missed opportunities because a leader has been reluctant to say anything, letting what should have been a teaching moment pass by. "No! You've got to do it at the time, when it's there—not a day later, a week later, or a month later," Bruce says. "It's got to be current, in the moment, and that's when the best things happen."[11]

Author and behavioral statistician Joseph Folkman offers a great analogy for the value of frequent feedback, explaining, "The advantage of receiving ongoing feedback is much like the advantage you gain from a GPS device as opposed to a paper map. Both provide directions about where you want to go. The GPS, however, provides the directions in the context of an accurate assessment of where you currently are."[12]

Clearly, making a conscious choice and commitment to regularly give honest feedback to those you lead is an excellent way to facilitate their growth and empower them to achieve greater success. However, feedback must be done well. Joseph Folkman makes the point that "Giving honest feedback is a fantastic gift," but, "people only experience it as a gift when it is delivered well. Giving honest feedback poorly, will, for most people, be viewed as a punishment—not a gift."[13] So how do you deliver feedback, especially corrective feedback, in a positive and constructive way? Here are some best practices:

> When done well and offered consistently, honest feedback is one of the most effective tools for facilitating growth and further empowering those you lead.

- **Be timely**. "Timeliness is critical in order for the recipient to associate the behavior with the feedback."[14] – *Lisa Petrilli*
- **Do it privately**. "[This] allows the employee to focus on the work they need to do, not what their coworkers think about them. Speaking privately also gives employees a chance to ask follow-up questions and bring up any issues affecting their performance."[15]– *Allison Gauss*
- **Watch your tone**. "Tone and phrasing are everything when giving feedback. Watch your tone for whining, sarcasm, judgmentalness, and other undermining messages."[16] – *Adele Margrave & Robert Gorden*
- **Be specific**. "[Feedback] must be specific so that the recipient has a clear understanding of the behavior or approach that they need to improve upon... Leaders should anticipate many questions and be prepared to give very specific and clear answers to help the recipient receive the feedback in the best light possible."[17] – *Lisa Petrilli*

- **Avoid exaggerating**. "[A] key mistake is using language like 'always' or 'never.' Hearing these words, people naturally get defensive as they can remember plenty of times when they did not do what you claim they did."[18] – *Center for Creative Leadership*
- **Keep it in perspective**. "Always describe behaviors, not traits. Don't dwell on the past; instead focus on what the employee can change in the future."[19] – *Amy Gallo*
- **Keep it brief**. "Oftentimes when people give other people feedback, they don't know when to stop. They give advice, describe personal experiences, and try to solve the other person's problem. People receiving feedback need time to digest and assimilate the information they have just received."[20] – *Center for Creative Leadership*
- **Offer help and support**. "We have a duty to help our staff develop and progress. We can do that by focusing on the way forward and on which steps they can take to improve—rather than criticizing them. If a team member is not performing according to the goals you have both set, DO be honest, but don't linger on the negative aspects. Help provide the stepping stones for the team member to progress instead."[21] – *Susanne Madsen*
- **Reaffirm their value**. "Reaffirming the person's value to the organization assures them of your desire to help them improve and to see them succeed to their greatest ability. In the end, isn't that what we all want for our teams, peers and the organization as a whole?"[22] – *Lisa Petrilli*

When done well and offered consistently, honest feedback is one of the most effective tools for facilitating growth and further empowering those you lead.

Build Confidence as Well as Competence

It should go without saying that *inspirational* leaders are *encouraging* leaders. Inspiration and encouragement go hand in hand, and nothing is more opposite inspiration than discouragement. It is virtually impossible for a person to feel both discouraged and inspired at the same time. So to inspire, a leader must also encourage. Encouragement boosts morale, motivation, and—most importantly—confidence. Inspirational leaders understand that confidence is just as vital for success as competence. Karin Hurt notes, "The good news is that building confidence and competence go hand in hand. Confident employees are more likely to try new behaviors and approaches, which breeds creativity and more success."[23] Andy Core echoes those thoughts, writing, "Self-confidence is one of those intangible traits that encourages an employee to do their work well. Confidence in what they are doing will lead to more productivity in the workplace."[24] Too often, smart, skilled people lack confidence in their abilities, and as a result fail to reach their full potential. Knowing this, inspirational leaders facilitate the growth of those they lead not only by helping develop competence, but also by helping instill confidence. As Lisa Hill said in an interview for this book, empowering people is about believing in them, challenging them, supporting them, and not micro-managing.[25] Those are the leadership habits that build employees' confidence.

> To inspire, a leader must also encourage.

My friend Clyde Pogson told me a story from the early days of his sales profession when he was first starting out as a sales clerk at the "CAT house" (CATERPILLAR® dealer) in Houston, Texas. After two years of working his way up in the sales department, Clyde got the opportunity to move into a sales role southwest of Houston. "So I packed my bags and moved to El Campo, Texas to begin my journey as a traveling CAT sales person." Clyde explained that it was there where he first met area manager Cliff Grissom, who immediately took Clyde under his wing and helped him grow in both competence and confidence:

> Here I was a green horn in the sales business, but Cliff took me under his wing and guided me to become a successful sales person. He explained to me that being successful took a lot of hard work and being honest to the company and to the customer. He advised me that there would not be any set hours, but to be flexible, and there would be some disappointments, but to keep plugging away and they could be overcome—and also to learn from them. After about two weeks Cliff left me alone to do my thing, but he

was always there if I needed any help, and we became very close friends.²⁶

Clyde explained that Cliff didn't do anything really extraordinary, but simply by leading by example and supporting and encouraging him, he made a huge difference in Clyde's early career. This is a great example of how one of the simplest but most powerful elements of inspirational leadership is empowering and facilitating growth by providing encouragement and support.

I keep returning to the example of Jack Lawless, who—as proven by the testimony of his colleagues and former direct reports—truly is an inspirational leader. During our interview, Jack mentioned one of his former direct reports, a woman named Kathy Dagg. Jack said, "Kathy was probably one of the finest directors of food nutrition services I ever had the opportunity to work with."²⁷ He then went on to describe how she had great potential as a leader, but lacked the confidence to step into a bigger role. However, over time and through encouragement and mentoring, Kathy gained the confidence to match her competence, and accepted a much-deserved promotion. Kathy herself told me the same story, attributing much of her career success to Jack's encouragement and support. She explained that Jack inspired her to take on the promotion to regional director: "Before Jack talked to me I would probably not have considered it," she said. "But over time, he led me to believe I could take on an advanced role in management and oversee and lead more than just one account."²⁸ Thanks to Jack's encouragement and belief in her abilities, Kathy is now a regional director overseeing over a dozen hospitals for Morrison Healthcare.

Another leader I can't help but mention again is Traci Bernard. During our interview I asked what her greatest joy as a leader has been. "Watching people grow and develop and move into leadership roles," she immediately responded, then added, "On the flip side—the more selfish side of it—seeing improvements in myself as a person and as a leader. Because isn't that why we're here, to keep getting better?"²⁹ Her colleagues and direct reports mentioned over and over again how much Traci helps make that growth happen by investing in and encouraging those she leads. Laura Wahl explained, "Traci empowers those around her by believing in them and giving them the tools they need to succeed. She is always lending encouraging words to *everyone* in every situation. Traci's belief in me empowers me to rise to every occasion to contribute to the success of THS."[30] Anthony Romero added, "Traci mentors and develops her team through challenging projects and assignments, and she never forgets to let us know how much she values us and our work."[31]

These two leaders—Jack Lawless and Traci Bernard—excel in the area of encouraging and building the confidence of those they lead. They value and respect each person who reports to them, and continually convey their admiration and appreciation for the work they do. As inspirational leaders, they understand and take to heart what the poet and philosopher Johann Wolfgang von Goethe once said: "Treat a man as he is and he will remain as he is. Treat a man as he can and should be and he will become as he can and should be."

PREPARE FOR FUTURE OPPORTUNITIES

Back in Chapter 11 we looked at the critical importance of investing in those you lead and how inspirational leaders do that. Investing in the life, wellbeing, and growth of those you lead is one of the greatest elements of inspirational leadership. However, some leaders are hesitant to really invest in their employees. Why? Because they're afraid they will lose their investment if that person chooses to leave their organization and pursue other opportunities. While that is arguably a valid concern (statistics indicate that the average job tenure of a typical U.S. worker is less than 5 years),[32] inspirational leaders see it a little differently. In a 2016 article, Inc.com columnist Tim Askew wrote, "While I see a multitude of articles written about holding on to great employees, I never see an article about celebrating an employee assuming greater leadership and greater personal growth by leaving." He went on to say, "There should be more discussion of this, particularly in the small business universe. I believe in supporting employee growth and fulfillment even to the point of their leaving your company."[33]

While letting go of a great employee might be a hard pill to swallow for some leaders, inspirational leaders understand from the very beginning that their job as a leader is to not just focus on the success of their business, but on the success of their people. If that means supporting a valued member of their team as he or she takes on a new role elsewhere—whether in a different department or outside of their organization altogether—so be it. My colleague Jim Wetrich, CEO of The Wetrich Group, put it simply: "I want everyone to be happy working in the field they enjoy." Jim explained, "As a leader I've helped others think about what it is they really love to do, and guided them toward that direction—even at the risk of losing great employees." He went on to give an example:

> I remember some time ago when I was speaking to my sales team, I urged them to do what they felt passionate about. At the end of my speech, one of our sales reps, a gentleman, came up to me and told me what he really wanted to do was become a teacher. His passion wasn't sales. His passion was teaching. So I told him, "Keep working; keep doing what you're doing, don't quit, but go get a teaching job." About nine months later, he found the teaching job he'd always been looking for and he went on to his career that he truly felt passionate about. That really makes you feel great as a leader when you can help people find what they're passionate about— what Bill George would call their "true north."[34]

Inspirational leaders like Jim Wetrich are not afraid of losing good employees, but rather, they understand the danger of trying to hang on to people who aren't pursuing what they're truly passionate about. They also believe in really investing in the growth and future success of each person whom they lead. One of Jim's colleagues and former direct reports, Sanchia Patrick Rasul, told me about how Jim, (known fondly as 'Big Red'), created an organizational culture committed to growth. "Simply put, Big Red is relentless about growth. He pushes leaders to see possibilities and refuses to tolerate excuses," she explained. "By observing his intolerance for the status quo, I learned how to push beyond my self-imposed boundaries. I grew immensely. My enhanced personal accountability for growth is, perhaps, the greatest gift Big Red gave me and to anyone who has had the opportunity to work for him."[35] Through gifts like that, inspirational leaders help prepare those they lead for future opportunities.

In an article titled "10 Things Only Exceptional Bosses Give Their Employees," author Jeff Haden wrote about another gift inspirational leaders give employees: "A chance for a meaningful future." Haden explains, "Every job should have the potential to lead to greater things. Exceptional bosses take the time to develop employees for the job they someday hope to land, even if that job is with another company." Haden goes on to address the question, "How can you know what an employee hopes to do someday?" The answer is simple: Ask! "Employees will only care about your business after you first show you care about them. One of the best ways is to show that while you certainly have hopes for your company's future, you also have hopes for your employees' futures."[36]

My friend and colleague Tod Jeffers, a national account manager responsible for federal government contracting with bioMérieux, made the point that leaders shouldn't be surprised when employees choose to move on to a new position or organization, because they ought to set those expectations up front. "What I mean by that is simply asking their employee where they want to go and what they want to do. 'Where do you see yourself in two to five years? How can we work together to help you achieve your potential, and what can I do as your manager to support your growth?' Those are great questions to ask at the outset or soon after an employee shows their worth," Tod explained. He went on to share a story about a colleague who had hired a young man with a lot of potential. The leader recognized the potential in this young man, who quickly became a valuable asset to his team and organization. When a promotion opened up for an overseas role in their organization, the leader didn't hesitate to recommend him for the position. The young man, questioning his own ability, was unsure, but his boss knew he had the skills to get the job done and encouraged him to accept the promotion, which he did. After three successful years in the new role, the up and coming leader was offered another promotion, which he respectfully declined in order to pursue a different opportunity. "That young man is now the CEO of another company, heading up an entire organization," Tod said.

> When amply equipped, frequently and positively critiqued, consistently encouraged, and fully supported in the pursuit of future opportunities, the people you lead will themselves become leaders who flourish and succeed.

"His former boss, my colleague, showed true leadership in not being afraid to promote his people and allow them to achieve their own success."[37] This is a great example of a leader who, instead of tightly hanging on to a high-performing employee, helped prepare him for future opportunities.

Ralph Nader once said: "The function of leadership is to produce more leaders, not more followers." Inspirational leaders do exactly that by facilitating the growth of those they lead. When amply equipped, frequently and positively critiqued, consistently encouraged, and fully supported in the pursuit of future opportunities, the people you lead will themselves become leaders who flourish and succeed.

KEY POINTS

To be a leader who facilitates growth:

- Equip your employees beyond the essentials required to do their job.
- Give frequent, consistent, and honest feedback.
- Build and value the confidence of those you lead as much as their competence.
- Prepare employees for future opportunities.

15

GIVE AUTHORITY

"Don't tell people how to do things, tell them what to do and let them surprise you with their results." – George S. Patton

Once equipped with the tools, knowledge, and confidence they need, to truly be empowered those you lead must also be given the authority to make decisions and take action. This is the area most people think of when they hear the word *empower*, and it is a vital component of inspirational leadership. As my colleague Jim Wetrich adamantly stated, "Empowering those you lead is one of the most critical aspects of leadership."[1]

Author and management consultant Mac McIntire defines empowerment as the extent to which a leader "has trust, respect, and confidence in an employee's ability to make appropriate decisions or to take appropriate action on work-related issues." He goes on to explain that when a leader "trusts the employee's judgment, respects the employee's opinion, and has confidence in the employee's decision-making abilities," he or she will be "more inclined to grant the employee the power to work free of close management scrutiny."[2]

None of us start out as experienced, senior leaders. Each of us has to start at the bottom and work our way up, gaining greater ability and authority as we go. But somewhere along the way, someone does recognize our ability and grant us that authority, enabling and empowering us to further innovate, experiment, make decisions, and achieve greater results. Inspirational leaders recognize the critical importance of giving that kind of authority to those they lead, empowering them to achieve greater success—personally, professionally, and organizationally! In this chapter we will look at how inspirational leaders give authority to those they lead by carefully avoiding micromanaging, encouraging appropriate independence and autonomy, and extending trust and grace.

Avoid Micromanaging

Micromanaging is one of those terms you most often hear in association with disliked bosses and disgruntled employees, and you hope it doesn't apply to you as a leader. The definition of *micromanage* is "to manage or control with excessive attention to minor details."[3] To put it bluntly, micromanaging is an indication that you do not really trust those you lead to do the work you've assigned them—or at least to do it well. For some leaders, relinquishing their hold on certain projects and tasks is very difficult. Greatly invested in the outcome, these leaders simply want to ensure that the work is done "right," (i.e. done their way), and thus they retain as much control as they can. Inspirational leaders, on the other hand, understand the incredible benefits of allowing those they lead to accomplish assignments in their own way. Jim Wetrich explained, "Inspirational leaders know that their direct reports and others within the organization will never do anything the same way the leader would do it. In fact, inspirational leaders know that it's often the case where the work being done is often *better* than what the leaders themselves may have been able to do." Jim went on to say,

> The vast majority of people are invigorated by an open environment where they can excel by doing the work the way that they want to do it... So let your people do the work the way they want to do it. It seems so simple, but many leaders have this expectation that "you've got to do it my way." I don't care how people do it. I really don't, as long as they get the work done, they enjoy doing the work they're doing, and they get the results they hope to get and were intended to get.[4]

Jim definitely has the outlook and approach of an inspirational leader! He understands that retaining a tight hold on delegated work is not only inefficient, but is a hindrance to the development of those you lead, ultimately leading to frustration on both ends. Inspirational leaders care deeply about the growth of those they lead, and recognize how micromanaging can quickly stifle and sabotage that growth. In a great article about avoiding micromanaging and helping your team members excel on their own, the editorial team at mindtools.com wrote:

> A truly effective manager sets up those around him to succeed. Micromanagers, on the other hand, prevent employees from making—and taking responsibility for—their own decisions. But it's precisely the process of making decisions, and living with the consequences, that causes people to grow and improve. Good managers *empower* their employees to do well by giving opportunities to excel; bad managers *disempower* their employees by hoarding those opportunities. And a disempowered employee is an ineffective one—one who requires a lot of time and energy from his supervisor.[5]

Inspirational leaders recognize these dangers of micromanaging and strive to avoid them, choosing instead to intentionally relinquish some measure of control and give authority to those they lead, giving them the opportunity to grow and improve.

Of course, avoiding micromanaging doesn't mean giving your employees free reign and being completely hands-off after delegating assignments—there is a balance between exercising excessive control and being completely unengaged and uninformed. Inspirational leaders find that balance—choosing to be involved and engaged with those they lead, but allowing them the freedom to take initiative, make decisions, and think outside the box. Bruce Lawrence, president and CEO of INTEGRIS Health, explained, "A leader must be engaged to the level that is necessary for the circumstances." Within the organization he leads, Bruce tells his team, "While I can't (and really don't need to) be involved in all aspects of your work, I do want to be kept informed of the most critical things going on in your area and how I can help you be successful and accomplish your role."[6]

> **Inspirational leaders find that balance—choosing to be involved and engaged with those they lead, but allowing them the freedom to take initiative, make decisions, and think outside the box.**

Inspirational leaders recognize the wisdom in always supporting and encouraging those they lead while giving them enough freedom and authority to do what they've been hired or assigned to do. Curtis Rooney is a great example of a leader who does just that. His colleague and former direct report Jennifer Bell explained, "Curtis is not a micromanager. He makes it a point to hire good people and then he gives them the freedom to do the job for which they were hired. This is not always the case with other bosses, and it's something that I know my teammates and I appreciated about Curtis."[7] Michael Payne echoed those comments, saying, "Curtis is very effective at empowering his staff to take responsibility, and provides them the authority and guidance to accomplish their goals. The tasks he assigns are clear, and then he allows them to go forward without micromanaging the process."[8] Curtis Rooney certainly lives out what Theodore Roosevelt once wisely said: "The best executive is the one who has sense enough to pick good men to do what he wants done and self-restraint enough to keep from meddling with them while they do it."

Encourage Appropriate Independence and Autonomy

Instead of micromanaging and focusing on minor details, inspirational leaders strive to give those they lead authority by encouraging an appropriate level of independence and autonomy. In his article "10 Things Only Exceptional Bosses Give Employees," author Jeff Haden explains, "Engagement and satisfaction are largely based on autonomy and independence. I care when it's 'mine.' I care when I'm in charge and feel empowered to do what's right. Plus, freedom breeds innovation: Even heavily process-oriented positions have room for different approaches."[9] When given the freedom to do it in their on way, employees feel a greater sense of ownership for their work, which in turn boosts morale and engagement. In contrast, when given responsibility but not corresponding authority, employees quickly become frustrated, discouraged, and disengaged. Clancy Hayes writes, "One of the most frequent complaints of team members is that they are given responsibility without corresponding authority. Leaders need to be willing to trust those they ask to do a job by giving them the authority necessary to do the job."[10]

Of course, just as the size, scope, and difficulty level of assignments should vary based on the experience and skill level of the individual or team, so should the degree of authority and autonomy given. Mac McIntire addressed this in an article titled "How to Empower Employees to Make Effective Decisions on the Front-Line." McIntire noted that some people cannot handle a great deal of responsibility and authority without becoming over-burdened and distressed—he likened this to trying to send a surge of power through a low-watt bulb. "Some employees cannot handle more than a few watts of responsibility and authority. Empowering these employees with a surge of new responsibilities may cause sudden spasms of anxiety and rapid burnout." He went on to say,

> On the other hand, if a manager sends 10 watts of empowerment through a 100-watt employee (one who is fully capable and willing to do more), the employee will never achieve his or her full potential. Highly capable employees who are underutilized become de-energized when their talents and abilities are not used fully. Eventually, 100-watt employees who are only given 10 watts of power either become 10-watt employees or they leave the company and go somewhere where they can reach their full potential.[11]

Knowing this, inspirational leaders carefully determine the appropriate level of independence and autonomy for the teams and individuals whom they lead, giving them the amount of authority best suited to their experience and skill level. Of course, this is a dynamic process—shifting as circumstances change, skills are developed, and people grow. Clancy Hayes suggests, "Increase authority when performance earns it and responsibility requires it. As people increase in skills and effectiveness, increase their authority. This will raise morale and increase the effectiveness of the team."[12]

Mark Dixon, president of The Mark Dixon Group, LLC, made a simple but profound statement during the interview he did for this book: "Empowering people is giving them the ability to be successful." To do that, Mark explained, you must "give the right level of authority, responsibility, and accountability—as well as resources to help accomplish what they need to

> "Empowering people is giving them the ability to be successful."
>
> – Mark Dixon

get done." He went on to talk about how one of the biggest problems leaders have when trying to empower those they lead is not being crystal clear on the desired outcome. "The outcome you're envisioning might be seen as a 20% improvement in something, but the outcome in their mind might only be a 2% improvement," Mark explained. "So you didn't really effectively empower them if you were hoping to get a transformational improvement, and in their mind they're seeking only an incremental improvement."[13] Like in so many areas, clear communication is essential to effectively empower those you lead!

While serving as the CEO and executive director of Mi Casa Resource Center in Denver, Colorado, Christine Márquez-Hudson strove to create a system where her staff really helped create the organization where they wanted to work. "At all different levels, my staff was providing input and leadership and really contributing to the implementation of the kind of organization that they wanted," Christine explained. She went on to say,

> I think that kind of autonomy is key. As a leader, I really see my job as being the one who holds the vision… I hold the vision for the rest of the staff to keep them on course, like the North Star. "Everybody, this is where we're going." When they start to veer, then we have a conversation about, "Well does it make sense to veer? Or shall we get back on course?" I feel like that's my job, but otherwise, they have a lot of autonomy. They're everything else; they're the rudders, they're the wind, they're the sails. They're doing all the other jobs that are making that ship move forward.[14]

Like Christine, inspirational leaders recognize the awesome power of their teams and the remarkable things that can be accomplished when they are given authority, independence, and autonomy. As Jeff Haden writes, "Whenever possible, give your employees the autonomy and independence to work the way they work best. When you do, they almost always find ways to do their jobs better than you imagined possible."[15]

EXTEND TRUST AND GRACE

Giving authority, refraining from micromanaging, and encouraging appropriate independence and autonomy are all things that require trust. Without trust, leaders are hesitant to delegate tasks, and try to retain as much control as possible—which not only causes them unnecessary work and stress, but also stifles the growth, development, and success of those they lead. Bob MacDonald does a great job of explaining the important role of trust:

> A leader empowers others by trusting others. Trust is built when an employee is assigned a task and then given the support, tools and authority to complete it. If a leader exhibits trust in the employees to do their job—by avoiding hovering over them and micromanaging—then the employee feels empowered to make a difference and has incentive to do the best job possible.[16]

Lorna Shaw, external affairs manager at Pogo Mine in Alaska, shared about how she has been given a lot of latitude in her current position, and how impactful her leader's trust and support has been:

> I'm grateful that I have a boss who believes in my abilities... I was given the opportunity to come here because they've seen what I have done with my previous employer. My boss knew what he was getting, and with that he said basically, "I trust you to do what you need to do. You tell me what you need from me." That is latitude that people are not often given. But one of the things that I see that he does is that he hires experts in their fields and he lets them do their jobs. And one of the things I most respect is that basically his attitude is "I am here to give you the resources you need to do your job." Instead of saying "I know what needs to be done, you need to do a, b, and c."[17]

Dr. Mark Kehrberg, former CMO at Ministry Health Care, described former president and CEO Dan Neufelder as a leader who also excels at empowering, giving authority, and extending trust. Mark related a story about when Dan first took the helm at Ministry Health Care: "Just after he arrived, the Chief Operating Officer of one of the hospitals—the one where I was a VP of Medical Affairs at the time—left, and Dan needed somebody to sit in that seat for awhile while he thought about his options, and he asked me to do it." Mark went on to explain that Dan clearly laid out what he needed for Mark to do in that role, then trusted him to go do it. "He ended the discussion by saying, 'Just let me know what you need, I'll sit down and talk with you any time you want. Call me any time you want,

I'm available.'"[18] With that kind of authority, trust, and support, Mark was certainly empowered to succeed—and he did!

In Mark's case, the trust extended to him to fulfill that role was repaid with positive results. But what happens when a leader extends trust and gives authority to an employee, and that employee stumbles—or fails completely? That's definitely a risk that comes with empowering those you lead; however, that risk of failure is itself a key component of empowerment. Mac McIntire explains: "To be truly empowered an employee must be free to make mistakes. One's most profound learning experiences often come when people make mistakes and are forced to learn from the consequences of those mistakes."[19] While this is a challenging element of empowerment for many leaders to accept, McIntire is right—some of the greatest growth comes as a result of mistakes and failed first attempts, and empowerment is all about growth and development. "Empowerment is what takes leadership learning out of the classroom and places it squarely in reality," writes Gary Runn. He continues:

> To empower an emerging leader is to risk. There must be permission to succeed and freedom to fail. Empowerment must include the transference of real decision-making authority, the allocation of adequate resources, and a healthy sense of accountability that focuses on leadership learning. Without these three aspects, there is no true empowerment.[20]

Inspirational leaders are not only willing to take on the risk associated with empowerment, but when mistakes *are* made, they respond with grace. Sandy Morford, CEO of Renovo Solutions, described his approach to giving authority, emphasizing how he handles employee mistakes:

> In my mind an individual in our company has to earn the ability to have authority, and they do that through their actions and they do that through their decisions. If they make the right decisions with the right amount of authority you reward that and you complement that. If by chance they happen to make the wrong decision, and that does happen, I'm not an individual that reprimands people in a negative reinforcement way. I'm more about "Okay, what can we learn from this? Let's all agree that you made the wrong decision. It resulted in the wrong outcome. Let's get past that. What's done is done. Now let's learn from that and decide how

you could or should handle it differently the next time something like that comes around." I want the granting of authority to be a learning experience for our team. I want them to learn from their successes as well as I want them to learn from their mistakes. I think over time by taking that approach to granting authority they learn quicker and they learn better.[21]

Like Sandy Morford, inspirational leaders see the great value in first extending trust to those they lead, and then responding with grace when mistakes happen or failures occur. They choose to view failure as a learning opportunity and growing experience, and they generously give second chances. As Clancy Hayes writes, "The only failure is one we do not learn from." Hayes goes on to suggest establishing some guidelines for failure:

> It is OK to make a mistake. It is OK to fail if we are doing our best. When we fail, we can talk about what went wrong, what we can learn, and how to do better. When team members know they are expected to succeed but that it is OK to fail, they are more creative and risk more. This is a positive environment for a team. When people experiment and take calculated risks in their responsibilities, morale increases and results are greater.[22]

Very few people thrive or grow in a micromanaged environment where the leader attempts to control the outcome by dictating behavior and actions to match his or her preferences. Inspirational leaders, while always engaged and supportive, know the value in giving authority, taking a step back, and trusting those they lead to make decisions and take appropriate risks. And when mistakes do happen, it's okay; they respond with grace and encouragement, offering another chance to grow and learn.

KEY POINTS

To be a leader who gives authority:

- Avoid micromanaging the work you've assigned.
- Encourage appropriate independence and autonomy.
- Extend trust and grace to those you lead.

PART IV
A CALL TO ACTION

16

LEVERAGE THE POWER OF HABIT

"We first make our habits, and then our habits make us" – John Dryden

Whether it's as simple as your daily routine or how you shake hands, or as significant as what words appear most in your vocabulary or how you respond to pressure in the workplace, habits control a very large portion of your daily life. Habits likely dictated when and how you went about reading this book, and habits will also heavily influence what you do once you finish reading. I urge you, as you read through this chapter on habits and the following chapter on creating a success system, to renew your commitment to take action on the concepts and principles held within this book. While I don't claim to be a preeminent leadership expert or offer the magic formula for success, I do believe nothing is as effective or influential as true inspirational leadership, and the key to becoming a more inspirational leader lies in your habits.

I have been writing a regular online column called "Tips for Greater Success" since early 2009. The very first article I wrote for the column was titled "Make Good Habits and Become Their Slave," which is an excellent success principle from the book *The Greatest Salesman in the World* by Og Mandino. Here is a brief excerpt from Mandino's fantastic book:

> In truth, the only difference between those who have failed and those who have succeeded lies in the difference of their habits. Good habits are the key to all success. Bad habits are the unlocked

door to failure. Thus, the first law I will obey, which precedeth all others is – I will form good habits and become their slave.[1]

I sincerely believe that nothing else has a greater influence on your success or lack of success than your habits. In that article I wrote back in 2009 I adamantly asserted, "The most imperative and proven success principle in the world is to better align your habits in support of that which you want to become, achieve, and leave as your legacy. Nothing has a stronger impact in your life than your habits. Absolutely nothing!"[2] I still firmly believe this. Habit is an incredibly powerful force in my life, your life—everyone's life! The good news is that the power of habit can absolutely be leveraged for greater success, and it is exactly that—the positive power of habit—which will help you become a truly inspirational leader.

> Nothing else has a greater influence on your success or lack of success than your habits.

So how do you leverage the power of habit? First, it helps to better understand how habits work and commit to being intentional about which habits influence your life. Then, you should identify the specific habits you want to eliminate, change, or begin. Next, you start with small steps and—most importantly—remain consistent! In this chapter we will look at each of those elements of leveraging the power of habit, along with some great examples from inspirational leaders.

Make a Commitment to be Intentional

Habits. We all have them. We're aware of many of our habits, but there are likely many more to which we haven't really given much thought. It's easy to take habits for granted and to just keep doing things the way we've always done them. But in doing so we miss out on the huge opportunity found in the power of habit. By becoming intentional about how we spend our time and what habits we allow to dictate our daily lives, we can accomplish so much more than we ever imagined.

To start with, it helps to better understand how habits work—how they are formed, why they are so powerful, how they can be changed, and, most importantly, how they can be leveraged to benefit our lives. In fact, at the core of Charles Duhigg's bestselling book *The Power of Habit*, is the argument that understanding how habits work is "The key to exercising regularly, losing weight, raising exceptional children, becoming more productive, building revolutionary companies and social movements, and achieving success."[3] Essentially, once you understand how habits work, you can leverage the power of habit to achieve just about anything! Of course, as Charles Duhigg has proven, an entire book could be written on how habits work and their power, but for the sake of space we're only going to briefly touch on the subject here.

In his book Duhigg outlines three basic elements of habits: cue, routine, and reward. He writes,

> This process within our brains is a three-step loop. First, there is a cue, a trigger that tells your brain to go into automatic mode and which habit to use. Then there is the routine, which can be physical or mental or emotional. Finally, there is a reward, which helps your brain figure out if this particular loop is worth remembering for the future. Over time, this loop—cue, routine, reward; cue, routine, reward—becomes more and more automatic. The cue and reward become intertwined until a powerful sense of anticipation and craving emerges. Eventually… a habit is born.[4]

Duhigg goes on to explain, "Habits are powerful, but delicate. They can emerge outside our consciousness, or can be deliberately designed. They often occur without our permission, but can be reshaped by fiddling with their parts."[5] To illustrate how the "cue, routine, reward" loop works and how a habit can be reshaped by "fiddling with its parts," Duhigg shares a personal example. He explains how he came to realize that he had developed an afternoon cookie-eating habit that he just couldn't muster the willpower to conquer. So he carefully examined and dissected that habit until he understood exactly what each of the three elements of the habit loop were. Then, with that understanding, he was able to ultimately reshape his habit into a healthier one. Duhigg explains that his first step in dissecting this habit was to isolate the cue that was triggering his afternoon routine. Was it his location, his activity, his mental state, the time of day, or something else? Within a few days of noting those different elements at play whenever he felt the cookie craving arise, Duhigg easily identified the cue as time of day—the craving always hit mid-afternoon, between 3 and 4. Next, he identified the specific routine, which is usually the most obvious aspect of a habit. In this case, it was getting up from his desk in the afternoon, walking to the cafeteria, buying a chocolate chip cookie, then eating it while chatting with colleagues. His last—and most challenging—step was to experiment in order to identify the reward that was really satisfying the craving driving his afternoon routine. Was it the sugary goodness of the cookie itself? Was it the physical activity of getting away from his desk for a few minutes? Was it the interaction with his colleagues in the cafeteria? By experimenting with the reward over a period of several days, Duhigg realized what he was craving wasn't really the sweet snack, but actually just a short break from his work to go chat with friends.

From there, it was a pretty simple matter of tweaking his routine in order to still respond to the same cue (a certain time of day) and enjoy the reward he was really craving, (interaction with others), but without the unnecessary cookie calories. Duhigg explains,

> Nowadays what happens is, at about 3:30 in the afternoon I absent-mindedly stand up, I look around the office, I see a friend, I'll walk over and we'll gossip for ten minutes, then I'll go back to my desk. The urge to go get a cookie has completely disappeared. The new behavior has become a habit. And I've lost about twelve pounds as a result.[6]

Is it really as simple as that? Yes and no. While virtually every habit can be broken down into that three-part loop, the three parts aren't always as easy to identify or change. Nonetheless, I have found that having that basic understanding of how habits work is extremely helpful for changing old habits or forming new ones. But the key is intentionality. Being intentional with your habits means being aware of what you're doing and having a plan for developing and nurturing positive habits. Stop taking your current habits for granted, and don't disregard the power of habit to help you achieve greater success as an inspirational leader. Commit to it. With determination and

> **The key is intentionality. Be aware of what you're doing and have a plan for developing and nurturing positive habits.**

intentionality, you can leverage the power of habit and become a more inspirational leader!

Identify and Select the Right Habits

Hopefully by this time you're already thinking about the habits in your life that you might want to change—or new habits you want to establish. I know writing this chapter certainly has made me think about it! Some habits are very easy to identify as "bad." For example, we all know smoking is bad for us, we shouldn't look at text messages while driving, and staying up watching late-night television instead of getting enough sleep isn't the best choice. By all means, work on eliminating or changing those habits! But we also all have a lot of habits that might not be all that bad per se, yet aren't necessarily good either—like hitting snooze two or three times every morning, running through the drive-thru close to your office for lunch during the week, or spending most of your evenings watching television or scrolling through social media. Are those routines the worst things ever? No. But they're also not adding a lot of value to your life. Sometimes there are even *good* habits in your life that might not be the best habits for achieving the kind of success you desire. An example related to the concept of becoming a more inspirational leader could be how you handle distractions. In order to limit distractions and boost their productivity, many highly successful people practice habits like keeping their office doors shut, the notifications on their phones turned off, or only checking their email a couple times a day. These are excellent habits. Yet, if one of your goals is to be a very approachable and responsive leader, these otherwise good habits might create barriers to approachability, and might hamper your ability to be responsive to those you lead and serve. So a key part of successful habits is identifying and selecting the *right* habits for you and for what you hope to achieve.

I believe it's most effective to start with the end in mind and with a positive mindset. So before you begin focusing on those habits that have slowly formed in your life that you would like to eliminate or change, first envision the end result you desire, and reflect on the habits that you want to strengthen or develop for the first time. Here are some examples of habits you might want to develop as part of your journey to becoming a more inspirational leader:

- To become a more *accountable* leader, make a habit of both shouldering responsibility and sharing credit by using "I" when taking blame and using "we" or "they" when accepting credit.
- To become a more *teachable* leader and a lifelong learner, incorporate a regular learning opportunity into your daily routine, like listening to a podcast or TED talk while getting ready for work or while driving to your office.
- To become a more *approachable* leader, dedicate thirty minutes of your mornings at work to simply walking the halls of your organization and chatting with the people you run into.
- To become a more *responsive* leader, consistently set reminders on your phone or make notes on your calendar to follow up with people who have approached you with a concern or request.
- To improve as a leader who *builds connections*, develop a habit of asking insightful questions during conversations and listening attentively to the responses.
- To improve as a leader who *makes investments*, make it a habit to genuinely thank your team members for their efforts and to frequently recognize them for their accomplishments.
- To improve as a leader who *demonstrates values*, commit to being respectful of everyone's time—consistently starting meetings on time, arriving early to appointments, and in general not making people wait for you.
- To improve as a leader who *facilitates growth*, develop the habit of giving frequent, constructive feedback to those you lead throughout the year, not just during annual performance reviews.

Obviously, there are countless more habits you could develop to help you implement the strategies and principles throughout this book and become a more inspirational leader—this is just a small sample. When I asked the leaders I interviewed for this book about their habits and any advice they have for other leaders, I received a wide variety of responses. Here are a few of them:

- **Be well informed.** "I read the three major newspapers first thing in the morning. CNN is always on in my office, and I find C-Span relaxing."[7] – *Curtis Rooney*

- **Take care of yourself**. "I try to do something physically for my body every day, and I like to read something spiritual every day as well. I find those habits help me continue to develop as a person in mind, body, and spirit."[8] – *Dan Neufelder*
- **Get out of your office**. "Get out of your office and meet with people at your level and below you in their offices. You'll learn more about how your organization really works."[9] – *Mark Dixon*
- **Be early and work hard**. "Always being early, working hard, long hours, and driving many miles helped me become a successful iron peddler!"[10] – *Clyde Pogson*
- **Be gracious**. "Saying 'Thank you' and 'You're welcome' is a habit that I have. I don't think you can do it enough. And handwritten thank you notes blow people away."[11] – *Tim Orellano*
- **Focus on serving**. "Focus on truly listening and understanding what others' needs are… once you do that, making the right decisions becomes so much easier because you're doing it for all the right reasons. You're doing it to help others get what they want."[12] – *Jack Lawless*
- **Smile**. "As a leader, I have always made it a point to 'just smile'— even in the midst of problems or difficult situations. When the tension in a room gets too high, it is important to take some time to just smile, maybe tell something funny, and get the participants to laugh. Laughter goes a long way in easing the tension and creating an atmosphere for compromise."[13] – *Richard Howe*
- **Have a firm handshake**. "Shaking hands is an important social gesture. I taught my daughters to make a firm handshake, because that's a good lesson for everyone."[14] – *Bill Keogh*
- **Don't confuse activity with accomplishment**. "I think most people don't plan their day accordingly, they just let it happen to them and the clock spins and then it is time to leave. They are exhausted, but what did they accomplish? I am quite guilty of this myself… and think 'why did I let myself get caught up in e-mail or non-productive tasks?' The time spent doing menial tasks pulled me away from what was really important and I didn't achieve success that day. There is always tomorrow, but if you allow this cycle

to continue it becomes routine and then a pattern forms."[15] – *Tod Jeffers*
- **Be consistent**. "Personal commitment and consistent actions from an inspirational leader are critical to his or her credibility and ability to motivate others."[16] – *Marc Reynolds*
- **Study others**. "I think that's where a lot of habits are developed—you learn from others and you admire others' habits and styles and management routines and you try to emulate that and create that for yourself."[17] – *Sandy Morford*

My hope is that as you have been reading through this book several things have jumped out at you—areas in which you'd really like to improve and strategies on which you intend to focus. I suggest flipping back through Part II and Part III of the book and skimming the Key Points at the end of each chapter to help you consider and identify some habits you would like to develop or strengthen. Don't be afraid to initially note several possible habits. Write them down, reflect on them, and ultimately select the ones you feel are most important and will bring the most value to you—personally, professionally, and organizationally.

Next, take some time for personal reflection to identify those areas in your life that have become controlled by habits that you'd like to change or eliminate. Be honest with yourself, and be thorough. Don't just limit your examination to your routines at work—take a look at your habits outside of work as well. Everything is intertwined; you might be amazed at how a simple change in your morning routine at home could drastically impact your leadership in your organization!

Once you have your two lists—the habits you want to develop or strengthen and the habits you want to change or eliminate—examine them side-by-side and look for ways those habits might overlap, with the idea being to replace some of the non-valuable (or even destructive) habits with the habits you really desire. As I'm sure you've heard it said before, the best way to overcome a bad habit is to replace it with a good one. It is very difficult—some would say nearly impossible—to eliminate or substantially change a habit unless you replace it. James Clear explains it well:

> Bad habits address certain needs in your life. And for that reason, it's better to replace your bad habits with a healthier behavior that addresses that same need. If you expect yourself to simply cut out

bad habits without replacing them, then you'll have certain needs that will be unmet and it's going to be hard to stick to a routine of "just don't do it" for very long.[18]

In his article Clear notes that most of our bad habits are caused by stress and boredom. "Everything from biting your nails to overspending on a shopping spree to drinking every weekend to wasting time on the internet can be a simple response to stress and boredom," Clear writes. "But it doesn't have to be that way. You can teach yourself new and healthy ways to deal with stress and boredom, which you can then substitute in place of your bad habits."[19] This is by far the most effective way to overcome bad habits.

For example, after some honest examination of your current habits, you might decide you really want to reduce the amount of time you spend scrolling through social media every day. And, after reflecting on the leadership habits you would like to develop and strengthen, you decide you would really like to become a more teachable leader, striving to retain the mindset of a beginner and truly be a lifelong learner. With those two habits in mind—one you want to change and one you want to add—you might discover an opportunity to replace the former with the latter. So instead of checking your Facebook newsfeed on your phone while eating breakfast every day, you could download the Kindle app and read a chapter in a non-fiction bestseller. Or instead of winding down in the evening with a scroll through Twitter or Instagram, you could listen to a TED talk on an unfamiliar topic while getting ready for bed. There are virtually unlimited possibilities and opportunities for changing or replacing your current habits in order to create greater value for yourself and for those you lead!

> There are virtually unlimited possibilities and opportunities for changing or replacing your current habits in order to create greater value for yourself and for those you lead!

Start Small but be Consistent

Of course, like with most worthwhile efforts, changing old habits and establishing new ones is much easier said than done. After reflecting on the various habits you'd like to change, eliminate, develop, or strengthen, you might be feeling overwhelmed. That's why it's important to start small—but be consistent. Consistency is key! In another article about habits I published a number of years ago, I wrote: "Twentieth century American philosopher Will Durant succinctly distilled a thought from the work of Aristotle in two short sentences: 'We are what we repeatedly do. Excellence, then, is not an act, but a habit.'" I went on to state that, "the power of habit can be harnessed and leveraged to our advantage," explaining:

> Through the right habits, we can achieve excellence. It will take effort, but with determination and perseverance, you can replace your poor habits with better ones… You can get one step closer to achieving your most important goals each day. You. Can. Do. It. It's the power of habit! Excellence is not something that just happens. Excellence is not a single act. Excellence is the result of good habits![18]

So what are some practical ways to start changing your habits and working toward excellence? In an article for *Forbes* magazine, contributor Amy Morin notes, "Self-discipline is the key to reaching your goals and creating a better life. The good news is we all have the ability to be self-disciplined—we just have to practice." She suggests six ways to help develop more self-discipline:

1. Acknowledge Your Weaknesses
2. Establish a Clear Plan
3. Remove the Temptations When Necessary
4. Practice Tolerating Emotional Discomfort
5. Visualize the Long-Term Rewards
6. Recover from Mistakes Effectively[19]

By focusing on developing greater self-discipline and consistently taking small steps in the right direction, you can and will master your habits and change your life and leadership!

KEY POINTS

To leverage the power of habit and become a more inspirational leader:

- Don't take your habits for granted—make a commitment to be intentional!
- Strive to better understand how habits work, why they are powerful, and how they can be changed.
- Identify and select the right habits for achieving the success you desire.
- Work on replacing non-valuable habits with better ones.
- Start small but be consistent—keep taking small steps in the right direction!

17

CREATE YOUR PERSONAL SUCCESS SYSTEM

"Dream big. Start small. Act now." – Robin Sharma

As we bring this study of inspirational leadership to a close, it is critical that you don't just leave what you've discovered and learned here on these pages to be forgotten and unused. For this book to actually be of any value to you, you must put its principles into action! In the previous chapter we looked at the power of habit and how it can be leveraged, and hopefully you've taken the time to reflect on your own habits and have identified and committed to making changes in order to become a more inspirational leader. In this chapter we're taking it one step further, looking at creating a personal success system in order to better use and leverage the concepts in this book.

In my first book, *Presidential Leadership*, which focuses on learning from the strengths of U.S. Presidents and identifying, improving, and leveraging your own strengths, I closed with a Call to Action that includes the following story:

> In the mid-1700s Benjamin Franklin developed a personal system for cultivating his character by focusing on improving in thirteen areas, or virtues. After selecting and defining each virtue, Franklin charted them out in a little book, which he kept with him at all times. He devoted one week at a time to each virtue, commit-

ting on a daily basis to focus on practicing that particular virtue throughout the day. At the end of each day, he would spend a few minutes honestly reflecting on whether or not he had truly adhered to that week's selected virtue. If upon reflection he found some fault in his behavior that day in respect to that goal, he would mark a small dot for that day on the chart in his book. He continued this process, day-by-day, week-by-week, for thirteen weeks, then began again, with the goal of decreasing the number of dots marked in his book until he could complete each week without adding any dots.[1]

We might not want to carry around a notebook full of dots, but I believe we can learn from Benjamin Franklin's personal method to improve in specific areas through very intentional focus and repetition. In that Call to Action I went on to explain:

> Similar to the concept of spaced learning, this careful and intentional repetition over an extended period of time is one of the most effective ways to absorb and internalize information and improve behavior and habits. Rather than try to accomplish something all at once or spend one extended period of time focusing on a task, it is far better to spend a shorter amount of time on it, take a break, and then return your focus to it again. Repeating this process over the course of the day, week, month, or year (depending on your goals) undoubtedly will produce the results you desire and enable you to become more effective and successful.[2]

This concept goes hand in hand with leveraging the power of habit. Thanks to the idea being rapidly spread on the internet, it has become a widely-held belief that it takes twenty-one days to form a new habit. The science behind that claim is lacking, but it is definitely true that it takes time—sometimes a lot of time. Habit formation is a process, not a one-time event. Changing old habits or establishing new ones requires intentional focus and repetition over an extended period of time. The truth is, every person is unique, as are the habits they form and goals they pursue. So while there are basic principles found within the habit process (i.e. the cue-routine-reward loop), there is really no one-size-fits-all system for establishing lasting, valuable habits and achieving your goals. However, there are definitely some general principles that can be helpful for creating and applying your own success system. Here are a few tips:

- **Write it down.** Writing down your goals makes them more real and tangible. Instead of just thinking about what you want to do, clearly articulate it in writing. That process alone will help you get started on your way to achieving those goals, and posting that written reminder somewhere—like by your desk or on your bathroom mirror—will help keep you on track.
- **Review daily.** Just as important as putting your plan in writing is to review it regularly—I recommend doing so every day. What aspects of inspirational leadership are you trying to further develop and strengthen? What habits are you trying to change or establish in order to achieve that goal? Have you been implementing those habits today? Frequently reviewing your plan and asking yourself those types of questions is an essential part of any success system.
- **Apply spaced learning.** Consistently working on new habits on a daily or weekly basis is the key to ingraining those habits long term. In an article titled "Spaced Learning and Repetition: How They Work and Why," Steven Boller of Bottom-Line Performance writes: "Rather than focusing on long periods of learning, we learn better when our brain cells are switched on and off, or with short periods of learning and breaks in between… By switching your learner's brain cells 'on' (during learning) and 'off' again (during breaks), the learner's unconscious has time to internalize the knowledge. Then the repetition of this process is what solidifies the information in long-term memory."[3]
- **Keep it simple.** Don't create a complicated system. While some people are great at in-depth tracking methods (like detailed calorie counting to achieve health goals), most of us lose motivation quickly when the process is too complicated. You need to reserve your energy and self-discipline for the habit you're trying to establish, not the system for tracking your progress. So something simple, like aiming for a brief time of personal reflection at the end of each day (like Benjamin Franklin), might be the most effective method for staying focused on your goals.
- **Make it measurable.** Even if your success system is as simple as a daily time of reflection, you should set measurable goals and

strive to track your progress. For example, in your quest to become a more approachable leader and build stronger connections with those you lead, you might set the goal that you will have at least one casual conversation with a team member every workday, and learn at least one new thing about a colleague every week. You can either mentally track these small objectives during your daily personal reflection, or you can jot yourself a note (physically or digitally) to help you measure your progress.

- **Stay accountable.** Without a doubt, one of the best ways to stick with a difficult task is to recruit the support, help, and encouragement of friends and colleagues. As life and business coach Sherry Collier explains, "When you are accountable to another living, breathing (and talking) human being, you are going to have access to objective opinions, feedback, gentle nudges to get back on track, and/or the proverbial 'kick in the pants' as needed."[4] So if possible, recruit a partner who will check in with you regularly and keep you accountable to working toward the goal(s) you have set.

The keys to creating an effective success system are commitment, simplicity, and consistency. Consider the above tips, find what works for you, and put it into practice! Don't just read this book, nod your head, and let the idea of inspirational leadership slowly fade away. With effort and intentionality, you, and all of those whom you directly and indirectly influence, can enjoy the unlimited, priceless, short-term and long-term benefits of inspirational leadership. Make the commitment. Choose one thing to start working on today—one habit to change or establish. Take action, and *Be an Inspirational Leader*!

> The keys to creating an effective success system are commitment, simplicity, and consistency.

Make the **COMMITMENT.** Take **ACTION.** *Be an Inspirational Leader!*

ACKNOWLEDGMENTS

As is true with every successful inspirational leader, I am forever indebted to hundreds—yes, even thousands—of incredible people who have contributed to my life, my work, and to my commitment to focus on leading and serving others with excellence. This includes my wonderful and ever-supportive parents, immediate and extended family, friends, colleagues, partners, and all those who have served so well in some capacity under my leadership. I am absolutely nothing without these priceless people! I am incredibly blessed in a million ways because of them. Thank you to each and every person who has contributed to my life, as that in turn has contributed to the creation of this book. Any good I may have done, any value I may have created, and any positive impact I may have made as an inspirational leader is directly attributed to each of you!

I would like to again mention two remarkable leaders, whose incredible, inspirational leadership has indelibly influenced my own leadership and positively impacted my life. **Max Coppom** and **Talmadge Johnson**, who each invested in me at different points in my mid to late twenties, are both absolutely superb at engaging, inspiring, and empowering the people, teams, and organizations they have led and influenced over the past 60 years. They are both among the best of the best of the world's inspirational leaders! I am forever indebted to these two men, who still greatly influence my values, best behavior, best thinking, and total commitment to inspirational leadership and serving others. Thank you Max and Talmadge for all you have done for me!

I also specifically want to thank the dozens of men and women who graciously answered my many questions and contributed their unique insights and perspectives on leadership. Without their contributions, this book would not exist. While their roles, titles, and/or organizations may have changed since the writing of this book—or even between interviewing them and publishing the book—the impact and legacy of each of these leaders' will always remain. So with heartfelt thanks, I'd like to acknowledge:

- **Harla Adams** – CEO, *National Institute for Healthcare Leadership*
- **Joel Allison** – CEO, *Baylor Scott & White Health*

- **Traci Bernard, RN** – President, *Texas Health Harris Methodist Hospital Southlake*
- **Kelly Breazeale** – Retired Senior Executive, *VHA (now Vizient)*
- **Sam Breneiser** – Executive Director, Contracting & Provider Relations, *Huntington Memorial Hospital*
- **Geoff Brenner** – President & CEO, *TPC*
- **Bill Brown** – President, *Bois D'Arc Management Group*
- **Celina Caprio** –Board Member & Volunteer, *MANA: A National Latina Organization*
- **Alan Cherry** – Editor & Content Creator, *Share Moving Media, Inc.*
- **Stephen Collins** – Retired Senior Executive, *VHA (now Vizient)*
- **Ed Crane** – Principal, *Edwin D. Crane Fundraising Counsel*
- **Mike Dewey** – President & Founder, *Hidden Star*
- **Mark Dixon** – President, *The Mark Dixon Group*
- **Cathy Eddy** – President, *Health Plan Alliance*
- **Peter Fine** – President & CEO, *Banner Health*
- **Bob Furman** – Retired Executive Director, *YMCA Camp Kitaki*
- **Tom Furman, DVM** – Veterinarian, *The Animal Center*
- **Kathleen Gallo, PhD, RN** – SVP & Chief Learning Officer, *Northwell Health*, Dean & Professor, *Hofstra Northwell School of Graduate Nursing and Physician Assistant Studies*
- **Marc Gelinas** – Healthcare Practice Area Lead, *Slalom Consulting*
- **Anne Granum** – VP, National & Strategic Accounts, *Renovo Solutions*
- **Lisa Hill** – Executive Director, *Invest In Kids*
- **Richard Howe, PhD** – CEO, *HCG*
- **Tod Jeffers** – National Account Manager, U.S. Federal Government & Premier GPO, *bioMerieux*
- **Sharla Jones** – VP, HR Learning & Development Manager, *PlainsCapital Bank*
- **Bill Keogh** – Retired Executive, *Hertz Corporation*
- **Eric Kugler** – Healthcare Executive
- **Jack Lawless** – Retired Division President, *Morrison Management Specialists*
- **Bruce Lawrence** – President & CEO, *INTEGRIS Health*
- **Brent Leisure** –State Parks Division Director, *Texas Parks & Wildlife Department*

- **Keith Lepak, MD** – Medical Director, *ER Centers of America*
- **Christine Márquez-Hudson** – President & CEO, *The Denver Foundation*
- **Ben McKibbens** – Retired President & CEO, *Valley Baptist Health System*
- **Sheleza Mohamed** – Department Manager, *UT Southwestern Medical Center*
- **Sandy Morford** – CEO, *Renovo Solutions*
- **Dan Neufelder** – Founder and CEO, *The Neufelder Consulting Group*
- **Tim Orellano** – President, *The Human Resources Team*
- **Andrea Overman** – Chief Marketing Officer, *Chief Outsiders*
- **Anne Pogson** – Retired
- **Clyde Pogson** – Retired Sales Executive
- **Marc Reynolds** – SVP, Payer Relations, *Scripps Health*
- **Curtis Rooney** – Founder & CEO, *Glen Echo Strategies*
- **Lorna Shaw** – External Affairs Manager, *Sumitomo Metal Mining Pogo*
- **Jane Shlaes** – Director, Learning & Organizational Development, *College of American Pathologists*
- **Dan Teeters** – VP Corporate Development, *Compass Group North America*
- **Chris Van Gorder** – President & CEO, *Scripps Health*
- **Hays Waldrop** – President & CEO, *Institute of Healthcare Executives and Suppliers*
- **Jim Wetrich** – CEO, *The Wetrich Group*
- **Buddy White** – Owner, *White & Associates Real Estate Services*
- **Mike Williams** – President & CEO, *Community Hospital Corporation*

In addition to interviewing each of the leaders above, I also reached out to some of their colleagues for further insights and comments—many of which I included in this book as well. So another big thank you to these individuals for taking the time to answer my questions:

- **Karen Adams**
- **Brad Beard**
- **Jennifer Bell**
- **Steve Boyd**
- **Michael Britton**

- Gary Brock
- Ron Bunnell
- Jonathan Camp
- Ed Clark
- Colleen Collarelli
- Kathy Dagg
- Karen Fox Elwell
- Jill Gable
- Richard Gonzales
- Chris Hammes
- John Hensing
- Bob Van Heuvelen
- Jessica Hill
- Spencer Jensen
- Mark Kehrberg
- Chris Kennedy
- Jeff Kirkham
- Becky Kuhn
- Scott Lewis
- Kathleen McComber
- Jay Niner
- Fred Pane
- Beth Pauchnik
- Michael Payne
- Wayne & Gladys Petersen
- Robert Pryor
- Sanchia Patrick Rasul
- Laura Redman
- Anthony Romero
- Marshall Snipes
- Bob Solheim
- Arthur Sparks
- Michael Svagdis
- Breda Turner
- Tom Veeser
- Laura Wahl
- Geoff Welch

ABOUT THE AUTHORS

Dan Nielsen is a successful leader, entrepreneur, teacher, author, and speaker. A perpetual student, Dan understands the incredible power of learning from successful leaders and strongly believes that leadership excellence is the key to all lasting progress and success.

Dan spent much of his career as a healthcare executive, serving for fifteen years as the President and CEO of Dallas-Fort Worth Medical Center, and nearly fifteen years as the lead executive responsible for the national education and networking strategies and activities of VHA (now Vizient), America's largest hospital and healthcare national alliance.

Dan is now a leader, speaker, and author with a broad area of interest. He is passionate about helping others reach their potential and achieve greater success, no matter who you are or how you define it. He regularly writes and speaks about achieving greater success, becoming a better leader, and living an inspired and joy-filled life. His first book, *Presidential Leadership: Learning from United States Presidential Libraries & Museums* was published in 2013 and is available via Amazon and other book retailers. To see more of Dan's writing and to learn about his dynamic, inspirational presentations, please visit his website, DanNielsen.com.

Whenever time allows, Dan continues to pursue two of his favorite hobbies: travel and photography. When not out traveling across America the Beautiful in his motorhome, which he fondly calls his "Inspirational Vehicle," Dan can usually be found getting some work done either in his favorite chair at Starbucks or while walking at the gym. Dan has two grown children and two grandchildren and lives near Dallas, Texas with his wife, Faye.

Emily Sirkel is a writer with a talent for providing written structure for Dan's vision, taking his big ideas and putting them into written form. Emily has worked with Dan since the beginning of 2012, serving as his coauthor, editor, collaborator, brainstorming partner, content developer, web admin, and "unrelenting taskmaster." This is her second book to coauthor with Dan, having worked with him on *Presidential Leadership* as well.

Emily has a bachelor's degree from Wayland Baptist University, and a unique background that includes diverse experiences such as being a homeschooled ranch-kid in eastern Montana and a camp food service director in central Texas. Though she didn't expect to become a writer, Emily has a talent and passion for communicating in written form and enjoys the opportunity to use that talent.

In addition to the writing she does with Dan, Emily sometimes finds time to pursue her other writing interests on her own website, EmilySirkel.com. When not writing, her "real job" is being a mom to her two beautiful little girls. Emily lives with her husband, Geoff, and their daughters near Dallas, Texas.

KEYNOTES

Dan Nielsen is an engaging and inspiring communicator and talented keynote speaker. With more than twenty-five years of experience delivering presentations, leading workshops, and facilitating meetings for groups of all sizes, Dan knows how to engage a room full of people—not merely entertaining them, but inspiring and equipping them to take action on the concepts he presents.

Dan's unique repertoire of keynotes and workshops leverages his extensive leadership experience as well as his hobbies and interests, and many keynotes feature his own beautiful photography, taken during his travels throughout America. Dan's refreshing and inspiring presentations include such topics and titles as:

- **Be An Inspirational Leader:** Engage, Inspire Empower (based on this book)

- **Lead With Your Strengths:** The Key to Leadership Excellence (based on Dan's first book, *Presidential Leadership*)

- **Achieve Greater Success:** Improve and Leverage Your Strengths

- **Sharpen Your Focus:** Achieving Clarity for More Effective Leadership

- **Be a Life-Long Learner:** Achieving Your Highest Priorities and Reaching Your Full Potential

- ***Critical Leadership Lessons from America's Healthcare Leaders***

For more information on Dan's keynotes and to inquire about his availability, please visit his website, DanNielsen.com.

RESOURCES

We hope you have found this book enjoyable, interesting, and—most importantly—valuable to your personal, professional, and organizational leadership development. If you would like more information and resources related to inspirational leadership, please visit the book website, BeAnInspirationalLeader.com. There you will find additional resources to help you on your journey to becoming a better, more effective inspirational leader.

For more valuable leadership content, we invite you to read *Presidential Leadership: Learning from United States Presidential Libraries & Museums*, and visit:

- PresidentialLeadership.com
- DanNielsen.com
- AmericasHealthcareLeaders.com

NOTES

Chapter 1

1. Jonathan Camp, comments from message to Bob Furman, shared with me in an email interview, received August 27, 2014.

2. Jonathan Camp, comments from email interview, received August 27, 2014.

3. Jill Gable, comments from email interview, received August 17, 2014.

4. Wayne and Gladys Peterson, comments from email interview, received August 15, 2014.

5. *Dictionary.com Unabridged*, s.v. "influence," accessed November 6, 2014, http://dictionary.reference.com/browse/influence.

6. Wayne Dyer, as quoted in "Interview With *New Age Retailer*," Wayne Dyer website, accessed October 7, 2014, http://www.drwaynedyer.com/press/interview-new-age-retailer/.

7. Alan Cherry, comments from email interview, received September 2, 2014.

8. Tony Hsieh, as quoted in "Grow Your Company as Big as Zappos.com: 7 Tips from Tony Hsieh," *Inc. Magazine*, accessed November 8, 2014, http://www.inc.com/allison-fass/tony-hsieh-zappos-growth-strategies.html.

9. Alan Cherry, comments from email interview, received September 2, 2014.

10. Geoff Brenner, comments from phone interview, conducted August 18, 2014.

Chapter 2

1. Marc Gelinas, comments from email interview, received August 19, 2014.

2. Brent Leisure, comments from email interview, received August 8, 2014.

3. Jim Clemmer, "Different Leadership Competencies for Each Organizational Level?" Clemmer Group website, accessed October 6, 2014, http://www.clemmergroup.com/blog/2014/09/04/different-leadership-competencies-for-each-organizational-level/.

4. Jack Zenger and Joseph Folkman, "What Inspiring Leaders Do," *Harvard Business Review*, accessed October 6, 2014, http://blogs.hbr.org/2013/06/what-inspiring-leaders-do/.

5. John C. Maxwell, "The Most Important Question a Leader Can Ask,"

Michael Hyatt website, accessed October 8, 2014, http://michaelhyatt.com/most-important-question-leader-can-ask.html.

6. John C. Maxwell, "A Minute With Maxwell: Inspiration," John Maxwell Team website, accessed October 9, 2014, http://johnmaxwellteam.com/inspiration/.

7. Celina Caprio, comments from phone interview, conducted August 21, 2014.

8. Dan Nielsen, "2 Keys to Inspiring Someone," Dan Nielsen website, accessed October 10, 2014, http://dannielsen.com/2013/01/31/2-keys-to-inspiring-someone/.

Chapter 3

1. "Don't Sell Your Hair to a Wig Shop," 2012 DirecTV Commercial, accessed October 15, 2014, http://youtu.be/KoG0O9xH6-U.

2. Kathleen Gallo, comments from phone interview, conducted August 18, 2014.

3. Harla Adams, comments from email interview, received September 11, 2014.

4. Dan Nielsen, *Presidential Leadership: Learning from United States Presidential Libraries & Museums*, (Dan Nielsen Company, 2013), 285.

5. Peter Drucker, *The Effective Executive*, (New York: HarperCollins, 2002), 71.

6. Jim Clemmer, "Review Of How To Be Exceptional: Drive Leadership Success By Magnifying Your Strengths," *The Leader Letter*, issue 114 (September 2012), page 5, http://www.clemmergroup.com/newsl/september2012.html.

7. Alan Cherry, comments from email interview, received September 2, 2014.

8. Jim Clemmer, "Exceptional Leaders Aren't Well-Rounded," Clemmer Group website, accessed October 16, 2014, http://www.clemmergroup.com/blog/2014/03/13/exceptional-leaders-arent-well-rounded/.

9. Marcus Buckingham, "Put Your Strengths to Work," *EntreLeadership Podcast*, episode 73 (May 5, 2014), https://www.entreleadership.com/podcasts/podcast-episode-73--put-your-strengths.

10. Dan Teeters, comments from email interview, received August 19, 2014.

11. Kathleen Gallo, comments from phone interview, conducted August 18,

2014.

12. Jack Zenger and Joseph Folkman, "Ten Fatal Flaws That Derail Leaders," *Harvard Business Review*, accessed October 8, 2014, http://hbr.org/2009/06/ten-fatal-flaws-that-derail-leaders/ar/1.

CHAPTER 4

1. *Dictionary.com Unabridged*, s.v. "integrity," accessed October 10, 2014, http://dictionary.reference.com/browse/integrity.

2. Dan Nielsen, *Presidential Leadership*, 156.

3. Ed Crane, comments from email interview, received August 13, 2014.

4. Michael Hyatt, "What My Dog Trainer Reminded Me About Leadership," Michael Hyatt website, accessed August 10, 2014, https://michaelhyatt.com/dog-training-and-leadership.html.

5. Ed Hansen, "'I Own It!' – The Single Most Powerful Thing a Leader Can Say," LinkedIn Pulse, accessed October 10, 2014, https://www.linkedin.com/pulse/article/20140609010846-251994533--i-own-it-the-single-most-powerful-thing-a-leader-can-say.

6. Stephen B. Collins, comments from email interview, received August 9, 2014.

7. Bill Brown, comments from email interview, received August 12, 2014.

8. Lorna Shaw, comments from phone interview, conducted July 23, 2014.

9. Harla Adams, comments from email interview, received September 11, 2014.

10. Mike Dewey, comments from phone interview, conducted August 21, 2014.

11. Hays Waldrop, comments from phone interview, conducted August 12, 2014.

12. Stephen M. R. Covey, *The SPEED of Trust: The One Thing That Changes Everything* (New York: Simon & Schuster, 2008), 26.

13. Amy Rees Anderson, "Success Will Come and Go, But Integrity is Forever," *Forbes Magazine*, accessed October 11, 2014, http://www.forbes.com/sites/amyanderson/2012/11/28/success-will-come-and-go-but-integrity-is-forever/.

14. Keith Lepak, comments from email interview, received August 6, 2014.

15. John Maxwell, "94 Leadership Quotes for You and Your Church," Sermon Central website, accessed October 12, 2014, http://www.sermoncentral.com/articleb.asp?article=John-Maxwell-94-Leadership-Quotes.

16. Dan Nielsen, *Presidential Leadership*, 277-278.

17. Bill Murphy, Jr., "7 Things Great Leaders Always Do (But Mere Managers Always Fear)," *Inc. Magazine*, accessed October 12, 2014, http://www.inc.com/bill-murphy-jr/7-things-great-leaders-always-do-but-mere-managers-always-fear.html.

18. Mark Dixon, comments from phone interview, conducted June 25, 2014.

19. Ibid.

20. Michael Hyatt, "The Top-10 Characteristics of Lousy Leaders," Michael Hyatt website, accessed October 13, 2014, http://michaelhyatt.com/lousy-leaders.html.

21. Bob Furman, comments from email interview, received August 9, 2014.

22. Celina Caprio, comments from phone interview, received August 21, 2014.

23. Jeff Haden, "10 Things Only Exceptional Bosses Give Employees," LinkedIn Pulse, accessed October 14, 2014, https://www.linkedin.com/pulse/20140630120036-20017018-10-things-only-exceptional-bosses-give-employees.

24. Ilene Muething, as quoted in "What My Dog Trainer Reminded Me About Leadership," Michael Hyatt website, accessed October 14, 2014, http://michaelhyatt.com/dog-training-and-leadership.html.

Chapter 5

1. Lisa Hill, comments from phone interview, conducted July 22, 2014.

2. Kelly Breazeale, comments from email interview, received August 7, 2014.

3. Marcus Buckingham, *EntreLeadership Podcast*, episode 73.

4. Christine Márquez-Hudson, comments from phone interview, conducted August 29, 2014.

5. Brent Leisure, comments from email interview, received August 8, 2014.

6. Kevin Cashman, "Five Enduring Leadership Lessons," *Forbes Magazine*, accessed December 18, 2014, http://www.forbes.com/sites/kevincashman/2014/09/05/five-enduring-leadership-lessons/.

7. Bill George, Peter Sims, Andrew N. McLean, Diana Mayer: "Discovering Your Authentic Leadership," *Harvard Business Review*, accessed December 18, 2014, https://hbr.org/2007/02/discovering-your-authentic-leadership.

8. Lisa Hill, comments from phone interview, conducted July 22, 2014.

9. Ibid.

10. William Shakespeare, *Hamlet*, Act 1, Scene 3, Lines 78-81 (Polonius).

11. Greg Schinkel, "Being an Approachable Leader," accessed December 31, 2014, http://www.uniquedevelopment.com/blog/being-an-approachable-leader/.

12. Brent Leisure, comments from email interview, received August 8, 2014.

13. Eric Kugler, comments from email interview, received August 21, 2014.

14. Anne Pogson, comments from email interview, received August 25, 2014.

15. Francisco Dao, "Without Confidence, There is No Leadership," *Inc. Magazine*, accessed November 13, 2014, http://www.inc.com/resources/leadership/articles/20080301/dao.html.

16. Lisa Hill, comments from phone interview, conducted July 22, 2014.

17. Lorna Shaw, comments from phone interview, conducted July 23, 2014.

18. Kathleen Gallo, comments from phone interview, conducted August 18, 2014.

19. Jim Wetrich, comments from phone interview, conducted May 30, 2014.

20. Sandy Morford, comments from phone interview, conducted May 8, 2014.

Chapter 6

1. Michael Josephson, "Eight Attributes of Great Leadership: What it Takes to Be an Exceptional Executive or Administrator," as published on Neal Beets' blogspot, accessed June 23, 2016, http://nealbeets.blogspot.com/2012/10/attributes-of-great-leadership-what-it.html.

2. Sandy Morford, comments from phone interview, conducted August 22, 2014.

3. Bruce Lawrence, comments from phone interview, conducted June 10, 2014.

4. Marshall Snipes, comments from email interview, received June 25, 2014.

5. Beth Pauchnik, comments from email interview, received June 27, 2014.

6. Christine Márquez-Hudson, comments from phone interview, conducted August 29, 2014.

7. Marc Gelinas, comments from email interview, received August 19, 2014.

8. Hal Urban, *Life's Greatest Lessons: 20 Things That Matter* (New York: Fireside, 2003), 42-43.

9. Jim Wetrich, comments from live interview, conducted in 2010.

10. Sanchia Patrick Rasul, comments from email interview, received July 8, 2014.

11. Michael Britton, comments from email interview, received July 14, 2014.

12. Bob Furman, comments from email interview, received August 9, 2014.

13. Mark Kehrberg, MD, comments from phone interview, conducted July 15, 2014.

14. Dan Neufelder, comments from phone interview, conducted May 28, 2014.

15. Dan Nielsen, "Leadership: What Is Your Greatest Failure?" *JHC* website, accessed December 8, 2014, http://www.jhconline.com/leadership-what-is-your-greatest-failure.html.

16. Sandy Morford, comments from phone interview, conducted August 22, 2014.

17. Kelly Breazeale, comments from email interview, received August 7, 2014.

18. Colleen Collarelli, comments from email interview, received August 3, 2014.

19. Kate Ebner, "Embracing the Beginner's Mindset," Life Reimagined website, accessed December 10, 2014, http://lifereimagined.aarp.org/stories/3251-Embracing-the-beginner-s-mindset.

20. Dan Nielsen, "Leadership Development – A Broader Perspective," *JHC* website, accessed December 10, 2014, http://www.jhconline.com/leadership-development-a-broader-perspective.html.

21. Celina Caprio, comments from phone interview, conducted August 2, 2014.

22. Cathy Eddy, comments from email interview, received August 6, 2014.

CHAPTER 7

1. Mark J. Campbell, "Approachability - The Key to Successful Communication as a Leader," Mark J. Campbell website, accessed December 29, 2014, http://www.mjcampbellassoc.com/articles/art-0076.htm.

2. Logan Chierotti, "Rethinking the Open Door Policy," *Inc. Magazine*, accessed December 29, 2014, http://www.inc.com/logan-chierotti/rethinking-the-open-door-policy.html.

3. Curtis Rooney, comments from phone interview, conducted June 6, 2014.

4. Cathy Eddy, comments from email interview, received August 6, 2014.

5. Logan Chierotti, "Rethinking the Open Door Policy."

6. Christine Márquez-Hudson, comments from phone interview, conducted August 29, 2014.

7. Jim Wetrich, comments from phone interview, conducted May 30, 2014.

8. Sanchia Patrick Rasul, comments from email interview, received July 8, 2014.

9. Bruce Lawrence, comments from phone interview, conducted June 10, 2014.

10. Sam Breneiser, comments from email interview, received August 23, 2014.

11. Cathy Eddy, comments from email interview, received August 6, 2014.

12. Tony Dungy with Nathan Whitaker, *The Mentor Leader: Secrets to Building People and Teams that Win Consistently* (Winter Park: Tyndale House Publishers, Inc., 2010), 90.

13. Ibid.

14. Jennifer Bell, comments from email interview, received June 23, 2014.

15. Michael Payne, comments from email interview, received June 18, 2014.

16. Fred Pane, comments from phone interview, conducted June 16, 2014.

17. Bob Van Heuvelen, comments from email interview, received July 9, 2014.

18. Jack Lawless, comments from phone interview, conducted July 24, 2014.

19. Michael Svagdis, comments from email interview, received July 28, 2014.

20. Ed Clark, comments from email interview, received July 29, 2014.

21. Arthur Sparks, comments from email interview, received August 8, 2014.

22. Jay Niner, comments from email interview, received August 18, 2014.

23. Scott Lewis, comments from email interview, received August 1, 2014.

24. Laura Wahl, comments from email interview, received May 28, 2014.

25. Jessica Hill, comments from email interview, received May 27, 2014.

26. Karen Adams, comments from email interview, received May 21, 2014.

27. Anthony Romero, comments from email interview, received May 19, 2014.

28. Laura Redman, comments from email interview, received May 23, 2014.

29. Stephen J. Meyer, "Study Shows Why 'Power Body Language' Could Make You A Less Effective Leader," *Forbes Magazine*, accessed January 2, 2015, http://www.forbes.com/sites/stevemeyer/2014/09/25/study-shows-why-power-body-language-could-make-you-a-less-effective-leader/.

30. Peter Fine, comments from phone interview, conducted May 19, 2014.

31. Beth Pauchnik, comments from email interview, received June 27, 2014.

32. Chris Hammes, comments from email interview, received July 7, 2014.

33. Christine Márquez-Hudson, comments from phone interview, conducted

August 29, 2014.

34. Cathy Eddy, comments from email interview, received August 6, 2014.

35. Sam Breneiser, comments from email interview, received August 23, 2014.

36. Lisa Hill, comments from phone interview, conducted July 22, 2014.

37. Jack Lawless, comments from phone interview, conducted July 24, 2014.

38. Bruce Lawrence, comments from phone interview, conducted June 10, 2014.

Chapter 8

1. Bill Treasurer, as quoted by BJ Gallagher, "Leaders Open Doors for Others," *Huffington Post*, accessed January 11, 2015, http://www.huffingtonpost.com/bj-gallagher/leaders-open-doors-for-ot_b_3281984.html.

2. Jack Lawless, comments from phone interview, conducted July 24, 2014.

3. Jennifer Bell, comments from email interview, received June 23, 2014.

4. Joel Allison, comments from phone interview, conducted May 21, 2014.

5. Mark Kehrberg, MD, comments from phone interview, conducted July 15, 2014.

6. Laura Wahl, comments from email interview, received May 28, 2014.

7. Steve Boyd, comments from email interview, received June 25, 2014.

8. Gary Brock, comments from email interview, received June 3, 2014.

9. Jack Lawless, comments from phone interview, conducted July 24, 2014.

10. Scott Lewis, comments from email interview, received August 1, 2014.

11. Arthur Sparks, comments from email interview, received August 8, 2014.

12. Bruce Lawrence, comments from phone interview, conducted June 10, 2014.

13. Lorna Shaw, comments from phone interview, conducted July 23, 2014.

14. Jeff Haden, "10 Things Only Exceptional Bosses Give Employees."

15. Traci Bernard, comments from phone interview, conducted May 9, 2014.

16. Harla Adams, comments from email interview, received September 11, 2014.

17. Marc Gelinas, comments from email interview, received August 19, 2014.

18. Sanchia Patrick Rasul, comments from email interview, received July 8, 2014.

19. Jim Wetrich, comments from phone interview, conducted May 30, 2014.

20. Tom Veeser, comments from phone interview, conducted July 18, 2014.

21. Michael Payne, comments from email interview, received June 18, 2014.

22. Bob Van Heuvelen, comments from email interview, received July 9, 2014.

23. Keith Lepak, comments from email interview, received August 6, 2014.

24. Curtis Rooney, comments from phone interview, conducted June 6, 2014.

25. Dan Nielsen, "What Energizes You?" Dan Nielsen website, accessed January 17, 2015, http://dannielsen.com/2013/05/14/what-energizes-you/.

26. Celina Caprio, comments from phone interview, conducted August 21, 2014.

Chapter 9

1. Steve Strang, "7 Inspiring Leaders and the Traits that Made Them Great," *Charisma Magazine*, accessed April 10, 2015, http://www.charismamag.com/blogs/the-strang-report/20298-7-inspiring-leaders-and-the-traits-that-made-them-great.

2. Jane Shlaes, comments from email interview, received August 18, 2014.

3. John Hensing, comments from email interview, received May 22, 2014.

4. Ron Bunnell, comments from email interview, received June 5, 2014.

5. Brad Beard, comments from email interview, received August 23, 2014.

6. Gary Brock, comments from email interview, received June 3, 2014.

7. Bruce Lawrence, comments from phone interview, conducted June 10, 2014.

8. Lorna Shaw, comments from phone interview, conducted July 23, 2014.

9. Buddy White, comments from email interview, received September 18, 2014.

10. Joel Allison, comments from phone interview, conducted May 21, 2014.

11. Lisa Hill, comments from phone interview, conducted July 22, 2014.

12. Sharla Jones, comments from email interview, received August 27, 2014.

13. Tim Orellano, comments from phone interview, conducted June 11, 2014.

14. Anne Granum, comments from blog comment on Dan Nielsen website, posted October 5, 2013, accessed September 10, 2016, http://dannielsen.com/2013/10/03/learning-from-jfk-be-an-inspirational-leader/.

15. Anne Granum, comments from email, received May 22, 2015.

16. Anne Granum, comments from email, received July 3, 2015.

Chapter 10

1. Dov Seidman, "To inspire others, it's how you do it that counts," CNN website, accessed June 3, 2015, http://www.cnn.com/2012/05/03/opinion/dov-seidman-oped/index.html.

2. Curtis Rooney, comments from phone interview, conducted June 6, 2014.

3. Christine Márquez-Hudson, comments from phone interview, conducted August 29, 2014.

4. David Bradford, "Leadership That Gets Results," Great Leadership website, accessed June 3, 2015, http://www.greatleadershipbydan.com/2014/05/leadership-that-gets-results.html.

5. Joel Allison, comments from phone interview, conducted May 21, 2014.

6. Jeff Haden, "10 Things Only Exceptional Bosses Give Employees."

7. Gary Brock, comments from email interview, received June 3, 2014.

8. Steve Boyd, comments from email interview, received June 25, 2014.

9. Sheleza Mohamed, comments from email interview, received September 1, 2014.

10. Jack Lawless, comments from phone interview, conducted July 24, 2014.

11. Richard Howe, comments from email interview, received August 8, 2014.

12. Harla Adams, comments from email interview, received September 11, 2014.

13. Celina Caprio, comments from phone interview, conducted August 21, 2014.

14. Tim Orellano, comments from phone interview, conducted June 11, 2014.

15. Jessica Hill, comments from email interview, received May 27, 2014.

16. Emma Seppala and Kim Cameron, "Proof That Positive Work Cultures Are More Productive," *Harvard Business Review*, accessed June 15, 2015, https://hbr.org/2015/12/proof-that-positive-work-cultures-are-more-productive.

17. Ibid.

18. Jennifer Bell, comments from email interview, received June 23, 2014.

19. Michael Payne, comments from email interview, received June 18, 2014.

20. Bob Van Heuvelen, comments from email interview, received July 9, 2014.

21. Sandy Morford, comments from phone interview, conducted August 22, 2014.

22. Jim Collins, *Good to Great: Why Some Companies Make the Leap… and Others Don't*, (New York: HarperCollins Publishers, Inc., 2001), 210.

23. Teresa Amabile and Steve Kramer, "To Give Your Employees Meaning, Start With Mission," *Harvard Business Review*, accessed June 17, 2015, https://hbr.org/2012/12/to-give-your-employees-meaning.html.

24. Marc Reynolds, comments from email interview, received August 19, 2014.

25. Ben McKibbens, comments from phone interview, conducted November 2011.

26. Eric Hellweg, "The Eight-Word Mission Statement," *Harvard Business Review*, accessed June 19, 2015, https://hbr.org/2010/10/the-eight-word-mission-stateme&cm_sp.

27. Dean Foods Company, as quoted by Teresa Amabile and Steve Kramer in "To Give Your Employees Meaning, Start With Mission," *Harvard Business Review*, accessed June 17, 2015, https://hbr.org/2012/12/to-give-your-employees-meaning.html.

28. Starbucks Coffee Company, as quoted by Teresa Amabile and Steve Kramer in "To Give Your Employees Meaning, Start With Mission," *Harvard Business Review*, accessed June 17, 2015, https://hbr.org/2012/12/to-give-your-employees-meaning.html.

29. Graham Kenny, "Your Company's Purpose Is Not Its Vision, Mission, or Values," *Harvard Business Review*, accessed June 19, 2015, https://hbr.org/2014/09/your-companys-purpose-is-not-its-vision-mission-or-values.

30. Harvard Business Review contributor, "Make Your Mission Meaningful," *Time Magazine* website, accessed June 20, 2015, http://business.time.com/2013/03/28/make-your-mission-meaningful/.

31. Warren Bennis, *Leading People is Like Herding Cats*, (Provo: Executive Excellence Publishing, 1999), 89.

32. Tamara Rosin, "A hospital worker has the most satisfying job in the world — You'd be surprised which one," *Becker's Hospital Review*, accessed October 20, 2015, http://www.beckershospitalreview.com/hospital-management-administration/a-hospital-worker-has-the-most-satisfying-job-in-the-world-you-d-be-surprised-which-one.html.

33. Ibid.

Chapter 11

1. Deborah Maher, "Invest In People, Create An Enlivened Future," DFM Consulting website, accessed April 26, 2016, http://dfmconsultinginc.

com/2014/02/24/invest-in-people-create-an-enlivened-future/.

2. Steve Chase, from his commencement address, "Be curious, open and flexible," at Georgetown University McDonough School of Business on April 27, 2014.

3. Sean Kelly, "9 Simple Ways to Invest in Your Employees and Combat Turnover," When I Work website, accessed April 27, 2016, http://wheniwork.com/blog/reduce-employee-turnover/.

4. Dan Neufelder, comments from phone interview, conducted May 28, 2014.

5. Laura Redman, comments from email interview, received May 23, 2014.

6. Traci Bernard, comments from phone interview, conducted May 9, 2014.

7. Sanchia Patrick Rasul, comments from email interview, received July 8, 2014.

8. Mark Dixon, comments from phone interview, conducted June 25, 2014.

9. Arthur Sparks, comments from email interview, received August 8, 2014.

10. Jay Niner, comments from email interview, received August 18, 2014.

11. Robert (Bob) Pryor, comments from email interview, received July 2, 2014.

12. Gary Brock, comments from email interview, received June 3, 2014.

13. Sheleza Mohamed, comments from email interview, received September 1, 2014.

14. Jeff Kirkham, comments from email interview, received July 8, 2014.

15. Brad Beard, comments from email interview, received August 23, 2014.

16. Celina Caprio, comments from phone interview, conducted August 21, 2014.

17. Jack Lawless, comments from phone interview, conducted July 24, 2014.

18. Arthur Sparks, comments from email interview, received August 8, 2014.

19. Kathy Dagg, comments from email interview, received July 31, 2014.

20. Ed Clark, comments from email interview, received July 29, 2014.

21. Scott Lewis, comments from email interview, received August 1, 2014.

22. Michael Svagdis, comments from email interview, received July 28, 2014.

23. Arthur Sparks, comments from email interview, received August 8, 2014.

24. Bruce Lawrence, comments from phone interview, conducted June 10, 2014.

25. Breda Turner, comments from email interview, received July 2, 2014.

26. Bill Murphy, Jr., "7 Things Great Leaders Always Do (But Mere Managers Always Fear)."

27. Dan Neufelder, comments from phone interview, conducted May 28, 2014.

28. Peter Fine, comments from phone interview, conducted May 19, 2014.

29. Traci Bernard, comments from phone interview, conducted May 9, 2014.

30. Karen Adams, comments from email interview, received May 21, 2014.

31. Anthony Romero, comments from email interview, received May 19, 2014.

32. Joel Allison, comments from phone interview, conducted May 21, 2014.

33. Jack Lawless, comments from phone interview, conducted July 24, 2014.

34. Arthur Sparks, comments from email interview, received August 8, 2014.

35. Celina Caprio, comments from phone interview, conducted August 21, 2014.

36. Tim Stevens, "The Best Strategy for Developing Leaders is No Strategy," *Entrepreneur Magazine*, accessed May 5, 2016, https://www.entrepreneur.com/article/247264.

37. Sasha Bricel, "Top 3 Reasons Why Employee Recognition is So Important," HR website, accessed May 5, 2016, http://www.hr.com/en/app/blog/2012/03/top-3-reasons-why-employee-recognition-is-so-impor_gzqy1ds1.html.

38. Michael Hyatt, "Four Characteristics of Inspirational Leaders," Michael Hyatt website, accessed May 20, 2015, http://michaelhyatt.com/four-characteristics-of-inspirational-leaders.html.

39. Jeff Haden, "10 Things Only Exceptional Bosses Give Employees."

40. Jack Lawless, comments from phone interview, conducted July 24, 2014.

41. Colleen Barrett, *Lead With LUV: A Different Way to Create Real Success*, (Upper Saddle River: FT Press, 2011), Kindle edition, chap. 2.

42. Sheri L. Dew, *Saying It Like It Is*, (Salt Lake City: Deseret Book, 2009).

CHAPTER 12

1. Dan Teeters, comments from email interview, received August 19, 2014.

2. Michael Hyatt, "Why Vision is More Important Than Strategy," Michael Hyatt website, accessed May 23, 2016, http://michaelhyatt.com/why-vision-is-more-important-than-strategy.html.

3. Saul Kaplan, comments in response to a question on the Quora website, accessed May 23, 2016, https://www.quora.com/Whats-the-difference-between-

vision-and-strategy.

4. Bill Brown, comments from email interview, received August 12, 2014.

5. Michael Hyatt, "The Top-10 Characteristics of Lousy Leaders."

6. Jack Lawless, comments from phone interview, conducted July 24, 2014.

7. Christine Márquez-Hudson, comments from phone interview, conducted August 29, 2014.

8. Michael Hyatt, "Four Characteristics of Inspirational Leaders."

9. Peter Fine, comments from phone interview, conducted May 19, 2014.

10. Marcus Buckingham, *EntreLeadership Podcast*, episode 73.

11. Mark Dixon, comments from phone interview, conducted June 25, 2014.

12. Ibid.

13. Thomas Furman, DVM, comments from email interview, received August 31, 2014.

14. Richard Howe, comments from email interview, received August 8, 2014.

15. Lisa Hill, comments from phone interview, conducted July 22, 2014.

16. Bob Solheim, comments from email interview, received July 13, 2014.

17. Mark Dixon, comments from phone interview, conducted June 25, 2014.

18. Bob Furman, comments from email interview, received August 9, 2014.

19. Lisa Claes, "Inspirational Leadership: Engaging Staff in Times of Change," The Adviser website, accessed June 5, 2016, http://www.theadviser.com.au/blog/30142-inspirational-leadership-engaging-staff-in-times-of-change.

20. Dan Neufelder, comments from phone interview, conducted May 28, 2014.

21. John Maxwell, *Sometimes You Win – Sometimes You Learn*, (New York: Center Street, 2013), Kindle edition, chap. 6.

22. Erika Anderson, "What Leading With Vision Really Means," *Fast Company*, accessed June 6, 2016, http://www.fastcompany.com/3003293/what-leading-vision-really-means.

CHAPTER 13

1. "About the IKEA Group," IKEA website, accessed June 21, 2016, http://www.ikea.com/ms/en_US/this-is-ikea/company-information/index.html.

2. Susan M. Heathfield, "Leadership Values and Workplace Ethics," Human Resources —About website, accessed June 21, 2016, http://humanresources.about.com/od/leadership/a/leader_values.htm.

3. Gary Peterson, "Three Reasons Why Values Matter, And I'm Not Talking The Money Kind," *Forbes Magazine*, accessed June 22, 2016, http://www.forbes.com/sites/garypeterson/2013/08/14/three-reasons-why-values-matter-and-im-not-talking-the-money-kind/.

4. Mike Williams, comments from live interview, conducted May 21, 2015.

5. Bruce Lawrence, comments from phone interview, conducted June 10, 2014.

6. "Mission, Vision and Values," INTEGRIS website, accessed June 22, 2016, http://integrisok.com/mission-vision-values.

7. Holly Lebowitz Rossi, "7 core value statements that inspire," *Fortune Magazine*, accessed June 23, 2016, http://fortune.com/2015/03/13/company-slogans/.

8. Ken Blanchard, "Lead with LUV," How We Lead website, accessed June 23, 2016, http://howwelead.org/2011/01/15/lead-with-luv/.

9. Bill Keogh, comments from email interview, received October 3, 2014.

10. Dov Seidman, "To inspire others, it's how you do it that counts," CNN website, accessed June 23, 2016, http://www.cnn.com/2012/05/03/opinion/dov-seidman-oped/index.html.

11. Michael Josephson, "Attributes of Great Leadership: What it Takes to Be an Exceptional Executive or Administrator."

12. Eric Harvey, Andy Smith, and Paul Sims, *Leading to Ethics: 10 Leadership Strategies for Building a High-Integrity Organization*, (Dallas: The Walk The Talk Company, 2003), 44.

13. Jeff Kirkham, comments from email interview, received July 8, 2014.

14. Bob Solheim, comments from email interview, received July 13, 2014.

15. Michael Hyatt, "Four Characteristics of Inspirational Leaders."

16. Scott Berkun, "Interview with Scott Berkun," Life Hack website, accessed June 24, 2016, http://www.lifehack.org/articles/productivity/interview-with-scott-berkun.html.

17. Harla Adams, comments from email interview, received September 11, 2014.

18. Dan Nielsen, "A Blueprint for Success: The Life, Leadership and Legacy of Marlowe Senske," *Tips for Greater Success*, accessed November 18, 2016, http://dannielsen.com/2009/06/30/a-blueprint-for-success-the-life-leadership-and-legacy-of-marlowe-senske/.

19. Bruce Lawrence, comments from phone interview, conducted June 10, 2014.

20. Anthony Romero, comments from email interview, received May 19, 2014.

21. Laura Wahl, comments from email interview, received May 28, 2014.

22. Jessica Hill, comments from email interview, received May 27, 2014.

23. Karen Adams, comments from email interview, received May 21, 2014.

24. Susan M. Heathfield, "Leadership Values and Workplace Ethics."

CHAPTER 14

1. Bob MacDonald, "Is the Power in You to Empower Others?" Bob MacDonald website, accessed July 6, 2016, http://bobmaconbusiness.com/?p=6719.

2. Ibid.

3. Lisa Quast, "6 Ways to Empower Others to Succeed," *Forbes Magazine*, accessed July 7, 2016, http://www.forbes.com/sites/lisaquast/2011/02/28/6-ways-to-empower-others-to-succeed/.

4. John Maxwell, "5 Ways to Equip During a Downturn," John Maxwell website, accessed July 7, 2016, http://www.johnmaxwell.com/cms/images/uploads/ads/5_Ways_to_Equip_During_a_Downturn.pdf.

5. Clancy Hayes, "10 Steps to Developing a Powerful Team," Global Christian Center website, accessed July 8, 2016, http://globalchristiancenter.com/administrative-leadership/church-leadership/24192-10-steps-to-developing-a-powerful-team.

6. Chris Van Gorder, comments from live interview, conducted May 27, 2015.

7. Ibid.

8. Jody Livingston, "Training – Equipping Your Team for Maximum Impact," The Longer Haul website, accessed July 8, 2016, http://thelongerhaul.com/training/.

9. The Mind Tools Editorial Team, "Giving Feedback: Keeping Team Member Performance High and Well-Integrated," Mind Tool website, accessed July 10, 2016, https://www.mindtools.com/pages/article/newTMM_98.htm.

10. Ibid.

11. Bruce Lawrence, comments from phone interview, conducted June 10, 2014.

12. Joseph Folkman, "The Best Gift Leaders Can Give: Honest Feedback,"

Forbes Magazine, accessed July 11, 2016, http://www.forbes.com/sites/joefolkman/2013/12/19/the-best-gift-leaders-can-give-honest-feedback/.

13. Ibid.

14. Lisa Petrilli, "Giving Constructive Feedback: Eight Leadership Essentials," Lisa Petrilli website, accessed July 12, 2016, http://www.lisapetrilli.com/2011/06/27/giving-constructive-feedback-eight-leadership-essentials/.

15. Allison Gauss, "4 Tips for Giving Effective Employee Feedback," Classy website, accessed July 13, 2016, https://www.classy.org/blog/4-tips-for-giving-effective-employee-feedback/.

16. Adele Margrave & Robert Gorden, *The Complete Idiot's Guide to Performance Appraisals*, (Indianapolis: Alpha Books, 2001), 220.

17. Lisa Petrilli, "Giving Constructive Feedback: Eight Leadership Essentials."

18. "Ten Common Mistakes in Giving Feedback," Center for Creative Leadership website, accessed July 14, 2016, http://www.ccl.org/leadership/pdf/publications/tencommon.pdf.

19. Amy Gallo, "Giving a High Performer Productive Feedback," *Harvard Business Review*, accessed July 15, 2016, https://hbr.org/2009/12/giving-a-high-performer-produc.

20. "Ten Common Mistakes in Giving Feedback," Center for Creative Leadership website, accessed July 14, 2016, http://www.ccl.org/leadership/pdf/publications/tencommon.pdf.

21. Susanne Madsen, in response to a comment on her article, "Top Tips for Providing Effective Feedback," Susanne Madsen website, accessed July 16, 2016, http://www.susannemadsen.co.uk/blog/top-tips-for-providing-effective-feedback.

22. Lisa Petrilli, "Giving Constructive Feedback: Eight Leadership Essentials."

23. Karin Hurt, "7 Ways to Build Your Employees' Self Confidence," *Success Magazine*, accessed July 16, 2016, http://www.success.com/mobile/article/7-ways-to-build-your-employees-self-confidence.

24. Andy Core, "The Importance of Confidence to Productivity in the Workplace," Andy Core website, accessed July 17, 2016, http://andycore.com/importance-confidence-productivity-workplace/.

25. Lisa Hill, comments from phone interview, conducted July 22, 2014.

26. Clyde Pogson, comments from email interview, received August 11, 2014.

27. Jack Lawless, comments from phone interview, conducted July 24, 2014.

28. Kathy Dagg, comments from email interview, received July 31, 2014.

29. Traci Bernard, comments from phone interview, conducted May 9, 2014.

30. Laura Wahl, comments from email interview, received May 28, 2014.

31. Anthony Romero, comments from email interview, received May 19, 2014.

32. Quentin Fottrell, "Typical U.S. worker now lasts 4.6 years on job," Market Watch website, accessed July 18, 2016, http://www.marketwatch.com/story/americans-less-likely-to-change-jobs-now-than-in-1980s-2014-01-10.

33. Tim Askew, "Why You Should Help Your Best Employees Leave You," *Inc. Magazine*, accessed July 18, 2016, http://www.inc.com/tim-askew/helping-your-best-employees-leave-you.html.

34. Jim Wetrich, comments from phone interview, conducted May 30, 2014.

35. Sanchia Patrick Rasul, comments from email interview, received July 8, 2014.

36. Jeff Haden, "10 Things Only Exceptional Bosses Give Their Employees."

37. Tod Jeffers, comments from email interview, received August 19, 2014.

CHAPTER 15

1. Jim Wetrich, comments from phone interview, conducted May 30, 2014.

2. Mac McIntire, "How to Empower Employees to Make Effective Decisions on the Front-Line," LinkedIn Pulse, accessed August 3, 2016, https://www.linkedin.com/pulse/20140618220758-20499125-how-to-empower-employees-to-make-effective-decisions-on-the-front-line.

3. *Dictionary.com Unabridged*, s.v. "micromanage," accessed August 3, 2016, http://www.dictionary.com/browse/micromanage.

4. Jim Wetrich, comments from phone interview, conducted May 30, 2014.

5. Mind Tools Editorial Team, "Avoiding Micromanagement: Helping Team Members Excel – On Their Own," Mind Tools website, accessed August 4, 2016, https://www.mindtools.com/pages/article/newTMM_90.htm.

6. Bruce Lawrence, comments from phone interview, conducted June 10, 2014.

7. Jennifer Bell, comments from email interview, received June 23, 2014.

8. Michael Payne, comments from email interview, received June 18, 2014.

9. Jeff Haden, "10 Things Only Exceptional Bosses Give Employees."

10. Clancy Hayes, "10 Steps to Developing a Powerful Team."

11. Mac McIntire, "How to Empower Employees to Make Effective Decisions

on the Front-Line."

12. Clancy Hayes, "10 Steps to Developing a Powerful Team."

13. Mark Dixon, comments from phone interview, conducted June 25, 2014.

14. Christine Márquez-Hudson, comments from phone interview, conducted August 29, 2014.

15. Jeff Haden, "10 Things Only Exceptional Bosses Give Employees."

16. Bob MacDonald, "Is the Power in You to Empower Others?"

17. Lorna Shaw, comments from phone interview, conducted July 23, 2014.

18. Mark Kehrberg, comments from phone interview, conducted July 15, 2014.

19. Mac McIntire, "How to Empower Employees to Make Effective Decisions on the Front-Line."

20. Gary Runn, "3 Critical Components for Developing Leaders," Gary Runn website, accessed August 5, 2016, http://garyrunn.com/2016/05/27/3-critical-components-developing-leaders/.

21. Sandy Morford, comments from phone interview, conducted August 22, 2014.

22. Clancy Hayes, "10 Steps to Developing a Powerful Team."

Chapter 16

1. Og Mandino, *The Greatest Salesman in the World*, (New York: Bantam Books, 1985), 54.

2. Dan Nielsen, "Make Good Habits And Become Their Slave," Dan Nielsen website, accessed August 17, 2016, http://dannielsen.com/2009/02/27/make-good-habits-and-become-their-slave/.

3. "The Power of Habit: Why We Do What We Do in Life and Business," Charles Duhigg website, accessed August 18, 2016, http://charlesduhigg.com/books/the-power-of-habit/.

4. Charles Duhigg, *The Power of Habit: Why We Do What We Do in Life and Business*, (New York: Random House, 2012), Kindle edition, chap. 1.

5. Ibid.

6. Charles Duhigg, comments from video, "How to break habits (from The Power of Habit by Charles Duhigg)," Charles Duhigg website, accessed August 18, 2016, http://charlesduhigg.com/books/the-power-of-habit/.

7. Curtis Rooney, comments from phone interview, conducted June 6, 2014.

8. Dan Neufelder, comments from phone interview, conducted May 28, 2014.

9. Mark Dixon, comments from phone interview, conducted June 25, 2014.

10. Clyde Pogson, comments from email interview, received August 11, 2014.

11. Tim Orellano, comments from phone interview, conducted June 11, 2014.

12. Jack Lawless, comments from phone interview, conducted July 24, 2014.

13. Richard Howe, comments from email interview, received August 8, 2014.

14. Bill Keogh, comments from email interview, received October 3, 2014.

15. Tod Jeffers, comments from email interview, received August 19, 2014.

16. Marc Reynolds, comments from email interview, received August 19, 2014.

17. Sandy Morford, comments from phone interview, conducted August 22, 2014.

18. James Clear, "How to Break a Bad Habit and Replace It With a Good One," James Clear website, accessed November 18, 2016, http://jamesclear.com/how-to-break-a-bad-habit.

19. Ibid.

20. Dan Nielsen, "Excellence – The Result of Good Habits," Dan Nielsen website, accessed August 22, 2016, http://dannielsen.com/2013/03/21/excellence-the-result-of-good-habits/.

21. Amy Morin, "6 Ways To Develop The Self-Discipline Necessary To Reach Your Goals," *Forbes Magazine*, accessed August 26, 2016, http://www.forbes.com/sites/amymorin/2014/10/03/6-ways-to-develop-the-self-discipline-necessary-to-reach-your-goals/.

Chapter 17

1. Dan Nielsen, *Presidential Leadership*, 286.

2. Ibid.

3. Steven Boller, "Spaced Learning and Repetition: How They Work and Why," Bottom Line Performance website, accessed September 17, 2016, http://www.bottomlineperformance.com/spaced-learning-and-repetition-why-they-work/.

4. Sherry Collier, "Accountability Works: Four Reasons and Four Tips," Sherry Collier website, accessed September 17, 2016, http://creativepathtogrowth.com/accountability-works-four-reasons-and-four-tips/.

Made in the USA
Lexington, KY
24 February 2017